WORK, WOMEN AND THE LABOUR MARKET

Edited by Jackie West

ROUTLEDGE & KEGAN PAUL
London, Boston and Henley

First published in 1982
by Routledge & Kegan Paul Ltd
39 Store Street,
London WC1E 7DD,
9 Park Street,
Boston, Mass. 02108, USA and
Broadway House,
Newtown Road,
Henley-on-Thames,
Oxon RG9 1BN
Printed in Great Britain by
The Thetford Press Ltd
© Routledge & Kegan Paul 1982

Library of Congress Cataloging in Publication Data
Main entry under title:

Work, women, and the labour market.

Includes index.
Contents: If it's only women it doesn't matter
so much/Peter Armstrong - Sex and skill in
the organisation of the clothing industry/Angela
Coyle - New technology and women's office work/
Jackie West - [etc.] 1. Women - Employment -
Great Britain - Addresses, essays, lectures.
2. Working class women - Great Britain -
Addresses, essays, lectures. I. West, Jackie.

HD6135.W64   331.4'0941   81-13856

ISBN 0-7100-0970-4   AACR2

CONTENTS

For Nancy

ACKNOWLEDGMENTS

My thanks to each of the contributors for making this book possible. They and many others encouraged me with the project, but in particular my thanks to Theo Nichols, Caroline Freeman, Angela Coyle, Alison Lever, Maralyn McDowell, Cleo Witt, Philippa Brewster, and above all to Will Guy. I am grateful to Doris Macey and especially Maralyn McDowell for typing so many of the articles and to such tight deadlines.

Jackie West

NOTES ON CONTRIBUTORS

Peter Armstrong is Lecturer in Industrial Relations at Huddersfield Polytechnic.

Angela Coyle is at the University of Warwick where she is completing a doctoral thesis on women's employment, and is researching women and unemployment for the EOC.

Rosemary Crompton is Lecturer in Sociology at the University of East Anglia.

Caroline Freeman researched and then set up the Barton Hill After-School and Holiday Playscheme at the Bristol Settlement, and is currently researching collective child care.

Barbro Hoel is completing a doctoral thesis on Asian women workers and the clothing industry at the University of Warwick.

Judith Hunt is Assistant Secretary (National Official with special responsibility for women) of the Technical, Administrative and Supervisory Section (TASS) of the Amalgamated Union of Engineering Workers (AUEW).

Gareth Jones is Lecturer in Sociology at the University of East Anglia.

Annie Phizacklea is a freelance researcher formerly employed at the SSRC Research Unit on Ethnic Relations at the University of Bristol.

Marilyn Porter has lectured in Sociology at the Universities of Bristol, Manchester and Newfoundland.

Stuart Reid is Lecturer in Sociology at Brunel University.

Jackie West is Lecturer in Sociology at the University of Bristol.

INTRODUCTION

Jackie West

There are, on official reckoning, well over 9½ million women
workers in Britain - in reality a good many more - and they make
up over 40 per cent of the entire labour force. But women work
overwhelmingly in specific areas of the economy and in a relatively
narrow range of occupations. Women's work is particularly low
paid, often poorly organised despite the increasing numbers of
women in trade unions, and women are a growing proportion of
the unemployed.

This book looks at women's employment in contemporary capitalism through closely researched studies of particular areas. It is
concerned with differences and similarities in women's and men's
experience in the labour market and as members of the working
class. It is about how and why women come to be in jobs typically
regarded as semi- or unskilled, and about women workers' consciousness as workers and as women. It looks at the role of trade
unions in relation to women and to sexual divisions, and at how
class and gender relations are woven together in the production
process. But first, something on the general contours of women's
employment.

A good deal of the increase in women's recorded employment in
the post-war period, as indeed of the labour force as a whole, is
due to the increase in part-time workers, most of whom are married women. Part-time workers are especially low paid, but this
is not the reason for women's generally low pay. For the differential in earnings between men and women - which in 1980 meant
that women's pay was less than two-thirds that of men - is a
differential which obtains between those who work full time. Part
of the difference arises from the greater contribution to men's pay
of shift, productivity and overtime premia, such payments accounting for around a quarter of male manual workers' pay and only a
seventh in the case of women. In white-collar jobs, apart from
differential promotion chances, women benefit less from discretion-
ary merit pay and from long-service premia which some unions
have negotiated. Even excluding the effects of overtime, from
which many women are effectively barred by domestic commitments,
full-time women workers' pay is still less than three quarters of
men's.[1] The gap now is less than it was in 1970, when equal pay
eventually reached the statute book, but improvements in earnings
reached their peak in 1976 and 1977. Since then women's position
relative to men has consistently declined.

One of the factors behind women's lower pay - though not the
reason for the decline - is their concentration in occupations which

1

are overwhelmingly female. It is catering, cleaning, hairdressing, bar work and other services which occupy over half of all women manual workers, and clerical and related work for a similar proportion of those in non-manual jobs. Women also work disproportionately in low-paid industries.

Struggles around equal pay showed that substantial gains could be made where women were involved in job evaluation (and hence the possibility of jobs being recognised as of equal value if not directly comparable to those of men) and where unions took strong action. But it is not only employers who have sought evasive action within the narrow terms of the Act, for male workers have often pressed for or colluded with measures which have protected their higher status and earning power (Snell, 1979). Measures such as the creation of 'de facto' women's grades in notionally unsegregated structures (with semi-skilled women at or just above the level for unskilled male labourers) or measures to increase basic or bonus pay for jobs done by men. Given greater union strength among men and already existing differences in men's and women's pay, it is no surprise that the gap has widened, following the restoration of free collective bargaining and percentage increases in annual pay awards. In the meantime the number of cases heard at Industrial Tribunals has fallen to a mere trickle and the success rate is now very low indeed (one-sixth of the 78 cases heard in 1979: EOC, 1980a). Improvements to legislation on equal pay and anti-discrimination are important but essentially a gloss on the structural causes of women's unequal position at work.

Women workers are a highly flexible as well as cheap source of labour in advanced capitalism. It is women's part-time work that has increased, often while full-time employment for men and women has declined, but part-time workers have also born the brunt of recessionary cycles in the 1970s – it is they who are drawn both in and out of the labour market most rapidly. Women's employment in manufacturing has also fallen more sharply than men's in all post-war recessions (Bruegel, 1979; Fonda and Moss, 1976). In early 1976 women made up 22 per cent of the registered unemployed. Just four years later this figure had risen to 31 per cent (EOC, 1980a, p. 78). The concentration of women in low-paid, labour-intensive work has never been a guarantee against disposability, although this has been masked by their growing employment in the expanding service sector – in health, education and welfare, the retail trade, the so-called 'miscellaneous services', public administration, finance – and office work in industry itself. The impact of 'new technology' here is already making its presence felt, however. And this aside from that of public expenditure cuts, which even in the late 1970s were slowing down the rate of employment growth.

As the current recession began to take a firmer hold, calls on women to return to the home have become more frequent and vociferous. In a radio interview in 1979, the Secretary for Social Services, Patrick Jenkin, stated that, given high unemployment,

the balance between the national need for women's work in the
economy and the need for them to look after their family was
shifting.

Such statements are highly invidious, first because they reinforce the notion that care of the nation's children should be the
exclusive responsibility of only one half of its adult members.
Second, because they reinforce exactly that which makes women's
place in the labour market so subordinate even when and where
there is a demand for women's employment. It is just because
women have to put the needs of their husbands and children first,
before their own needs for autonomy and economic independence,
that women can, for instance, be recruited into jobs paying a
'supplementary wage'.

Nineteenth-century attempts to relegate women to the home and
restrict their employment merely served to marginalise women's
position in factory work and further concentrate women in low-
paid, badly organised sectors such as the sweated trades, outwork
and domestic service. The extent but also diversity of women's
industrial employment is only now being rediscovered. Apart from
unsupported women, working-class wives continued to work depending on local opportunities, family circumstances and the level
and regularity of the male wage, even among skilled workers
(Alexander, 1976; Alexander, Davin and Hostettler, 1979).
Increases in women's 'economic activity', particularly this century,
reflect in part its greater visibility. Women have been drawn into
the expanding sphere of commodity production. This has not sub-
stantially reduced women's domestic responsibilities – men help
with rather than share these. But women have been increasingly
employed to assemble, pack or sell things – clothes, textiles,
food, drink – 'consumer goods' once provided within the home.
Women also now perform services, such as cleaning, cooking,
washing, and teaching and health care too, for organisations
rather than private individuals.

There are of course many other considerations in the rising
numbers of women workers, including the growth of new consumer
goods and engineering industries and the hitherto enormous expansion of the service sector itself. But among them must be counted
the importance of married women's earnings to the maintenance of
families' standard of living. It is not simply that aspirations may
have risen, but rather that it is the income of wives which keeps
many families above the poverty line, and there is a clear relationship between high household income and married women's employment.[2]

Even official figures reveal that seven in ten married women
between the ages of 35 and 54 are 'economically active', that is in
paid work or seeking it. Many women are the sole economic providers for their children or other dependent relatives. Their
poverty reflects in particular the low wages they – as women – can
command in the labour market and the way this and their domestic
responsibilities often force them to rely on supplementary benefit
(Land, 1978a). The idea, reinforced by the state, that women are

or should be dependent on a male breadwinner legitimises lower pay for all women and their lesser claim on scarce resources. The belief that women's wages should supplement, but not substitute for men's, also reinforces lower wages for men, their work incentive and belief in the adequacy of the wage system as such. In any case the ideal of the family wage - earned by men - is the incompatible with equal pay for women (McIntosh, 1978; Barrett and McIntosh, 1980).

What I have sketched above are some of the broad outlines of women's place in the labour force. The contributions here, taken as a whole, explore these and more specific questions in the context of detailed case studies.

The book begins with analyses of job segregation along the lines of sex. Such labour-market segmentation into primary and secondary jobs, and for instance between the skilled and unskilled, cuts across most areas of employment within industries and firms as well as between them. It has been a major theme in recent theoretical work. Dual labour market models, in both their classic and radical forms, essentially locate the causes in the requirements of production itself. Marxist feminist perspectives, by contrast, draw attention to the ways in which the specific advantages of women workers are determined by the sexual division of labour, by women's role in reproductive, domestic and productive work as a whole. There is concern, for example, with how the material relations of the family and the subordination of women to men enables women, rather than others, to be drawn into deskilled, low-paid and insecure jobs and to be excluded from others, and how patriarchal relations are directly implicated in the struggle between capital and labour over control of the labour process. Although there is a far-from-resolved debate on these issues (see, for instance, Barrett, 1980; Beechey, 1979; Hartmann, 1979b), attention too has been drawn to how the exclusionary practices of men combine with the 'needs of capital' to reinforce women's subordination in work and also undermine the interests of male workers and the working class as a whole.

The two articles which open this book address these issues through concrete investigations of sexual divisions and their development in specific manufacturing industries. They look, too, at the significance of the sexual division of labour for production within the context of capital's 'economic' imperatives, the need to examine which has become urgent in the present period.

Angela Coyle, in her discussion of the clothing industry, analyses the concentration of women in low-paid work in terms of the deskilling of the labour process and labour resistance to that. Her starting point is the economic constraints, particularly in the post-war period, which have shaped the industry's reliance on relatively labour-intensive processes and particular categories of labour. She shows how transformations of the production process have destroyed male craft skills and allowed greater 'substitution' of semi-skilled female labour. But she demonstrates that distinctions of skill in men's and women's work have much less basis in the content of jobs than in male workers' resistance to loss of control and status. The organisation of the industry has structured deteriorating wage and employment levels for all workers but for women this is combined with the effects of the union's defence of male jobs and wages. She identifies, however, the ways in which this coincides with management avoidance of equal pay and needs for cheap labour, and also how women are used to undercut men and depress their rates of pay. In conclusion, she discusses the kinds of new strategies which are needed to overcome women's inequality.

Peter Armstrong's article is based on fieldwork in two factories, one producing footwear, the other electrical goods. He takes issue with dual labour market models on various counts, in particular that distinctions between semi-skilled men and unskilled women reflect real differences of skill. There is however a material and significant difference in terms of capital-and labour-intensive processes. He locates the development of this recent pattern of segregation in the two factories in relation to changing management strategies, preferred sources of labour and the influence of worker reactions and legislation. He analyses the particular vulnerability of women in labour-intensive work and the ways their role in the family is used by management. But he makes clear the extent to which men's 'privileges' are earned through overtime and shiftwork and the conditions to which they are tied by the need for a family wage. Finally, he explores the divisions between workers and argues for the viability of alliances which would challenge segregation and positively benefit both women and men at work.

Questions about skills in 'women's work' are also taken up in the two articles on clerical work. Until recently women in the office have been virtually ignored in social research. This invisibility is at last being corrected. McNally (1979), for example, has charted the influence of jobs themselves and the labour market on women's attitudes to work and challenged the stereotype of the passive female office worker. Barker and Downing (1980) have identified the relations of the social office as the key to both women's place in the hierarchy of mental labour, and to a 'feminine' culture of resistance to alienating work, but they also argue that micro electronic technology is replacing patriarchal with more specifically capitalist forms of control. Nevertheless secretarial rather than other forms of clerical work has been the main focus of recent studies and it is important not to lose sight of certain other basic ways in which women's role structures their location and functions in the office.

Drawing extensively on their research in local government, Rosemary Crompton, Gareth Jones and Stuart Reid ask why women are concentrated in clerical jobs and what is the nature of the work they do. They reveal the only partial truth that women fail to gain promotion because of poorer qualifications. They explore the similarities and contrasts between men and women in terms of these as well as the diversity between distinct groups of women

workers themselves, and argue that women are particularly disadvantaged in the promotion stakes because of the constraints
imposed by family commitments. They also challenge stereotypical
assumptions about the nature of clerical work, identifying factors
which have inhibited deskilling in local government, and show how
the availability of married women often obscures the real content
of low-grade jobs. At the same time they indicate the future implications of changes in women's qualifications and some implications
too for recent sociological studies on social mobility.

Jackie West looks at the impact of new technology on women
clerical workers. Through a critique of the dominant orthodoxy,
which sees the introduction of microelectronics as benign, I show
that women's clerical work in certain key sectors of the economy
is highly vulnerable to a real contraction of job opportunities,
although the process is concealed in many ways. There is also
greater polarisation both within the general office as well as the
secretarial hierarchy. I am sceptical about deskilling as such but
suggest that reskilling is little in evidence and that much depends,
as does the extent of labour displacement, on the trade union
response. In discussing the nature of 'new technology' agreements,
and some of the conditions won for those whose jobs are being
transformed, I maintain, however, that particular constraints are
posed by the recession and by management objectives to cut costs
and increase efficiency.

New technology and greater office rationalisation have important
implications for the 'proletarianisation' of clerical workers in so
far as they further undermine the conditions, relative autonomy
and especially job security which have conventionally made office
work for women a meaningful alternative to work on the shop
floor - although, as the previous paper indicates, there is need
for more detailed research on the impact of computerisation. New
technology is also displacing semi- and unskilled workers in manufacturing and women are highly vulnerable here as well, particularly in the electronics industry itself (Incomes Data Services,
1980: Bruegel, 1979).

The multinational microelectronics industry, whose products are
being deployed in the restructuring of western capitalism, are
dependent on the gross exploitation of women workers in South-
East Asia in microprocessor assembly (Grossman, 1978). Within
advanced capitalist economies themselves low-wage sectors are
also continually reproduced and a vital source of cheap, docile
and flexible labour has always been that of immigrants, or migrants
including women. Women have formed a significant proportion of
workers in, for instance, the Irish, Spanish, Cypriot and
Philippino labour migrations to Britain and the Yugoslav and Greek
migrations throughout Western Europe (Phizacklea, forthcoming).
In Britain, especially since the 1960s, Asian and West Indian
women have been increasingly drawn upon. As the two articles
here make clear, their position as wage workers is both similar to
and in many ways distinct from that of women workers generally.

The focus of Barbro Hoel's paper is the ways in which Asian

women are exploited in the sweated clothing trade and the limits
and possibilities of resistance. She documents their use as cheap
and disposable labour and shows how this is actively shaped by
their vulnerability as immigrants and as women, as well as by the
organisation of the trade itself. She describes how the work force
is divided by the payment system and employers' strategies of
control which both use and reproduce the more general subordination of Asian women. Her rich ethnographic account of their
conditions as wage workers is complemented by an account of
their struggles for trade union recognition in the late 1970s. The
general difficulties that women workers face of sustaining industrial organisation and militancy are posed particularly acutely for
such women, for they are more vulnerable than most to employers'
power. It is sometimes assumed that the weakest workers do not
organise, a notion challenged by women's struggles both in the
past and today (Alexander, Davin and Hostettler, 1979; Parsons,
1974). These women, at least at this point in their lives, are not
isolated part-timers, nor outworkers whose dependence on their
employer is secured by the way, as women, they are tied directly
to the home by their children. But for these Asian women unionism
and autonomy are new phenomena and they demonstrate women's
resilience and determination in the face of considerable obstacles.

Consciousness and action are also taken up by Annie Phizacklea
in her discussion of West Indian women. She considers first the
economic, political and ideological relations which structure their
specific position within the working class and their employment·
post-war economic demands, racial discrimination and their role
as working mothers in the West Indies and in Britain. She indicates how both their position as women and as black migrant labour
shapes their subordinate place in the labour force, and reveals
the insights and complexities of seeing West Indian women and
migrant women generally as a form of reserve labour. Drawing
on her research in west London she looks at West Indian women's
relation to work, trade unionism and industrial action. She identifies in many respects a more radical consciousness as workers
than among West Indian men and English men and women, and concludes by looking at the influence of their position as black women
on forms of political action.

It has been stressed that women's position in the labour market
and at work is structured by their particular situation as women
and by their actual or expected role in the family. The following
two articles explore more directly the ways in which personal life,
the sexual division of labour and work experience are interwoven
for women. This involves looking in detail at the reality behind,
for instance, statistical figures on women workers with dependent
children. It involves looking at how the ever-present demands of
maintaining husbands and children are reflected in consciousness,
in the necessity rather than choice of paid work for many married
women, and in the foreclosing of employment options and conditions.

Marilyn Porter is concerned with how the connections between
wage labour, sexual divisions and the structure and ideology of

the family in capitalism are actually experienced in the lives of
working-class women. She explores the relationship of women's
ideas about work and collective action to their understanding and
experience of their place in the family. We see how the material
conditions of their lives influence women's relation to domestic
work and childcare, and how these structure the distinct terms
on which women with young children are employed, their part-
time jobs and their expectations. It is their position and immediate
interests as housewives which shape their largely negative per-
ceptions of unions, of claims to equal pay, and of strikes, although
their husbands are also seen to play a part in reinforcing their
distance from the workplace and from politics. But she reveals too
the complexities and ambiguities in women's views on industrial
action and their critique of politics. She thus explores, through
extensive interview material, the contradictions and potential in
the women's consciousness and also the way that solidarity between
working-class women and men is inhibited by the objective and
ideological division of their worlds.

The sexual division of labour is also the focus of Caroline Freeman's article which looks at the direct effects of women's responsibilities for children on their position in the labour market and
exploitation as workers. Beginning with the nature of childcare
provision, she documents, using case material, the complex
arrangements of working mothers. It is these which underpin the
distinct patterns in their working lives and the particular dis-
abilities of their part-time jobs. She considers the economic and
ideological factors which lead employers to discriminate against
women workers, those which underlie concessions and the use of
part-time labour. She shows how individual bargains benefit
'understanding' employers and how the price women pay is determined not by preferences but by the material circumstances of
their lives. She concludes by discussing the significance and
limitations of fighting discrimination in the workplace using
legislation. Arguing that union struggles and reforms based on
concessions to women's role consolidate it, she indicates the kind
which are needed to undermine the sexual division of labour and
open up the possibility of transforming the family in the interests
of men and children as well as women.

If the root cause of women's unequal relation to paid work is
the sexual division of labour, this also means challenging the way
trade union practices reinforce the more general subordination of
women. Women's direct experience of unionism has often left them
disenchanted, and participation has frequently been restricted or
prevented by both the burden of the 'double shift' and by union
neglect, nationally and at shopfloor level, of their specific
interests as workers and as women. Derogatory attitudes, not
simply indifference, to women and to 'women's work' are not confined to management but often permeate women's relations with
their union officials and male shop stewards. Male-oriented in their
organisation as well as their policies or priorities, the unions'
structure has sometimes inhibited the activism of women stewards

too (Pollert, 1981; Coote and Kellner, 1981). But if women have always had to struggle to get their voices heard within the labour movement, there are signs that their presence is increasingly permanent and effective.

Judith Hunt, in the final contribution to this book, explores recent developments within the trade union movement as a whole. She begins with the heritage and contradictions of separate organisation among women workers in the face of exclusion, but also the historical lessons of denying women separate representation in unions once they were accepted. Highlighting the significance of the recent growth in women's membership, she shows how increased discussion on women's rights is due to the particular impact of the contemporary women's movement, and charts its influence on the development and widening of trade union policies. While stressing the importance of union organisation to improving women's pay and conditions, she documents the inadequate representation of women within the unions and the various steps that have been taken to redress this inequality. And while identifying the changes which indicate a more serious concern with women's issues, she concludes by emphasising the continuing need for action to ensure participation and the recognition of women's demands.

NOTES

1   Women's average gross hourly earnings, excluding the effect of overtime, were, in 1980, 73.5 per cent of men's - little better than the 73 per cent for 1979. The peak in 1977 was 75.5 per cent. See EOC Fifth Annual Report, 1981.
2   EOC, 1980a, p. 86. The Royal Commission on the Distribution of Income and Wealth (Research Report 6, 1978) reported that the chances of a family being in poverty were roughly 1 in 14 where wives were employed, but almost as much as 1 in 3 where they were not. See also L. Hamill (1976).

1 SEX AND SKILL IN THE ORGANISATION OF THE CLOTHING INDUSTRY

Angela Coyle

INTRODUCTION

This article looks at the clothing industry, which has a larger concentration of women employees than any other industry. In asking the questions, why are women still concentrated in un-skilled and low paid work, and why hasn't anti-discrimination and equal pay legislation changed that, it would appear that some answers lie in the forms of organisation of the labour process itself. To perceive women's marginalised relation to production as a consequence of their 'dual role' and a discriminatory labour market is not enough, and here the concentration of women in low-paid work is placed within the context of the deskilling of the labour process. Such changes in the organisation of the labour process have created the unskilled jobs which women undertake, but it does not explain why women's wages are so persistently lower than men's, nor the blanket categorisation of women's work as always being of lower skill value than men's work. Deskilling is not an abstract formula, and in clothing, as elsewhere, the range of strategies available to management to effect the cheapen-ing of production occur in the context of economic constraints and labour resistance. What is shown here is that strategies employed by management to exert a downward pressure on wages (and along the way avoid equal pay), combine with union strategies to resist that, to have the effect of reinforcing sexual divisions within the labour process. So that although the actions of manage-ment and male workers derive from quite different imperatives, they can have a short-term coincidence of interests in keeping female labour segregated in certain jobs. It does raise questions about traditional forms of trade union strategy, especially trade union sectionalism, and just how women can get out of the low-wage ghetto.

The clothing industry has an exceptionally high reliance on female labour, about 80 per cent of the total labour force. Being a labour-intensive industry, it is particularly dependent on cheap labour. With a wide-ranging product - light and heavy clothing, men's, women's and children's wear - the methods of production are diverse and unevenly developed. Sweatshop and modern factory exist alongside each other. It is traditionally a craft-based industry but skilled work and particularly men's work has been undermined through rationalisation. It is now women who are employed on the main assembly processes as semi-skilled and unskilled labour, whilst men hold on to an ever-diminishing

range of jobs which are accepted as skilled work and men's work.
Union organisation has not been particularly effective in preventing the deskilling of labour and, rather, the main limits to that
have been imposed by the limited capital available to the industry.
Production is still based on human labour rather than machines
and for this reason labour costs are the main costs of production.
In turn, it is precisely because of these costs that labour productivity has to be extended and 'rationalised' to its full potential
through work study and it is not without reason that the industry
has not entirely lost its sweatshop associations (North Tyneside
Community Development Project, 1978, p. 41).

Precisely how deskilling occurs will depend on the specific
conditions that exist within an industry. There are variations
from industry to industry and from firm to firm but, within a
range of strategies available to management, there are two possible
emphases. One is to exert pressure on labour itself and to maximise
efficiency of effort through reorganising work methods and extending the division of labour. Skilled work is broken down into a
series of simplified routinised processes which can be undertaken
by less skilled, and cheaper, labour. As a managerial strategy,
this was developed by Frederick 'Speedy' Taylor whose 'scientific'
approach to the division of labour laid the basis of work study as
it is employed today. The second possibility for management is to
replace human labour by machines. The use of work study and
the mechanisation of production are strategies often employed in
conjunction with one another, but the weight of emphasis will be
determined often by factors outside of management control. Sometimes labour organisation is so strong that it can make work study
almost impossible (Goodrich, 1975) and labour control of production can only be significantly broken by the introduction of new
machinery (as for example in the printing industry). The use of
machinery, on the other hand, is governed by how much capital
is available for such investment and whether it is adequately
compensated by reduced labour costs. Where particularly cheap
labour is available there may be no particular incentive to replace
labour with expensive machines (Marx, 1976, pp. 515-16). De
skilling as a range of managerial strategies, occurs in an uneven
and eclectic way, rather than as a pervasive and driving logic.
Old methods will do for as long as they remain profitable.

This is certainly demonstrated in the clothing industry where
a characteristically low capital investment contributes to the
industry's hand-to-mouth existence, whilst, at the same time,
narrow profit margins, a changing product and highly competitive
markets often militate against further investment. It is still true
that if wages can be kept at rock bottom levels, small producers
can be very competitive and profitable (Roche, 1973, p. 203).
Fashion and seasonal changes and an unstable market means that
there are regular changes in production methods. The clothing
industry needs a rapidly adaptable labour process and human
labour is more adaptable than machinery. Technical change and
rationalisation first occurred in the inter-war period, and in the

context of the relatively reduced availability of cheap labour, the streamlining of the product and market stability. The industry's reliance on cheap labour was upset both by the introduction of the Trades Boards which set minimum wage rates for the industry and by restrictions imposed on the early wave of immigration from Eastern Europe (Wray, 1957 pp. 19). This forced changes in production methods, most notably in men's wear which employed a higher proportion of skilled male labour and which was far less subject to fashion changes. (It forced changes in fashion itself, so that intricate processes such as tucking and pleating were rarely found on mass-produced garments.) Developments in production coexisted with the expansion of retail outlets and fuelled the development of each other. Department and chain stores tendered contracts directly with manufacturers. Some manufacturers moved into retail as well - Burton the Tailor being probably the most well-known example. Once producers had more reliable markets for their product they were prepared to expand the scale of production to meet larger production runs. The Board of Trade study into the industry in 1947 considered that the expansion of retail outlets led to the 'revolutionising (of) manufacturers' methods of production', and noted that for the first time factory production had become more profitable than production based on either homeworkers or sweatshops (Board of Trade, 1947, pp. 8-9).

Since the war, the developments of the clothing industry have been very uneven. The technical basis for development exists, but mostly the industry cannot afford it. Large-scale production units do exist, as, for example, Levi Strauss in Scotland where over 1,000 workers are employed using advanced technology and producing the ultimate streamlined product - jeans of one style and one size. It is equally true however, that the late 1970s have seen the return of production based on the labour of homeworkers (Campbell, 1979). Whilst the industry remains so labour intensive it is particularly vulnerable to competition from low-wage economies in South-East Asia and India. A Korean Airlines advertisement taunted the British clothing industry: 'For the cost of manufacturing two shirts in Korea, this is what can be manufactured in Great Britain. . . .' The picture showed one shirt sleeve ('Garment Worker', November, 1975). Not only do rival producers have significantly lower wage costs, they are often using the most advanced technology available to the industry. In 1975, the setting up of an Economic Development Committee for the clothing industry marked the beginning of £20 million government assistance to invest in advanced machinery. Where it has occurred such investment has had the effect of significantly increasing productivity, but still the industry relies on squeezing labour. Mostly it can, and wages are amongst the lowest in the manufacturing sector. Women are particularly vulnerable to this pressure and trade union organisation has not protected them.

DESKILLING: A CHANGING LABOUR PROCESS
AND A CHANGING LABOUR FORCE

The traditional method of production is known as 'making through' and this was defined by the Board of Trade in 1947 as 'the making of a garment by a single skilled worker'. Under the 'making through' system it was often the case that the main assembly was undertaken by a single skilled worker (male), whilst less skilled operations, such as the sewing of button holes and pockets, were undertaken by 'assistants' (men and women). The variations within this system hinged on differences of control. The master tailor system, for example, originated from Jewish tailoring workshops. Under this system the master tailor, who was often paid by contract, performed the skilled operations in making up the garment, and then himself recruited and employed less-skilled labour as assistants. This 'set system', as it is sometimes referred to, was carried over into factory production. In a factory a head machinist was responsible for organising and supervising his bench of machinists. Production was essentially controlled by the craftsman, who in turn was serviced by less-skilled workers, and the factory owner or manager exercised only the most general supervision. Craftsmen controlled productivity, the allocation of work and payment. It was a system which was increasingly attacked by management who sought to control the labour process and by workers themselves, for it was very exploitative of less-skilled labour. Most union agreements after the war included the ending of the set system. 'Making through' is now extremely unusual, but where it does occur it is without anything like a comparable degree of autonomy and control.

The range of producers and the range of products make it difficult to typify contemporary production methods; there is a wider division of labour than that which occurs in the factory. A great deal of the clothing produced in Britain today comes from the labour of women working at home or in small 'sweatshops' for very low rates of pay. However, this chapter concentrates on the medium sized factories (of approximately 150 workers) which became typical of the industry as it developed after the war. Deskilling aims to destroy comparability between complex and simplified tasks, between skilled and unskilled work, and hence between men's work and women's work. Yet because of the uneven development of the industry, the sexual segregation of labour in these factories is not complete. Men and women may perform different jobs but they are part of the same production process, where the interplay of deskilling with the reinforcement of sexual divisions is particularly apparent.

Men's skills were significantly attacked during the inter-war period with the transition from craft workshop to factory production. The extensive sub-division of processes, combined with technical change, not only attacked the skills of previously very highly skilled men but provided the basis for substitution. 'Mechanisation is making garment making a mass production industry,

it is substituting female machine minders for male craftsmen'
(Hamilton, 1941, p. 130). The introduction of new machines has
reduced both the skill level which the industry requires and the
quantity of labour, so that 'the use of these machines enables
one semi-skilled operative to replace three skilled machinists'
(Wray, 1957, p. 81). Moreover, the intensification of labour since
the war has particularly affected women and work study has been
employed to speed up machinists' operations (Wray, 1957, p. 91).
Deskilling is an ongoing imperative for management. Most processes have now become mechanised and each has been broken
down into operations of the simplest form and the shortest time.
The assembly of a garment is now based on a series of short
simple operations for which operators can be trained very quickly.
Despite these changes, however, the level of mechanisation still
renders clothing dependent on labour. It is not an automated
labour process - 'what still counts in the fashion trade is the hand
that guides the pieces of limp cloth through the classically simple
sewing machine' (Campbell, 1979).
   Increased mechanisation and the displacement of men from most
assembly work has not changed the proportions of men to women
that much. It has been estimated that four in every ten jobs in
the industry have been lost between 1951 and 1976 and women
have been affected almost as badly as men (National Union of
Tailors and Garment Workers, 1978). In 1951 men were 21.4 per
cent of the labour force whilst women made up 78.6 per cent, by
1976 this had changed to 18.9 per cent men and 81.1 per cent
women (National Union of Tailors and Garment Workers, 1978).
What such figures conceal is the concentration of women onto
assembly processes, the concentration of men in the cutting room
and the stock room, and the absolute mushrooming of managerial
and supervisory jobs for men (a reflection of the extent of deskilling and the growth of managerial control). Once men were involved
in the making of the garment but, now deskilled, it has become
'women's work'.
   The sewing machine has become a sophisticated and fast piece
of equipment. Straight seams can now be stitched automatically so
that this operation amounts to machine feeding rather than sewing.
Similarly there are machines for basting, fixing buttons, stitching
button holes, zips and trimmings. Ideally the machine paces production, but, in clothing, machine processes are mostly not automated processes, they still rely on labour to operate them and
piecerate incentive payments and time and motion study become
vital forms of control. Most firms have their own time and motion
teams. Operations are carefully timed and the standard rate set
is very fast indeed. Most operations have a cycle time of under
one minute. High productivity is essential but for the women concerned it can mean 'sweating golfballs' and still being unable to
reach management's production targets (North Tyneside Community
Development Project, 1978, p. 40). Despite the innovations made
by work study methods there are processes which still require
skill and judgement (Kynaston Reeves, 1970, p. 122). This is

true of the stitching of pockets, sleeves and collars, where the
operator has to position and manipulate the fabric as it is stitched.
These operations have a longer training period than any other
machining operation, and although they have a longer cycle time
of three minutes, the women have to work just as fast and just as
intensively, and it can take up to six months to reach required
production speeds. The ability to work at high speed is a skill
inadvertently created by deskilling. It is informally recognised
as such through the particularly long training period for some
operations, yet is not explicitly acknowledged through gradings
or wages. Women's work comes under the generic category of
semi-skilled and covers a vast range of operations.

In looking at men's jobs in the clothing industry, it becomes
apparent how skill is socially constructed in the context of changing technology. Skill is as much about job control and wage levels
as it is about technique. Men in the industry are now employed
in the cutting room, the stock room and in supervisory roles.[1]
The cutting room is a male stronghold. Men lay the cloth, lay the
pattern on the fabric, mark the fabric and cut the fabric. The
craft basis of these operations was undermined by the introduction
of machines in the inter-war period, notably the bandsaw. The
bandsaw requires a great deal of concentration, certainly looks
dangerous and an error would be expensive since several layers
of cloth are cut in one operation. It is a moot point, however,
whether its operation requires the three-year apprenticeship
(once seven years) which the NUTGW insist upon. (Women have
done this work, but informally, and usually in small non-unionised
factories.) The technical basis of men's skills has been eroded
in the cutting room by certain machines, but the relative level of
technical development is quite low, and elements of job control
remain. As other men's jobs have been deskilled and lost, the
cutting room has become a kind of retreat. Inside the cutting room
men defend their wages and skill differentials. Unlike women, men
are employed on time rates and largely determine their own pace
of work. Recruitment and training of cutters operates informally
through men already in the industry, a form unthinkable for
women's work. Up until recently, management have had to put up
with this level of labour control in the cutting room, but have
avoided comparability with the rest of the shopfloor through the
isolation and segregation of higher paid workers.

Once a factory has been rationalised, or 'engineered', it is an
anomaly in the extension of managerial control to have certain
groups of workers outside that system of control. Potentially the
cutting room can now be drawn into the rationalisation process.
Micro-technology has revolutionised the possibilities of the cutting
process. Equipment now exists which will perform the entire laying
and cutting operation automatically. Such equipment is too great
a capital investment for an average-sized firm, but it does lay
the basis of future amalgamations and concentration of capital,
both of which are inevitable for future development ('Garment
Worker', August 1972; Roche, 1973, p. 208). Such new technology

has deep implications for skilled men's jobs, as the union journal, 'Garment Worker', indicates (January 1979): 'The Leeds and Doncaster factories (of the Burton Group) will have a cutback in the cutting rooms, the most serious being at the latter where the entire cutting force will be made redundant.' At Hepworths a cutting system costing £250,000 'has meant that a team of girls is now doing jobs which were traditionally a male preserve' as well as destroying fifty men's jobs. The girls take twelve weeks to train ('Guardian', 8 July, 1980). One firm in the North of England cannot afford such a capital outlay but has removed the wall between the men in the cutting room and the women on the shopfloor, at least preparing the way for future changes.

These technical changes and the rationalisation of the labour process have occurred in the context of the relative availability of cheap labour, which in turn effects changes in the kind of labour required by the industry. In the post-war period many clothing factories were set up in government-designated Development Areas which had 'the only major source of relatively cheap female labour available to an industry where the prevailing trend was towards the creation of larger units, using less skilled and hence cheaper labour' (Hague and Newman, 1952, p. 58). Moreover skilled workers are not just expensive, but resistant to change. So that one firm's labour policy was not just concerned with cost per se but with control as well:

It was rather the impossibility of adapting a labour force from traditional methods to mass production line operation. For cost reasons such a system was becoming vital to our future well being. We had attempted to introduce it and had been forced to abandon it, partly because of our inadequate premises, but chiefly because of worker resistance. Our labour experience probably holds for the clothing industry in general; in traditional clothing centres it is very hard to break with traditional methods (Hague and Newman, 1952, p. 54).

The industry's endemic labour shortage is actually a shortage of cheap labour, and a more or less permanent feature since the war. The war period actually created the conditions upon which the industry could stabilise and develop[2] and yet after the war the industry faced acute labour shortages, particularly of female labour, who were reluctant to return to the industry when better work and pay was available elsewhere ('Garment Worker', May 1970).

The ideal labour recruit has always been a school leaver: quick to learn, not resistant to new work methods and not eligible for an adult wage rate. The reliance on school leavers has not been without problems however, especially in terms of labour turnover. Many leave before they fully train or reach full pay rates. On average a trained operator stays in the industry for three and a half years (Clothing and Allied Products ITB, 1972, p. 4). Increasingly, school leavers are hard to recruit, although girls

between the ages of 15-19 make up approximately 20 per cent of
the female labour force (Census 1971). The raising of the school
leaving age has reduced the number of school leavers available
to the industry, but moreover the industry is not a very attractive one and parents are reluctant to see their children enter the
industry (Winyard, 1977).

The industry employs a lot of married women (60 per cent) but
they tend to be women who have worked in the industry for many
years. Despite labour shortages there has been resistance to
recruiting them as part of any positive employment policy. Peter
Potts of the NUTGW makes the same point: 'I do not think that
the industry as a whole has investigated sufficiently the possibilities and prospects of older married women. There seems to be
a mental block when it comes to the question of training the older
married woman' ('Garment Worker', November 1974). In 1973,
the Industrial Training Board for the clothing industry introduced
its document 'In Lieu of School Leavers' with a reconsideration of
the employment of married women for unskilled work. 'Until
recently it has not been thought possible to train anyone over the
age of twenty five as a flat machinist if she has never before used
an industrial machine' (Clothing and Allied Products ITB, 1973).
These moves were further endorsed by the Industrial Training
Research Unit, who developed a series of tests to be used in the
recruitment of older women to assess suitability for training, when
skill was no longer a relevant criterion, but rather speed, dexterity and the ability to receive instruction (Industrial Training
Research Unit, 1975, p. 3). Despite these moves, the recruitment of
married women has not been taken up in any significant way. Few
'concessions' are made to married women. Although some firms
will grant time off during slack periods there is little part-time
work available. Approximately 12 per cent of the total labour force
is employed on a part-time basis which is lower than the average
for manufacturing as a whole, 20 per cent (Department of Employment, 1974), and extremely low for such a female-dominated
industry.

Immigrant labour has always been important to the industry.
From the late nineteenth and early twentieth centuries, immigrants
from Eastern Europe supplied the industry with a great deal of its
skilled male labour, and, Birnbaum suggests, were responsible
for establishing the difference between men's and women's work
as the difference between skilled and unskilled work (Birnbaum,
undated). Now it is female immigrant labour only which is significant as a distinctive labour force. West Indian, Filipino and
Asian women are employed in a new kind of sweatshop that has
grown up in the inner ring areas of large cities, and are a particularly vulnerable and cheap source of labour (Williams, 1972; and
see Barbro Hoel's paper in this volume).

Finally, it is worth noting, in relation to the industry's labour
force, that the use of homeworkers is a traditional resolution of
the search for cheap labour. Technically self-employed, their
wages are low and unprotected by either union organisation or

wages council orders (Brown, 1974). Economic recession and
competition from foreign markets has once again made production
based on the labour of homeworkers more economical than factory
production. This is particularly true for London, the traditional
site of women's wear production, where it is estimated that half
the fashion trade's output is produced by homeworkers (Campbell,
1979). The number of homeworkers employed is difficult to estimate, but it is clear that rapid loss of jobs in the industry is not
entirely due to increased efficiency and increased labour productivity, and some clothing firms have chosen to move out of
manufacture and into the business of orchestrating the labour of
homeworkers (Campbell, 1979).

TRADE UNION ORGANISATION: LABOUR'S RESPONSE
TO DESKILLING

Employment conditions in the clothing industry have worsened
through the intensification of labour and a continued downward
pressure on wages (Winyard, 1977, p. 19). Jobs are being lost
by about 2 per cent a year. The labour force has been reduced
from approximately half a million in 1951 to approximately 300,000
in 1976 (National Union of Tailors and Garment Workers, 1978).
Unemployment amongst clothing workers is higher than average
('Garment Worker', January 1980). Absenteeism and a high labour
turnover – as high as 75 per cent for some firms – have become
characteristic features of the industry, and symptomatic of the
poor conditions of employment. Although the industry 'lives or
dies on its ability to attract and keep labour . . . labour turnover
is sometimes regarded as being like the weather, to be talked
about but beyond control' (Clothing and Allied Products ITB,
1974, p. 2). The industry is caught in a paradoxical situation
where deteriorating profits in a highly competitive and unstable
market force a downward pressure on wages, but which creates
in turn an expensive labour cost. The industry does not fully
benefit from its investment in training and the labour turnover
is estimated to cost £15,000,000 a year (Roche, 1973, p. 202).
Yet this is a vice which is difficult to get out of since individual
firms will see the necessity of reducing wage costs in terms of
their own immediate survival.
    Relative earnings in the industry have declined since the 1950s.
The continuation of government controls on clothing production in
the early post-war period meant that in 1950 the industry could
attract labour by offering rates of pay that were above the manufacturing average, but particularly since 1971 there has been a
continual decline of earnings in clothing relative to manufacture
as a whole. By 1979, the average manual wage for men in clothing
was £80 per week, as against a national average of £96, and for
women the average weekly manual wage was £50, as against a
national average of £58 per week (Department of Employment,
October 1980). The fact that clothing is a wages council industry

has done little to improve wages, for although the council sets
the minimum rates, they often do little more than ratify 'voluntary'
agreements made between the union and the employer (North
Tyneside Community Development Project, 1978, p. 42).

The NUTGW has not been very successful in protecting either
jobs or wage levels in the industry. It is certainly the case that
the kinds of labour employed are notoriously difficult to organise,
but even where labour is organised the unions have seemingly
little power. The labour force remains divided and competitive.
Deskilling as a system of new work methods and new productivity
payments can be mystifying (Powell, 1976), and the NUTGW admit
to not having coped with it ('Garment Worker', March 1964). It is
quite common, for example, for workers not to know how their
wages are calculated. Moreover a system of payment based on an
individual productivity bonus,

> is perhaps the major force mitigating against the union's attempt
> to build up a cohesive and organised workforce. The management
> has its greatest stronghold and the most powerful weapon in the
> bonus; the union is powerless to break it and the workforce
> desperate to achieve it (North Tyneside Community Development
> Project, 1978, p. 43).

A combination of basic wage and piecework bonus makes up an
economic formula presented by management to provide incentive
and maximise productivity. It is mostly women's work that is
subject to this form of payment. Basic rates are kept low and
women find that in order to maintain their wages they have to
work harder and harder. They cannot win. Piecework is not a
system of reward for increased productivity – it is a way of pushing
wages down. Payment decreases proportionately as output rises
and women receive only a portion of their increased productivity
(Alexander, 1980, p. 27; Royal Commission on Equal Pay, 1946,
p. 50).

Rates for every job are negotiated between management and
unions, but there is considerable scope for variations. The NUTGW
negotiates nationally with firms within the clothing manufacturers'
federation. It also makes individual agreements with firms outside
of that and, perhaps most relevant for women workers, productivity
agreements (bargaining over the rates for new work methods)
which are made locally and voluntarily. Rates of pay are always
being renegotiated in the clothing industry because of regular
changes in the product – different styles and different fabric can
be more, or less, easy to work – as well as changes in work
methods. Because of male domination of the union structure,
women's rates of pay are usually negotiated for them by men, who
may not themselves be subject to the productivity deal under
negotiation. Where elements of craft control have so far been
retained, management have been able to exert only minimal control
through payment incentives. Skilled men are paid on time rates,
since their work is not easily measurable by work study, with

bonuses negotiated over different fabrics and styles. Organisation
is an important distinction in the determination of men's and
women's pay. Whereas men organise collectively for a collective
weekly bonus for the entire cutting room, 'the women we can pick
off one by one' (Managing Director of a garment factory). The
difficulties of confronting aggressive managerial control should
not be underestimated but the tendency for skilled men to view
their interests as separate from the rest of the labour force does
leave women wide open to attack.[3] The clothing industry does not
see a great deal of female militancy, but in the Leeds clothing
strike, 1970, women's anger was directed not just against their
employers, but also against male trade unionists who they felt
were not representing their interests (Rowbotham, 1973, p. 94).
    Women's membership of the union is uneven. About half the
industry's workforce is unionised and women make up about 90
per cent of the membership. The organisation of female labour
has tended to occur in those branches of the industry where men
and women are employed, whilst branches such as light clothing,
which has an almost entirely female labour force, remain slow to
unionise ('Garment Worker', May 1970). Men dominate the union
hierarchy both in the National Executive and at a local level
(Toynbee, 1980; 'Garment Worker', January 1976). The scope for
women's participation is limited even if they were interested. As
well as branch meetings being held at times which are difficult
for women to attend, the Community Development Project study
of North Shields noted that although five clothing firms in the
area had 900 union members, there was no union branch in North
Shields. Not surprisingly therefore, 'the union, despite membership, is weak, and on the whole makes little difference to these
women's working lives' (North Tyneside Community Development
Project, 1978, p. 42).
    At an official level the problem of low pay for women has not
gone unnoticed:

> Low pay for women is still regarded as being inherently a less
> serious problem than low pay among men, despite the fact that
> average earnings for women remain substantially below that for
> men. The assumption underlying such a view, that the man
> should be the major breadwinner in the household, is not com-
> patible with any belief in equal rights for everyone irrespective
> of sex ('Garment Worker', February 1977).

The NUTGW recognises the social problem of low wages amongst
women, the inadequacy of Equal Pay legislation, and how female
wages depress wage levels generally. All through the 1960s the
union put resolutions to the Trades Union Congress urging equal
pay for equal work, it has also been noted that 'the implementation
of the (Equal Pay) Act could often upset traditional differentials'
('Garment Worker', April 1975). Yet the only real strategy that
has developed against deskilling has been for skilled male labour
to struggle to differentiate itself from less skilled labour, to defend

skills by preserving pay differentials. Paradoxically, it is management who are undermining the difference between the pay of men
and women. This process, though, is occurring not through any
re-evaluation, or upgrading of women's work, but through technical innovation and the reorganisation of the labour process to
attack the skills of previously highly skilled men. The NUTGW
cannot both *significantly* improve women's pay rates and maintain
men's pay rates by maintaining differentials. Its commitment to
the latter implicitly accepts the distinction of men's and women's
rates and management's definition of women's work as being of
low skill value. Such a short-term strategy has long-term effects
for both men and women in the industry. If the union accepts the
rate for the job as, in effect, a 'woman's rate', it usually means
that the rate for the job has been set at a particularly low level,
and it becomes immaterial to management whether that job is performed by a man or a woman. As the NUTGW general secretary
(Jack MacGougan) recognised,

> If the reclassification of jobs in the industry brings about a
> situation where you have a rate per hour against an operation,
> be it male or female, as a minimum rate, then I think you could
> have this tendency, especially where there is a shortage of
> female labour and a paucity of male employment, for men to come
> into jobs now looked upon exclusively as women's ('Garment
> Worker', July 1970).

Pressing is an example of where this can happen. In factories
which have introduced automated pressing machines, pressing is
undertaken by both men and women earning equal rates of pay.
Yet this 'equality' comes about through a rather complex process.
Once pressing was men's work, but as it was rendered less skilled
through the introduction of machinery it increasingly became work
performed by both men and women - only women's rates of pay
were lower. Legislation for Equal Pay forced some rethinking of
this situation. Men were removed from the job, but then automated
pressing machines were introduced which 'killed' any basis for
comparison with the job of pressing as it had been previously
undertaken. These machines render pressing a machine-paced
operation which involves little more than machine feeding. Once
new gradings and new rates of pay were set for an essentially
new job, management re-established pressing as a job for both
men and women. In this instance, Equal Pay legislation has provided the imperative for new levels of rationalisation and further
deskilling.
    Equal pay legislation cannot be fully operable when it rests on
the principle of comparability alone. The NUTGW recognises the
inadequacy of legislation for securing equal pay for women and,
rather, argues that women's wages have to be improved through
collective bargaining ('Garment Worker', October 1977). Such
legislation assumes a levelling up with men, whereas the trend in
clothing has been to effect a levelling down of all labour to minimum

skill and wage rates. Employers need a formally segregated work force for as long as there is the possibility of comparability between low paid and high paid workers. Once rates have been set at low levels then segregation is not important. The clothing industry could not have afforded the implementation of equal pay in any real sense. At its present level of technical development it only survives because it can pay low wages. Equal pay, rather, has meant, for a time at least, a loss of men's jobs where men and women might have been employed alongside each other, for example on pressing, trimming and hand sewing (Roche, 1973, p. 204) and indicates some reasons for male trade unionists' apparently low commitment to equal pay for women.

Tracing the broad developments of the clothing industry in this way, indicates not only that a craft-based industry has been deskilled, but also how that has happened. The economic structure of the clothing industry has limited the choice of strategies open to management; the form of deskilling is specific to the industry. Or at least to industries with similar economic and structural features. Women are employed in the context of the cheapening of labour and the demand for female labour arises precisely where there is a greater than average demand for cheap labour - on those processes which are relatively labour intensive. This is certainly true for clothing (see also Peter Armstrong's discussion in this volume) and becomes almost a general criterion for locating women's work. Even in highly capitalised industries, such as engineering, women are to be found on those jobs which are difficult, or expensive to automate. Deskilling has occurred in the clothing industry, so far, without a major transition from a labour-intensive to a capital-intensive industry. The industry has always relied on women as cheap labour, but they have also been a direct agency of deskilling. As a form of female 'takeover' it gives rise to direct and obvious hostility towards women, and historically men have organised to keep women out of the industry (Taylor, 1979) and out of certain jobs. In some industries men's strategies of exclusion have been more 'successful' especially in those with high capital investment, although this may be because management can employ technical means for deskilling, whereas in clothing cheap labour has been the obvious and only management strategy. Early strategies of exclusion employed by male clothing workers (Boston, 1980, p. 164) have given way to unionisation but still men's defence of their skills is a contradictory procedure. As real skill differences are eroded, other forms of differentiation from unskilled labour are sought. Gender becomes a most obvious form of differentiation.

A NEED FOR NEW STRATEGIES

The failure of Equal Pay legislation is perhaps a false trail, with the more important question being why trade union organisation has not improved women's wages, either through active support

of the Equal Pay Act or through collective bargaining. Women
are drawn into production as cheap labour and in competition
with men. Women enter into a relation which not only exploits
their labour power, but which places them in an antagonistic
relation to men. Women enter production to perform the unskilled
and semi-skilled jobs that have been created by the extension of
the division of labour. The division of labour is not just a convenient separation of tasks but, as Braverman (1974, p. 125)
notes, 'divided and hostile' and men have always opposed and
sought to restrict the conditions of women's employment.' The
development of capitalist production on the basis of gender divisions has meant that no workers' struggle has ever been free of
these sexual politics' (Taylor, 1979, p. 33).

While there is mostly no real question of women directly replacing men in their jobs, there is an indirect process whereby, as
the labour process is restructured and transformed, there is
little comparability between old and new work methods, between
skilled and unskilled work, and between jobs which have been
traditionally designated as men's and women's work. As this transformation is brought about in part by the introduction of new
machinery, which changes the technical basis of the labour process, it appears to be the machine that eases women into men's
jobs. The typewriter enabled women to be employed to do much of
the work previously performed by male clerks; the introduction
of computer-based typesetting and compositing machines means
that women typists can do the work previously performed by
craftsmen printers ('Guardian', 9 July 1980).

In the clothing industry, skilled labour has tried to resist the
process of deskilling by resisting the introduction of less-skilled
labour, and sought to preserve skills and maintain wage differentials in the face of a trend which has the distinctive effect of
the homogenisation of labour. From this specific example more
general points can be made and particularly to question the value
of 'orthodox' strategies. Craft skill provided the basis for strong
labour organisation, but it is organisation, not skill per se, which
provides the possibilities of workers' control. As craft skill has
been undermined labour has had to find new bases for organisation.
High wages reflect some regaining of control, and strong organisation can survive the obsolescence of skills on which it is based
(Rubery, 1978, pp. 28,31). Exclusion and the preservation of
sectional interests, the defence of skill and differentiation, have
always been ways in which skilled workers have organised to
protect themselves. As a form of job control it is conservative
and gained at the expense of others. As Rubery points out, 'a
worker's main concern under competition is to obtain and keep a
job. Workers act defensively to protect themselves from the competition of the external labour market, to obtain job security and
higher wages, to the exclusion and detriment of those remaining
in the unorganised sector' (Rubery, 1978, p. 34).

As a strategy it has not been particularly effective, and, as
management take the offensive, skilled labour is increasingly under

threat from low-paid labour (Braverman, 1974, pp.392-95).
Paradoxically sectional union practice can facilitate this;

The *normal* activities of unions which necessitate established
bargaining relationships with employers, conciliation and compromise and the division of the working class along the lines of
sectional interests, clearly serve to strengthen rather than
weaken, capitalist relations of production (Clarke, 1977, p. 18).

It can be the case that organised labour endorses the creation of
a cheap, unskilled labour reserve (Herding, 1977, p. 260), out
of a short-term and contradictory strategy.

The use of women as a cheap labour reserve does give added
mileage to the struggle between management and skilled male
labour. Gender divisions outside of production already place wome
in a subordinate position to men, and this inequality gets reproduced within production itself where, albeit for different reasons,
both management and male labour have sought to preserve sexual
divisions. Skill is a social construction as well as being founded or
expertise, and when the differentiation of skilled and unskilled
labour is posed in terms of male and female labour, it has a particularly wide socal validation. Such differentiation has been a
form of trade union organisation by which male trade unionists
have both sought the restriction of women's employment and the
maintenance of a larger 'breadwinner's' wage for men (Barrett
and McIntosh, 1980; Humphries, 1977; Land, 1980; Rubery, 1978)
Certainly the differentiation of men as breadwinners has often
been a distinctive form of labour organisation in clothing (Taylor,
1979), an industry which rests on traditional attitudes, and,
even where there have been equal pay rates in operation, it has
been the criterion for the allocation of *more* work to men (Cunniso
1966, p. 195).

Once created as an extraneous category of labour, women can
be slipped onto certain jobs - unskilled, 'women's' jobs. It would
seem that organised male labour was content to see women con-
tained within an unskilled, low-paid and subordinate female ghetto
and to defend skills on the basis of the preservation of masculine
skills (Phillips and Taylor, 1980). The ghettoisation of female
labour, in the long term, facilitates a more general undermining
of skills and wage levels. Deskilling extends the possibilities of
using women's labour when they have already been established as
a low-waged group. This is partly why trade union strategies of
exclusion can be seen to give way to the extension of organisation
to the semi-skilled (Rubery, 1978, p. 31). Although women's
membership of trade unions is increasing, there is a big differenc
between membership and participation (as Judith Hunt stresses in
this volume), and it is increasingly clear that men in trade unions
are still primarily concerned with men's interests, rather than
women's or collective ones. As Rowbotham has stressed, 'the whol
orientation of the trade unions is masculine. It is only by a specia
effort that men remember women. The only guarantee women have

that their own interests will be considered is to organise as
workers and as women' (1973, p. 96).

The ethic of the survival of the fittest which seems to inform
much of trade union practice has led to a serious questioning of
what women can gain from trade union organisation and collective
bargaining (Campbell and Charlton, 1978). It has been suggested
that only a feminist incomes policy, specifically aimed at reducing
differentials and guaranteeing a basic wage, can really improve
women's economic position (Campbell, 1980). Although in principle
the trade union movement has not been opposed to a socialist
wage and a guaranteed minimum wage for all, under competitive
conditions it slides back into short-term strategies which gain for
some, the most strongly organised, the best, immediate deal.
Additionally, incomes policies since the war have actually been a
form of incomes control (Panitch, 1976, p. 4) and have not
challenged differentials (Pond, 1977), and it is not without reason
that the trade union movement remains resistant to the idea.

The causes of women's low pay do not really lie within the inad-
equacies of the Equal Pay Act 1975 as a piece of legislation, nor
within collective bargaining as a form of organisation. The problem
lies in a sexual division of labour that places women in a subordinate role. Whilst the material fact of women's dependency is
undermined by participation in paid work, it is ideologically reproduced within the organisation of the labour process itself.
Employers are keen to define women as dependent, marginal
labour as a justification of low wages, whilst organised male labour
preserve their 'breadwinner's' wage in relation to women's inadequate one. Women are employed on terms which place them in an
antagonistic relation to men, and yet men's defences against the
threat of cheap female labour operate divisively and *precisely*
reinforce the conditions which make women such a threat. It is
unlikely that skilled labour will subordinate their 'sectional
interests to wider class and social interests in the absence of an
alternative economic and social policy' (Eaton et al, 1975, p. 2).
Yet such alternatives do not materialise out of thin air but from
practices which do not accept such sectional interests but, rather,
challenge them. It is for women not just to challenge their subordination, but to develop a political practice which is not rooted
in conservative defences (women have little to defend) and which
will form a cohesive organisation against the creation and reproduction of those divisions that set men and women in opposition
to one another.

ACKNOWLEDGMENTS

I should like to acknowledge Tony Elger for his helpful comments
on earlier drafts.

NOTES

1   In the 1971 Census, 10 per cent sample, 'managers, foremen
    and supervisors' accounted for one quarter of male employees
    in the clothing industry.
2   Extensive changes in production methods were brought about
    by the war. The industry was required to make vast numbers
    of uniforms by government contract which brought about pre-
    viously unknown stability of demand. Rationing and the Govern-
    ment Utility Scheme meant that even 'civilian' garments were
    sufficiently streamlined to suit mass production. The labour
    supply was stabilised by the deployment of labour from less
    crucial industries (often married women). Government controls
    between 1942 and 1949 provided the basis for further develop-
    ments in work organisation and the use of machinery. The
    removal of controls by 1952 returned the industry to its charac-
    teristic state of crisis and instability (see Wray, 1957, pp.
    43-64).
3   The National Board for Prices and Incomes noted in 1968, 'our
    case studies have provided particularly striking evidence that
    management control of PBR (Payment by Results) is notably
    tighter where women predominate in the labour force. It
    appears that women have not subjected such systems to the
    same degree of pressure as have men'.

2 'IF IT'S ONLY WOMEN IT DOESN'T MATTER SO MUCH'

Peter Armstrong

Clive, the manager of Lancashire Electrical Fittings' moulding shop was watching a fitter put the finishing touches to a new machine for punching the flash from electrical socket mouldings. Not unaware of the implications of his work, the fitter looked up and asked, 'How many will this put out of work?' On being told that it would 'save' the work of two women the fitter consoled himself with the thought which forms the title of this paper 'Oh well, if it's only women it doesn't matter so much'.

A little later the six women who still performed flash removal operations by hand looked up from their work with some anxiety as the machine was lowered in position. 'You watch' said Clive in a confidential aside, 'they'll all work a bit faster now. They'll think their jobs might be automated too'. Sure enough one of the women subsequently asked 'They couldn't automate this, could they?' 'I don't know' replied Clive, clearly unwilling to drop a tactical advantage, 'you think of biscuit factories'.

What the women (and the fitter) were thinking of was not hypothetical biscuit factories but the flash trimming line itself. Over the last year the number of women employed there had been reduced from 35 to 6 ('He gets a feather in his cap upstairs for that'). Those who had left the line had either 'naturally wasted' or accepted alternative work in the firm's large (and exclusively female) assembly department. Of course the work previously done by 29 women had not simply vanished. Most of it was now performed automatically - and deafeningly - by vibratory flash removal machines and these, like the moulding machines themselves, were operated exclusively by men. Ironically the task of sorting batches containing defective mouldings which had previously been done by these women had recently been added to the workload of the male moulding operatives who had seemed uninvolved when the trimming line was originally run down. There were protests, of course, but they were ineffective. As one of the female trimmers put it - herself a former moulder and shop steward - 'They're bloody clueless. They just do anything they're told'.

In miniature this sequence of events involves the three themes which will be developed in the body of this paper. These are:

1 The segregation of work on the shopfloor, more especially the nature of recent developments.

2 The different characteristic deprivations of male and female work which arise from the pattern of segregation.

3 The implications for women's efforts to achieve equality at the workplace.

The information on which the discussion of these themes is based was originally gathered for a project on shopfloor industrial relations and therefore has its limitations. In total the author spent seven months in 1978/9 on full-time observational fieldwork in two factories in Greater Manchester: 'Moulded Footwear Limited' (MOFOL), which employed 350 manual workers in the manufacture of slippers, and 'Lancashire Electrical Fittings' (LEF) were 650 shopfloor workers produced light electrical fittings. In both factories women formed a two-thirds majority of the shopfloor workforce and although, as remarked earlier, their particular problems were not the primary topic of the research, one aspect of their situation was immediately apparent. Out of 1,000 shopfloor jobs in both factories only a dozen or so (the formation of aeriels at LEF) was performed by both men and women.

THE PATTERN OF WORK SEGREGATION

In both factories, then, three years after the passing of the Sex Discrimination Act, the segregation of manual work was virtually complete and constituted a taken-for-granted feature of factory life. At MOFOL, for example, it sometimes happened that one or two of the men who ran the automatic presses which moulded the soles onto the slippers would fail to turn up. This could cause the women who processed the men's output to run short of work and they were then either redeployed or sent home without pay, depending on the states of other departments. Even though the men's work was, by common consent, unskilled, no one raised the possibility of a woman taking over one of the presses (though, as will be seen, there were reasons why such a proposal would probably have encountered management resistance in any case). As Hakim (1979, p. 45) has observed, industry level statistics on the proportions of men and women engaged in various occupations very much understate the extent of segregation in individual establishments. Moreover they also fail to illuminate the important attitudinal question of how far different tasks have become identified as characteristically male or female.

The allocation of different types of work to men and women suggests the kind of differentiation of the workforce which has prompted the development of dual labour market theories. These theories visualise workers as confined to one of two distinct labour markets with little mobility between them. 'Primary sector' jobs require skill, dependability, or both. They are relatively secure, offer the possibility of promotion and are comparatively well paid. For some writers (e.g. Piore, 1975; Reich, Gordon and Edwards, 1980), the primary sector also includes an upper 'independent' sector consisting of clerical, technical and professional employees but since this paper is concerned only with conditions on the shopfloor, white-collar workers will be excluded from consideration.

In contrast to the primary sector, jobs in the 'secondary sector', are unskilled, without prospects, insecure and badly paid. In its original formulation (Gordon, 1972), dual labour market theory was used to explain the exclusion of the urban poor from primary-sector employment since these lacked, or were supposed to lack, the required skills and qualities of dependability. Later, Barron and Norris (1976) adapted the same argument to explain the fact that women too were excluded from the primary sector, adding that in their case the supposed option of depending on a husband's wage could be used to legitimise the low pay and insecurity characteristic of the secondary sector. 'If it's only women . . .'

Views differ on the origin of labour-market segmentation. According to dual labour market theories proper, it arose from the ability of large firms to invest in advanced technology and to exert substantial control over their product markets. What such employers required from their workers above all was stability and dependability. Their workers, being comparatively skilled, represented a considerable manpower investment and additionally (or alternatively, cf. Rubery, 1978), they controlled strategically vital processes. On this view the comparative security of primary-sector workers, their chances of promotion and their high wages relative to the secondary sector were seen as attempts by the employers, to 'buy' co-operation. No such strategy was necessary in relation to secondary-sector workers. Indeed, insecurity followed directly from the employers' need to adjust the labour force to an unstable product market. Moreover secondary-sector workers were unskilled and therefore easily replaceable from the ranks of the unemployed. On this view, the differentiation of the workforce results in the first place from a difference in their power in the market place, a view which is also consistent with the observation that, on the whole, it is primary-sector workers who possess the trade union strength to defend their interests.

What Rubery (1978) called the 'radical' view, however, also stresses the divisive potential of labour-market segmentation. In this aspect it serves the interests of capital by isolating secondary sector workers (who have the problems) from those in the primary sector (who have the strength) (Gordon, 1972; Reich, Gordon and Edwards, 1980). Again, writers such as Edwards (1975; 1980) and Friedman (1977), perhaps reacting to the artificiality of considering market relations in the abstract, have located the origin of segmentation in the different control strategies pursued by capital at successive stages of development. Whereas secondary-sector conditions correspond to a coercive strategy aimed simply at securing obedience, primary-sector conditions represent part of an attempt to enlist the workers' active co-operation under technical and economic conditions such that mere obedience is no longer enough. Although writers who take this approach are clearly observing the same phenomenon as dual labour market theorists, their work serves to emphasise that it is a change in the techniques of control which is at issue, not a diminution in its extent.

A final variation in interpretation is specific to the analysis of female subordination. Thus Rubery (1978) and Beechey (1978) propose an analysis of dual labour markets which pays far more attention to the role of male-dominated trade unionists in placing constraints on the pursuit of profit. On this view, segregation is seen partly as the outcome of attempts by men to defend themselves from the threat of competition from the potential 'reserve army of labour' constituted by women. In the work of Hartmann male trade unionists appear in a rather more offensive role. From the premise that the theoretical tendency of capitalism would be to reduce all labour to the same level, she deduces that it is largely men who are responsible for segregation as a result of their efforts to secure their own relatively favoured position (Hartmann, 1979a, p. 207).

Perhaps an inevitable feature of any debate conducted at such a level of generality is a certain confusion as to what are the actual characteristics of primary- and secondary-sector work - and, by implication, what types of work are denied to women. Whereas secondary-sector work is, by general consent, assumed to be unskilled, Piore (1975) has noted an association of secondary sector conditions with labour-intensive processes, which is not at all the same thing. It has also been noted (Piore, 1975; Edwards, 1980) that there is a correspondence between primary-sector conditions and capital-intensive processes, whereas the view that primary-sector workers represent a substantial manpower investment implies a differentiation by skill. Barron and Norris (1976) tend to use both defining characteristics as if they were interchangeable. More sensitive than most to the potential difference between skill and employment on capital-intensive operations, Rubery (1978) has argued that, in consequence of the overall tendency of machine technology to depress skill levels (cf. Braverman, 1974), the bargaining power of the skilled worker is being replaced by that of the controller of machines (both, presumably male). However, more may be involved here than the simple replacement of one source of bargaining power by another. These are, in principle, quite different bases of occupational segregation and might well be different in their consequences. Perhaps it is at this point that fieldwork at the shopfloor level can make a contribution.

In MOFOL a large majority of the men and in LEF a substantial minority of them could fairly be described as unskilled or, at most, semi-skilled machine operators. 'I could train a pair of chimpanzees to do this job' was one MOFOL foreman's way of encouraging two hard-pressed operatives, an anthropoid view of the work echoed by a shop steward who thought that 'One day they'll train baboons to do this job'. The case of the LEF moulding operatives was less clear-cut: although the moulding manager had created a short promotion hierarchy based on experience, the senior management, for obvious reasons, continued to maintain that all of the jobs were unskilled, as did the craft stewards who,

on one occasion, contemptuously put down the aspirations of the
moulders with the flattening comment, 'Get away with you, there's
a difference between skill and experience you know'. Objectively
the market situation of the LEF moulders was very different to
that of the craftsmen: whereas it was comparatively easy for the
management to recruit moulding operatives (for the dayshift at
least), the firm had (perhaps unwisely) offered a bounty to any
craftsman giving information which led to the recruitment of
another.

Thus although nearly all the male manual workers in both
factories (with the exception of a few labourers) could be classed
as primary-sector workers (in that their jobs were fairly secure
and comparatively well paid), they could nevertheless be classed
into two groups according to the basis of their 'privileged' position.
The first group were what might be called a 'traditional' male
elite of time-served craftsmen whose position was based on the
possession of a recognised skill. Alongside these was a group of
semi-skilled machine operatives whose relatively privileged position
appeared, as Rubery (1978) suggests, to be based on their control
of machine operations. In contrast to both groups of men, the
women in both factories were secondary-sector workers (relatively
low paid and insecure), employed for the most part on unskilled
operations which required only simple hand tools. The major –
and revealing – exception was in MOFOL's machining room where
120 women were employed on stitching together the upper parts
of slippers. In a purely technical sense the machines used by
these women were a good deal more complicated than the hand
presses operated by some of the men in the same factory. Besides
performing more demanding work than the other women, the
machinists were also better paid on the average and were, on the
evidence of the author's stay in the factory, rather less vulnerable
to redeployment, short time and redundancy. Moreover there
were, at the time of the research, other factories within fairly
easy reach advertising for 'skilled machinists' – despite the MOFOL
management's conviction that the work was not, in fact, skilled.

Superficially all this points to the conclusion that those engaged
in the traditionally female occupation of machining (cf. Goodman
et al., 1977, pp. 40-1) share some of the characteristics of primary-
sector workers. A comparison with the men in the same factory,
however, quickly dispels this illusion. Machinists are pieceworkers
and average wages can be deceptive. Although the quickest of
them might earn £80 per week (comparable to the male operatives
on 8 hour days) the slowest earned only £42 (comparable to women
elsewhere in the factory). Being in demand, no machinists were
made redundant or laid off during the research. On the other
hand, they had little job security in the sense that they were
moved about from task to task within the department, completely
at management discretion and despite any protests they might
make. Moreover it turned out on close examination that there *was*
an important difference between the work of the women machinists
and the male pressmen: despite the comparative simplicity of the

men's hand presses, just one of the eight moulds used in each
one of them cost more than an entire sewing machine. Generally
speaking, of course, the cost difference between the machinery
or tools used in other 'male' and 'female' processes was much
greater.

This points towards a reconsideration of the distinction between
primary- and secondary-sector work. Whilst it is perfectly true
that women tend to be excluded from work which is formally recognised as skilled (i.e. craft work), they are nevertheless to be
found performing work which is skilled in a real sense. And
whilst they also tend to be excluded from machine processes,
there are exceptions where the machinery involved is relatively
cheap. The segregation of shopfloor work would therefore appear
to have two aspects which have tended to become confused in the
literature on the segmentation of the labour force. Firstly there
is segregation by formally recognised skill. Secondly there is
segregation according to the level of capital investment involved.
Indeed at the industry level this has been confirmed by Bridges's
(1980) survey of American industry. Men tend to monopolise both
craft work *and* capital-intensive processes, whatever the level
of skill involved in the latter. Correspondingly women's work
tends to be unrecognised as skilled (whatever the actual levels
of skill) *and* of a labour-intensive kind (implying that complex
equipment may be involved, providing only that it is cheap).
Whereas segregation by formally recognised skill is more or less
traditional, in both factories there had been fairly recent inten-
sifications of segregation according to the level of capital investment per worker.

RECENT DEVELOPMENTS IN SEGREGATION

MOFOL's chief engineer could recall a time when the hand presses
were operated by women. Later, as business expanded, the output of the presses was increased by introducing a permanent male
nightshift thus increasing the return on the capital outlay represented by the presses. Later still 'The blokes got fed up with
working nights all the time so the women were phased out.' Mean-
while the labour-intensive operations of trimming and packing the
output of the presses continued to be performed by female dayworkers since more women could be employed with only a small
additional expenditure on equipment. In this instance the development of work segregation evidently followed from the firm's drive
to maximise the return on capital investment combined with the
constraints represented by 'protective legislation' on the one hand
and the unwillingness of the men to work permanent nights on the
other.

In LEF too the segregation of work in the moulding shop had
occurred within the memory of some of the workers. At one time
women had operated the moulding machines alongside men. Then,
as in MOFOL, output was expanded by operating the machines on

shifts and the female moulders were transferred to other departments ('We were told it was the morals law'), albeit retaining
their original grades. The pattern at LEF, however, differed
from that in MOFOL since it still included a permanent male nightshift. Obviously the removal of the women from the moulding
operation could not, in this instance, be attributed to male insistance on a share of the daywork. In these circumstances, why
should it still benefit an employer to move women off the dayshift?

In this connection official and semi-official publications on the
organisation of shiftwork reveal a significant change of heart
over the last few years. Thirteen years ago a government publication advocated, as a means of 'tapping' female labour, the use
of a double dayshift coupled with a permanent male nightshift
(Ministry of Labour, 1967, p. 6). Eleven years later, however,
the attractions of this arrangement had evidently declined, as
witness an Institute of Personnel Management publication (Walker,
1978, p. 5):

> Sometimes a group of male permanent night workers man
> machinery, which is operated during the day by women on
> a double day shift. *This leads to problems of equal pay for
> equal work.* (Emphasis added)

As Hakim (1979) has acidly observed, 'The extent to which it
has been possible to adjust pay structures and jobs to reduce the
effects of the (equal pay) act on women's earnings whilst, at the
same time, staying within the act is indeed noteworthy.' A number
of commentators (e.g. E.O.C., 1978a, p.11) have suggested that
equal pay legislation has contributed to occupational segregation,
and one can see what is meant, although it seems rather unfair
to blame the law for the consequences of the measures taken by
employers to evade it. As to why they should be particularly keen
to do so on capital-intensive processes, it will be recalled that it
is the reliability of the worker which is a priority here and it is
by now well established that employers believe women to be less
reliable than men (A. Hunt, 1975, pp. 13, 94).

Overall, then, the patterns of segregation in the two factories
had a great deal in common. Alongside the 'traditional' exclusion
of women from craft work there had recently developed, or intensified, a segregation in which men worked on capital-intensive
processes whilst women were relegated to labour-intensive operations. The dynamics of the process are fairly clear-cut. When
markets allow, the economics of any capital-intensive process
clearly favour a move to shiftwork, a pressure which is much less
where labour-intensive operations are concerned. Protective
legislation (or the unwillingness of employers to apply for exemp-
tion orders and thereby expose themselves to equal pay claims)
perhaps coupled with a disinclination on the men's part to work
permanent nights, then ensure that women are excluded from
capital-intensive operations.

THE INSECURITY OF WOMEN'S WORK

The redeployment of the women from the capital-intensive processes in LEF's moulding shop had its counterpart in MOFOL.
Indeed there were a dozen 'redundancies' on the day the author's
fieldwork started. These came about as a result of the closure of
a department employing mostly women on a labour-intensive process in which the sole of the slipper was cemented, rather than
moulded, onto the upper. In the words of a senior manager, 'They
priced themselves out of the market. I ask you; women like that
earning £80 per week?' and it was clear that in future the firm
intended to concentrate resources on the production of footwear
with moulded soles. 'All they see is those machines' grumbled one
of the older managers who had been heavily involved with the
cementing process. Whereas in LEF (and earlier in MOFOL itself)
the women had been moved directly off a capital-intensive process,
in this instance they had been displaced as a result of a rundown
in a labour-intensive process. Thus even at this stage one can
see two different sources of insecurity which disproportionately
affect women. Firstly they are vulnerable to removal from capital-
intensive operations, a process which by the time of the research,
had been virtually completed in MOFOL and LEF. Secondly, once
women are employed only on labour-intensive operations, they
become vulnerable to any switch of resources into existing or
additional capital-intensive operations. In the MOFOL case quoted
above, this came about as a result of disinvestment in a labour-
intensive operation but it could, as illustrated by the instance
with which this paper began, come about as a result of the replacement of a hand process by machinery. Notice that in LEF the flash
removal machines, which had eliminated most of the work previously done by 29 women, were operated by men.
    Besides their quite realistic fear of redundancy, the women on
MOFOL's trimming lines were subjected to short-term insecurities
which were clearly related to the labour-intensive nature of their
work. Within wide limits of output, most capital-intensive processes, if they run at all, need the same manning levels. However,
the volume of the labour-intensive work of processing the output
of capital plant varies, sooner or later, with the level of output.
In MOFOL, for example, there had to be enough women on the
trimming line to cope with the full output of the moulding machines
in case urgent orders were received. However, it quite often
happened that the machines ran under capacity. There might be
a shortage of orders, a machine could break down or, as one of
the men put it, 'Boddington's Ale wouldn't let me get up'. When
this happened, the women on the trimming lines would be redeployed or, more often, sent home without pay. In consequence
it was noticeable that the women would keep careful count of the
number of men coming on shift to see whether there would be
enough work to carry them through the afternoon.
    In fact short-time working is fairly common in the shoe industry
and there is provision for it in the relevant National Agreement.

In essence this states that the time lost need not be paid for,
provided that notification is given before the end of the previous
working day. Otherwise the affected workers are supposed to
receive their basic rates.

In MOFOL, however, the women were never paid for the lost
time even though the typical notice given was about half an hour.
But then most of the women were glad enough to get away on any
terms, especially on Friday afternoons since 'It gives you a lift
with the housework'. So any theoretical rights they had under
the National Agreement were of little account. Nevertheless supervisors had developed an elaborate ritual to ensure that the voluntary nature of the short time was well understood on all sides.
'What I do is I ask them if they want to go. Then I'm not telling
them, see?' explained one of them. Any remaining pockets of
resistance presented little problem. One manager outlined his
tactics thus, 'Right, she's playing awkward now so the next time
she wants to go along with the rest, I'll not let her'. 'It must be
a great sensation of power', grumbled one of the women when she
was 'kept in' in this manner. Evidently the mobilisation of women
workers against such short-term insecurities is considerably
handicapped by the pressure of their outside commitments (see
the chapters in this volume by Caroline Freeman and Marilyn
Porter) whilst the position of any individual dissidents is decisively
undermined by the acquiescence of the majority.

This, then, points to a third form of insecurity suffered by
female workers, which corresponds in some degree to their role
as an irregularly employed 'stagnant reserve army of labour' (cf.
Simeral, 1978, p. 176). Whereas short-run fluctuations of production or demand may have relatively little effect on the capital-
intensive operations run by men, the women's labour-intensive
operations bear the full brunt. Note, however, that this kind of
insecurity will remain latent where, as at LEF during the research,
production levels remain stable.

Much of the vulnerability of women workers clearly derives in
the first place from the imperatives of capital. Thus the relegation
of women to labour-intensive processes results from the push to
maximise the return on capital invested as refracted by protective
legislation, by men's unwillingness to work permanent nights and
fuelled by a belief on the part of managers that, if wages are to be
equal, male workers on capital-intensive processes are likely to
offer greater reliability for the money.

Once women are confined to labour-intensive processes, they
will then be disproportionately exposed to their employers'
attempts to minimise wage costs. It is here that employers can
least afford to 'carry' workers if there is a temporary or longer-
term downturn in the market. It is here, where wage costs comprise a high proportion of the total, that the impact of competition
from low-wage countries (a problem both for MOFOL and LEF)
will be felt most keenly and it is this sector which is permanently
vulnerable to the threat of further mechanisation (see Angela
Coyle's discussion of these constraints in the clothing industry).

The pressure to minimise wage costs in labour-intensive processes was well illustrated by another aspect of management policy common to both factories: that of maintaining their freedom to move female workers wherever and whenever they choose. Thus in MOFOL a manager expostulated, '"My work?" There's no such thing as "my work"', and in LEF one explained that, 'We won't recruit anyone from F - if we can help it. You've practically got to fill in a form to move anybody there'. Indeed this aspect of female workers' insecurity could fairly be described as a self-conscious management policy.

It is not, of course, being argued that segregation by skill, differences in trade union strength and an ideology legitimising insecurity for women workers are not also important. The point being made is that even if none of these other factors existed, the continuing development of segregation according to the level of capital investment per worker would still create disproportionate insecurity for women workers. It is therefore a problem which needs to be recognised and dealt with.

It is interesting in the light of these observations to return to the question of the security of male primary-sector workers. The conventional view is that this arises from the employers' need to 'buy' co-operation since primary-sector workers are either skilled or responsible for expensive plant and are, in any case, organised into strong trade unions. However, it has already been suggested that the bargaining power of controllers of machines is not equivalent to that of skilled workers, as Rubery (1978) implies. Whereas skilled men can be difficult to replace (remember the 'head hunting' bonus at LEF), the operators of complex machinery may not be ('I could train a pair of baboons to do this job'). Once a clear conceptual distinction has been drawn between skilled work and that involved with the operation of capital plant (which may or may not be skilled), it will be realised that the employers' priority in relation to the latter is to keep production going, not necessarily to retain the worker's loyalty or even the worker himself. And whilst high wages, security and generally favourable treatment *may* be an appropriate tactic (cf. Blauner's (1964) account of minimally alienated *male* process workers), it will also be realised that there are more ways of killing a cat than choking it with cream. In the short term, for example, some of MOFOL's reluctant moulding operatives may have been amused and flattered by the firm's practice of sending surplus foremen round to their homes in order to cajole them into work. In the longer term, however, the firm guaranteed their 'security' of employment by insisting that they sign new contracts of employment in which they undertook to work 12-hour shifts and nights as and when required. Two men who refused on the grounds that they had 'gentlemen's agreements' that they would only be required to work days were promptly made redundant.

The same unattractive face of employment 'security' threatened to appear at LEF where the sporadic attendance of some of the men on nightshift was causing problems for the moulding shop manager. 'I can only think they're paid too much if they can afford to stop off' he mused on one occasion, half to himself. Later he flirted with the idea of 'reinterpreting' the nightshift allowance as an attendance bonus, although this particular proposal was quietly dropped after a very oblique exchange with the senior steward. What these thoughts indicate is that the manager's priority was to ensure that the men worked as and when the economics of his capital plant dictated and that buying their loyalty was only one means of achieving this. Although kindness may occur, simply because it is a less costly option on a capital-intensive process than on a labour-intensive one it is important not to lose sight of management's ultimate interests in the matter.

A NOTE ON DIFFERENTIALS

These thoughts on the nature of the employment security enjoyed by unskilled male plant operatives prompt a parallel re-opening of the question of their pay differentials over women workers. Before proceeding it should be pointed out that comparisons of pay rates within the two factories are necessarily imprecise due to individual variations. In MOFOL most of the workers were on piecework and, in the extreme case of the machine room, there could be a two-to-one variation in earnings between women working side by side on the same job. Variations in LEF were on a smaller scale and derived from a measured daywork system based on time study (except - perhaps significantly - in the moulding shop where men were employed; there the manager had excluded the time-study engineers and job grading was by management discretion).

With the foregoing reservations then, the wages of full-time female workers in LEF ranged from £46.50 to £52. The male moulding operatives took home between £72 and £108 and craftsmen earned about £90 (all figures exclusive of bonus). However, the women's and the craftsmen's earnings both refer to a 39-hour week and the craftsmen's differential was explicitly justified (or rationalised) by a claim of skilled status. The moulding operatives, on the other hand, earned their £72 by working four 12-hour day-shifts or their £108 by working four 12-hour (permanent) nights. Since LEF operated a grading system, it is readily possible to calculate the notional wage for a moulding operative on a standard 39-hour week. When this is done the notional wages lie between £47.37 (for a new recruit) to £53.50 (for an experienced man, able to set and adjust moulding tools). Although these figures are not very different from the women's actual wages, the calculation is *not* claimed to demonstrate the absence of discrimination since it might well be argued that the overtime and nightshift premiums are excessive and, in any case, are not available to women as a result of the firm's policies and/or protective legislation. What the figures *do* demonstrate is the extent to which the wages of the

unskilled or semi-skilled operators of capital plant have been
made conditional on the acceptance of overtime and shiftwork. At
the price levels of 1978/79 the only shopfloor workers in LEF who
could reasonably expect to keep a family on the wage earned in a
39-hour week were the craftsmen. As Beechey (1978) has pointed
out, the prevalent definition of the female wage as secondary
allows employers to pay a wage below the amount required to keep
a family. But by the same token the notional 39-hour wage for a
male moulding operative (a wage moreover which was actually
received by at least one day labourer), was also below that required to keep a family. That was one reason why the 39-hour
wage for the operatives is notional. The other reason, of course,
was that as in MOFOL, the men were simply not given the option
of working a flat week on days.

To a lesser extent the same pattern could be discerned at
MOFOL, though in this case it was partially masked by the piecework payment system and the consequent large variations in individual earnings. Whereas the women on the slipper trimming lines
earned between £38 and £55 for a 40-hour week, those in the
machining room earned anywhere between £40 and £80. A flat
week's wages for maintenance craftsmen was £78 whilst the craft
workers on piece rates in the 'clicking' department, where the
upper parts of the slippers were stamped from rolls of synthetic
material, could earn between £90 and £120, both for a 40-hour
week on days. The semi-skilled men operating either the hand
presses or the automatic presses which moulded the soles onto
the slippers took home between £85 (for a 40-hour week on dayshift) and £140 (for a 56-hour week on nights). On paper the
semi-skilled men's dayshift wage represents a considerable differential over most of the women since only £3 of the £85 was paid
as a shiftwork premium. However it needs to be remembered that
this figure could only be earned by undertaking to work 12 hour-
shifts and nights as required. Despite the rulings of industrial
tribunals that shiftworking by men does not itself justify a differential on basic rates, the true differential 'earned' by the pressmen as a result of their commitment to shift work can only be
realistically ascertained by comparing male dayworkers of the
same skill level elsewhere in the same factory. Here there were
two options; the £45 earned by day labourers or the £60 earned
in the hot, dusty conditions of the firm's compound mixing room.
Clearly the first option was impossible and the second, as was
forcibly pointed out to the author, was very marginal as a wage
on which to keep a family. In this connection it was noticeable
both in MOFOL and LEF that the low-paid day labourers tended
either to be young men still living at home or elderly men whose
children had left home. Unlike LEF then, MOFOL's male operators
of capital plant received a considerable differential over most of
the women. However, an examination of the non-shiftwork alternatives available within the same firm to men of comparable skill
level makes it clear that the acceptance of 12-hour shifts and
nightwork whenever management required was these men's only

means of earning a living wage within that firm. At the same time
it should also be pointed out that for all but a handful of the most
skilled machinists, the women had no means at all of earning a
living wage within that firm. Moreover it was clearly going to stay
that way as was emphasised by 'remedial' action taken by the
management when a woman about to be married pulled out all the
stops in an effort to save something for the occasion and suc-
ceeded in earning roughly the same as the pressmen. ('We'll have
to look at this piece-rate of yours again Mary. We can't have a girl
of 21 earning £120 per week'.)

Overall it is reasonably clear that whilst the craftsmen's differential over women workers is a real one, that of the unskilled or
semi-skilled operators of capital plant depends on working shifts,
nights, long hours of overtime or a combination of these. Nor is
the differential an option as far as most of the men are concerned.
The same sexist ideology which legitimises the payment of low
wages to women on the grounds that they should depend on their
husbands for the main wage also saddles their husbands with the
task of earning that main wage. For those lacking craft skills
this responsibility has become a means of binding them to the time
scale dictated by the economics of the capital-intensive operations
on which they are employed. In that respect it is simply another
aspect of the 'security' discussed earlier.

RELATIONSHIPS WITHIN THE WORKFORCE

All theories of the segmentation of the labour force agree that it
serves to undermine the workers' potential for solidarity. But
whereas dual labour market theories emphasise the *divergent*
interests of the two sectors in relation to capital, feminist writers
tend to stress the *conflicting* interests of men and women in the
competition for primary-sector work (e.g. Hartmann, 1979a, p. 230).
The one perspective implies a basic relationship of indifference
and the other, one of hostility.

Provided hostility is understood in this sense of conflicting
interests, rather than as an actual attitude, there is little doubt
that it played some role in the recent intensification of segregation
at MOFOL. There the men on permanent nights, through the
intermediary action of management, gained for themselves the
women's dayshift on a capital-intensive operation. In LEF, on
the other hand, the men's role seems to have been more passive
since a permanent male nightshift remained in operation.

For what it is worth, indifference rather than hostility best
describes the prevailing current relationships between men and
women in the two factories. For example the fitter who thought
that 'if it's only women it doesn't matter so much' was reasoning
his way out of an uncomfortable concern that his work was being
used to destroy women's jobs. He was not congratulating the
management for doing so. However, it needs to be stressed that
this lack of overt hostility towards women existed in a context

where segregation was already an accomplished fact. Neither of
the managements had made any move to change this state of
affairs and nor would it have been in their interests to do so.
There is therefore no way of knowing how the men might have
reacted.

In both factories the segregation of work and the men's lack
of concern with the women's problems (despite overlapping union
membership) was so taken for granted that it took some effort of
imagination to visualise the possibilities for solidarity which
remained unrealised. In MOFOL's 'clicking' department, for
example, the male craftsmen had evolved a one-out-all-out rule
in order to cope with short-time working, and a rota for transfers
out of the department. They explained with some pride that these
restrictions forced the management to organise the work more
efficiently and also prevented victimisation. Yet the male clickers
were laid off and transferred far less frequently than the women
alongside them who sorted and packed their output and it occurred
to no one that the protection of the one-out-all-out rule should
extend to them. Thus one of the clickers could boast that 'We're
our own union down here', whilst his female colleagues continued
to be laid off or redeployed entirely at management discretion.

Here the indifference was that of primary-sector workers, as
conventionally understood, towards the secondary sector. However,
once it is clear that the part of the primary sector which consists
of the semi-skilled operatives of capital plant has its own characteristic problems, it will be realised that indifference can cut two
ways. Although MOFOL's pressmen were uninvolved whilst the
women who processed their output were repeatedly laid off or
transferred to other departments, they had difficulties of their
own. Their nightshift consisted of four 12-hour nights ending
at 6 a.m. on the Friday. They were then required to come in for
a further 8 hours from 2 p.m. to 10 p.m. on the same Friday.
'Everyone hates the doublers', explained their shop steward. 'By
the time you've got home and had something to eat you only get
four hours' sleep before it's time to get up again. You come in like
a zombie.' However, his efforts to mobilise on the issue were
entirely confined to the pressmen themselves, despite the fact that
the support of the women (machinists in that instance) had, in the
past, proved decisive for a group of low-paid male workers who
had walked out of the firm's millroom in a pay dispute. Perhaps
because of the pressmen's sense of isolation, the steward was not
finding it easy to get them to act on the issue. 'All they've got
to do is not come in one Friday' he explained, 'No strike or anything - but they won't see it.' In other words, whilst the women
suffered from the characteristic insecurity of labour-intensive
processes the men were subject to the characteristic demanding
time scale of capital-intensive operations. Neither party was
involved in the other's problems or even gave much sign of being
aware of them. Whereas craft workers might be seen as a privileged
stratum in relation to women and therefore as lacking an interest
in mutual support, the semi-skilled plant operatives can also be

seen simply as another group of workers with their own characteristic problems. This points towards the possibility of sharing
the problems and thereby minimising them as well as to the possibility of combining against employers to overcome them.

Before pursuing this line, it is worth looking at another possibility opened up by the complex nature of contemporary work
segregation: namely that women might advance their interests
by an alliance with one category of male workers against the
other. In fact this happened at LEF and it well illustrates the
possibilities and limitations of such an approach. The occasion
was a disproportion in the bonus payments received by craftsmen
on the one hand and by women and semi-skilled male plant operatives on the other. As it happened the women and the semi-
skilled plant operatives were also organised by the same trade
union (GMWU) whereas the craftsmen were members of AUEW.
Thus the alliance depended on a somewhat fortuitous coincidence
of interests and in any case was on an issue some way removed
from the fundamental problems of work on labour-intensive
operations.

To begin more or less at the beginning, the firm's bonus system,
based on the output of assembled units, had been introduced in
three stages: the first for assembly workers (all female), the
second for the sections which manufactured certain components
for assembly (predominantly female but with a minority of male
moulding machine operatives) and the third for craftsmen (all
male). Principally through a management miscalculation, the
craftsmen's bonus was soon running way ahead of the others
(typically £15 per week as against £2). Eventually this provoked
a stoppage by the female assembly workers 'to show that lot in
there who earns the bonus'. This prodded management into re-
opening the bonus as an issue and, as a result, the craftsmen
were persuaded that all three schemes should pay into a common
'pot' which would then be shared out again on the basis that
craftsmen would receive a 90 per cent differential over the rest.
Although this was still a considerable differential, the craftsmen
had, as they saw it, voluntarily given something up since the
pooling agreement meant a reduction in their own bonus payments.
Accordingly they were later disgusted when the 90 per cent differential itself was challenged.

The occasion of this was a threat of industrial action from the
white-collar staff whose (separate) bonus scheme had failed to
pay out. The company then proposed to unravel the whole situation by renegotiating a factory-wide bonus scheme on a common
footing. In the run-up to this negotiation the forceful, influential
(and female) senior GMWU steward widely propagandised the idea
of a flat-rate bonus, in which demand she was supported by the
men in the moulding shop. Thus the craftsmen, who were initially
adamant in their insistance on retaining the 90 per cent differential, found themselves confronted by an alliance between female
workers and the male moulding shop operatives (not to mention
the white-collar staff). In view of their earlier concession the

craft stewards saw this as a stab in the back. 'WE HELPED YOU', shouted one of them in one of the negotiations and the issue quickly became defined in wholly divisive terms. The craft stewards' 'I don't care what the bonus level is, we're going to keep that differential' was matched by almost identical statements from the senior GMWU steward in favour of flat-rate distribution. In this context it was a simple matter for the personnel director to sit back and enunciate the then fashionable philosophy of kitty bargaining - 'OK it's your bonus, how you divide it is up to you' - and later to present his own preference for a payout proportional to each person's earnings as a reasonable compromise. Despite their solidarity, the craftsmen were always on a loser. Whereas it was strategically rumoured that the firm was thinking of contracting out the craftsmen's work, they could scarcely contemplate accumulating a pile of unassembled components, still less could they afford to have the expensive moulding machines standing idle. Though the male moulders were few in number, their support considerably reinforced the women's position.

From the women's point of view this was undoubtedly a victory, for whilst the settlement fell short of their stated aims they nevertheless achieved an increase in bonus. However, they did so wholly at the expense of the craftsmen who, on this occasion, had originally been no more than the innocent beneficiaries of a management error. Throughout many weeks of negotiation, the only person who raised the possibility of repairing the management error by increasing the overall size of the bonus 'pot' was the GMWU district official, but the on-site representatives were, by then, too concerned with the question of distribution to take up this additional theme. On this occasion at least, the idea that women should use the potential of an alliance with male plant operatives to mount an attack on the 'privileges' of male craft workers seems to have served the interests of capital quite as effectively as labour-market segregation itself. Apart from which, such an alliance depends on a chance coincidence of interests and cannot, therefore, concern the problems which are characteristic only of the unskilled, labour-intensive work performed by women. There is however the possibility of a more fruitful form of alliance.

It seems clear that the mutual ignorance and indifference which exists between semi-skilled male plant operatives and women workers stems ultimately from the fact that neither group directly experiences the characteristic problems faced by the other. If this is the case the obvious way of creating a natural solidarity on these issues would be to ensure that both groups *do* share the other's problems and this in turn implies some form of work sharing. Short of some cataclysmic transformation of family life, it seems unrealistic and unreasonable to propose that women should take a share of night work. Equally it is unrealistic to call for a total abolition of shiftwork this side of the abolition of competitive capitalism (cf. Coyle, 1980, pp. 10, 11). What does seem possible in the short term is for men to run the capital plant during the night and to transfer onto labour-intensive operations for their dayshifts.

Women could take over the capital plant for a double dayshift, working a rota system with labour-intensive operations, assuming, as seems typical, that the number of jobs of this latter type is greater than those on capital plant. This would offer women at least a share in the security of capital intensive work whilst the female double dayshift would open up the possibility of a normal existence to some men presently working permanent 12-hour nights - and if that arrangement exposed the fact that the rates of pay for such work were really quite low, that might not, in the long run, be such a bad thing.

Despite the rhetoric of job enrichment, employers might well resist work-sharing proposals on these lines. Depending on the actual skill level of the jobs involved there would be extra training costs, as against which the employer would gain considerable insurance against turnover and absenteeism. Then again there might be 'problems with equal pay' but so, if the act is ever to mean anything, there should be. From the point of view of this paper however, the real point is to press for some reversal of the recent increase in work segregation before the sex-typing of light assembly work and the operation of heavy plant takes too firm a hold.

ACKNOWLEDGMENTS

The fieldwork for this paper was performed during a project on shopfloor industrial relations sponsored by the SSRC and directed by Professor J.F.B. Goodman to whom thanks are due. Thanks are also due to Theo Nichols.

3 CONTEMPORARY CLERICAL WORK: A CASE STUDY OF LOCAL GOVERNMENT

Rosemary Crompton, Gareth Jones and Stuart Reid

INTRODUCTION

In this chapter we examine aspects of the work and work situation of female clerical workers.

It is important, but obvious, to note that our work does include women. Lockwood's classic, 'The Blackcoated Worker' (1966) gives them little attention; women clerical workers are excluded from Stewart, Prandy and Blackburn's (1980) study, and Goldthorpe's (1980) detailed study of social mobility, occupational and class structure. This is surprising, for while male clerks in 1951 were 143 per cent of male clerks in 1911, female clerks in 1951 were 781 per cent of the 1911 figure. Further, by 1951 women constituted 58.8 per cent of all clerks (Routh, 1980). Stewart and his colleagues estimate that this figure has risen to 70 per cent (p. 93). In 1971 clerks and cashiers made up 17.5 per cent of all working women, while typists, shorthand writers and secretaries made up a further 8.7 per cent (Bird, 1980). These changes have been taking place against a background of increasing numbers of women in employment. Women clerical workers seem to deserve some attention, not only because they constitute a large and growing section of the workforce but also because their experience of work must relate to important questions in class theory, the study of social mobility and the sociology of occupations.

Secondly, we should note that initially our emphasis was on women while employed and in particular on the nature of the tasks they carried out. There is a general scarcity of empirical material in this area. However, women's domestic roles have a major impact on their employment, and so far as clerical work is concerned this relationship has two elements. Firstly, it affects the patterns of grading and career development, such that women are disadvantaged in the pursuit of promotion by their real and felt domestic commitments. Secondly and partly in consequence of the first relation, the type of work they carry out is also affected. However, this latter relationship is complex. While it is probably true that women often perform fairly routine and menial clerical tasks, close examination of their work demonstrates that women also carry out more responsible and diverse work while occupying low clerical grades. We will try to illustrate these two relations in our analysis of the empirical material.

The data we use was collected in 1980 as part of a larger project on the contemporary work situation of clerical employees. Our method was that of the intensive case study. We studied clerical

employment in four departments of a provincial local authority.
We obtained basic data on all 358 employees in these departments,
including clerical, administrative and managerial employees, giving
details of age, gender, length of service, grade, job moves with
their current employer, level of pre- and post-entry qualifications
and previous employment.[1] Secondly, we carried out unstructured
interviews with managerial and administrative personnel in each
department. These supplied a managerial account of the way each
department functioned and the place of clerical workers within
this context. We also obtained the 'official' account of promotion
prospects for clerical workers. Finally, we carried out interviews
of about 40 minutes, using a schedule, with 86 clerical workers,
53 of whom were women. The selection of interviewees was not
random but reflected the grading structure of each department.
The interviews covered the nature of the work, promotion, supervision, impact of mechanisation and trade unionism. We concentrate
here on two themes: the nature of the work and the question of
female promotion. The former raises questions about occupational
classifications, and in particular the problematic nature of the label
'clerical work' which we take to be important in the context of recent analyses of clerical workers referred to earlier. The latter
highlights a central theme of this volume: the extent to which
women are seriously disadvantaged as employees. Clearly, a number
of other issues and questions remain unexamined, for example, the
effects of mechanisation and computerisation on clerical work, and
the extent of women's involvement in union affairs. (Aspects of these
topics are discussed by Jackie West and Judith Hunt in this volume.)

A method such as ours has both advantages and disadvantages.
We feel that we have a fairly full and detailed picture of the nature
of clerical work in this organisation; of career expectations, career
realities and of the place of women in the social organisation of the
clerical work. However, our focus in this paper is rather narrow,
our respondents are located in one particular section of economic
activity, and are public rather than private sector employees. (In
the absence of complete figures, NALGO estimate that 70 per cent
of Clerical grades in local government are filled by women). Our
study is also located in a particular local labour market, in a
regional centre in the East of England. In many respects the labour
market is rather like that in other provincial centres (Bird, 1980,
p. 29, Table 10).[2]

The following discussion will show that, in the main, women
clerks are not promoted and that the grading structure works
against certain categories of women workers. However, in the
context of this book, we would stress that our respondents constitute a relatively advantaged section of the female labour force.
Despite the scale of government cuts, jobs in local government are
still relatively secure. Further, there is some pressure on public
employers to act in accordance with current employment legislation,
to honour nationally agreed salary rates and to enter into negotiation with a union which represents a large proportion of clerical
workers in local government.

The first section of our analysis deals with the recruitment of clerical workers and a comparison of the career-potential of men and women.

RECRUITMENT, QUALIFICATIONS AND CAREERS

The 358 employees for whom we gathered some information were almost evenly divided on the basis of gender (52 per cent men, 48 per cent women). However, whereas 78 per cent of the women were on Clerical grades, this applied to only 29 per cent of the men. The first task we set ourselves, therefore, was to give an account of the processes which resulted in this particular gender/ grade structure. In all of the departments we studied a full career hierarchy was available - that is, it was (theoretically) possible to rise from Clerical Officer (CO) to Principal Officer (PO). Why, therefore, had women not experienced this career progression?

Three major factors were associated with promotion to higher- graded posts. These were firstly, formal qualifications (both pre- and post-entry into full-time employment); secondly, length of (unbroken) service with the local authority - this was especially important at the Administrative, Professional and Technical (AP) grades; and thirdly, geographical mobility - this was especially important at PO grades. Although some women did complain of overt discrimination, the possible effect of this seemed relatively insignificant when compared to the impact of the three factors noted above. It was apparent that many women found it impossibly diffi- cult to combine what may be termed 'promotability' in the work role with the domestic roles of wife and mother.

Qualifications
Recent research indicates that, when career progression is taken into account, income levels vary positively with educational levels attained (Stewart et al., 1980 - it should be noted that this evidence relates to men only). If we take grade as an approximate indicator of income, Table 3.1 demonstrates that levels of pre- entry qualification rise steadily with grade.

What also emerges very clearly is that women are less well- qualified than men, and their concentration in the Clerical category - indeed, no women had achieved PO level and only four Senior Officer (SO). The association between grade level and post- entry qualifications is even more marked, as can be seen from Table 3.2.

The proportions with no post-entry qualifications decline sharply from Clerical through to PO grades, and 68 per cent of PO grades (all of whom are men) have professional or equivalent qualifications Women are much less likely to possess post-entry qualifications than men, and where they do occur, these are likely to be secretarial.

It would appear, therefore, that the lower grade levels charac- teristic of the women in our study may effectively be 'explained'

Table 3.1   Grade by highest pre-entry qualifications: men and women (%)

| Grade: | Men | | | | Women | | |
	Clerical	AP	SO	PO+	Clerical	AP	SO * (numbers)
None	11	5	6	3	24	20	0
CSE	3	5	0	0	18	0	0
GCE 'O'	44	41	18	20	29	27	0
GCE 'A'	17	16	24	23	13	13	(2)
Degree	0	2	29	20	1	7	(2)
School Certificate	17	30	18	26	0	20	0
Higher School Certificate	3	0	6	3	8	0	0
City and Guilds/OND	–	0	0	3	2	0	0
Other	6	2	0	3	5	13	0
No.	100 (36)	100 (44)	100 (15)	100 (35)	100 (84)	100 (15)	(4)

* There were no women in the Principal Officer (PO) category.

Table 3.2   Grade by post-entry qualifications: men and women (%)

| Grade: | Men | | | | Women | | |
	Clerical	AP	SO	PO+	Clerical	AP	SO (numbers)
None	67	38	25	12	64	42	(2)
Local government clerical	3	2	31	3	1	0	0
Secretarial	–	–	–	–	18	42	0
Clerical (RSA, etc.)	–	5	–	–	8	8	0
ONC, CMA, etc. (non-professional)	8	30	19	18	8	8	0
HNC, CIPFA, etc. (professional)	3	13	13	68	0	0	(2)
Further academic	11	8	13	0	1	0	0
Services qualifications	8	5	0	0	0	0	0
Total	100	100	100	100	100	100	100

by their lack of qualifications. This kind of evidence would seem to confirm suggestions that women, qua women, are effectively part of a 'secondary' labour force, recruited to carry out 'the most menial clerical tasks with limited opportunities for promotion' (Stewart et al., 1980, p. 94). This explanation, although valid to a certain extent, is not, however, sufficient. For various reasons – which we discuss below – women clerks do not achieve promotion, but to describe their work as 'menial' is – in the local authority context at any rate - seriously mistaken.

Recruits to local authority Clerical grades at or about the
school-leaving age are normally expected, though not required,
to have at least three 'O' levels, or, less frequently, 'A' levels.[3]
In practice, departmental managers expressed a preference for
five 'O' levels in recruits of school-leaving age. The young recruit
with a number of 'O' levels - or possibly 'A' levels - is normally
expected to make a career in local government service.

In fact, the proportion of boys and girls achieving five or more
'O' level passes is, and always has been, relatively similar (Byrne,
1978). Among our population there were as many well-qualified
young women (17 with 'O' level and 7 with 'A' level aged under
25) as young men (12 with 'O' level and 10 with 'A' level under
25). In addition, there were no gender variations by grade
amongst this younger, qualified age group - that is, young women
were not doing noticeably worse (and if anything slightly better)
than young men in career terms. In respect of the labour pool
which may be described as 'the bright school leaver', young
women do not, on our evidence, comprise a 'secondary' labour
force.

However, we did identify one clear example of the recruitment
of young women which would correspond to what Gordon (following Kerr) has termed 'balkanisation' - that is 'defining different
clusters of jobs for which they (the employers) establish quite
different entry requirements' (Gordon, 1972). This was in data
preparation, i.e. keypunch operators. Although data preparation
'girls' need not necessarily be young, in practice the majority
were. Formal academic qualifications were regarded as largely
unnecessary (the most common was CSE) - what mattered was
whether or not the girl had the mechanical aptitude to enable her
to maintain the required rate of depressions per hour. Recruitment was highly informal, often through friendship and family
networks. Indeed, of the 10 data preparation operators and supervisors we actually interviewed, 6 had obtained their jobs in this
way. The women recruited to these jobs did not expect any promotion, neither were they expected to be promoted. Some women
saw the situation very clearly:

'[There's] not much chance of promotion in our office - elsewhere
staff can go on day-release and so on, get promoted that way.
[Here you] have to wait till someone leaves.'

The women's expectations reflected the reality of the situation -
only 2 of the 10 we interviewed actually *wanted* to be promoted,
the others making comments such as:

'I have had the chance (because the supervisor left) to become
senior operator - but no one was keen to take it - senior operators *have* to be in at certain times.'

'I'm not adventurous - the sort of person who just rides along
with the tide - I can't be bothered.'

Moving up from the youngest age group, however, the picture
changes considerably. Firstly, whereas women outnumbered men
in the under-25 age category (43 women as opposed to 27 men),
men predominate in the 25-35 age group (44 men as opposed to
20 women). This reflects, of course, the fact that women of this
age are less likely to be in paid employment because of child-rearing.
Secondly, men begin to draw ahead of women in terms of qualifications (particularly at degree level). In this age group, 20 men
had 'O' levels, 11 'A' levels, and 8 a degree, whereas the numbers
of women were, respectively 9, 7 and only 1.

These characteristics reflect the different levels of formal
educational attainment between the sexes in the population as a
whole. Boys take more subjects than girls at 'A' level, and proportionately more boys than girls proceed to university education
(Byrne, 1978). There are, therefore, more men than women available in the 'degree pool'. We have already noted that the association between grade levels and post-entry qualifications (which
are invariably taken part-time) was even more marked than that
between grade and pre-entry qualifications. The importance of
part-time further education (FE) to what may be loosely termed
'middle-class' career development is being increasingly recognised
(Stewart et al., 1980; Raffe, 1979). Although more women than
men participate in FE as a whole, this participation is overwhelmingly restricted to typing and secretarial training – which, as we
have seen in Table 3.2, hardly constitutes a passport to upward
job mobility (see also Benet, 1972; McNally, 1979). It is the
'courses for intermediate and advanced diplomas and certificates
in insurance, banking, accountancy, (and) business administration' which 'depend on day release *over eighteen;* and here
men outnumber women by up to 100 to one . . . men receive
proportionately more release by employers from 18-21 for *career-
based* vocational courses while investment in young women over
eighteen drops dramatically and proportionately more, for the key
years of 19-20 – and thereafter' (Byrne, 1978, p. 197).

Again, these features are reflected in our sample, for only 2 of
the women had obtained relevant post-entry qualifications (i.e.
Clerical examinations, ONC Business Studies, Accountancy, etc.),
as opposed to 29 of men aged between 25 and 35. This doubtless
contributes to the fact that it is here that we begin to find systematic gender variations in the grading of men and women, even
when *pre*-entry qualifications are the same. Seven of the 9 women
with 'O' levels in this age group were still on Clerical grades, as
against only a quarter of the men, and whereas none of the men
with 'A' level were on Clerical grades, 6 out of the 7 women were.

Given the importance of post-entry, part-time qualifications to
career development, it is unfortunate that we did not ask our
respondents about this. Possibly many women consciously or un-
consciously anticipate their leaving in order to have children – in
these circumstances, the effort involved in taking further qualifications might well seem not worthwhile. As far as we were aware,
managers did not discriminate against young women in respect of

day release for further education, indeed, some managers
suggested that more women were taking advantage of day release
than had done so in previous years. In fact 36 per cent of the
women in the under-25 age group had achieved post-entry qualifications (i.e. Clerical examinations, ONC in Business Studies,
etc.), a percentage which, although lower than the men's (48 per
cent), stands in sharp contrast to the very low proportion of
women in the 25-35 age group (8 per cent) who had done so.

As we are here working with very small numbers, considerable
caution should be exercised in the interpretation of this data.
However, if this evidence is indicative of a trend towards the
increased acquisition of post-entry qualifications by women, it
could have interesting implications for the future. Forty-eight per
cent of all people on Clerical grades were aged 35 or more. Some
were long-service clerical workers, but most had been recruited
directly into these grades - from a very different labour 'pool'
from that of the 'bright school leaver'. For them, formal qualifications were not particularly important - clerical recruits in the
older age ranges were not, on the whole, considered as promotion
prospects. Indeed, 31 per cent of those on clerical grades aged
35 or more had no formal academic qualifications at all, and only
a tiny minority (6 per cent) relevant post-entry ones. A majority
(65 per cent) of older clerical workers were women - many returnees
to wage work after time spent rearing a family. As we shall see
in the final section of this chapter, many of these older women
are engaged in work tasks which, although graded as 'clerical',
demanded considerable responsibility and initiative. The present
generation of young women under 25, however, would seem to be
increasingly better qualified - especially in respect of post-entry
qualifications. Our evidence is only suggestive, hardly conclusive.
Whether they will be willing, on their return to the labour force,
to take up the kinds of clerical positions at present occupied by
older women is a question for the future. Much will depend on the
relative impact of the two other factors we found to be highly
significant in relation to career prospects - length of service and
geographical mobility.

Length of service
The relation between a woman's domestic role (and the ideology
which serves to enforce it) and her participation in the labour
market has been well chronicled in the growing literature on women
at work (Barker and Allen, 1976). We asked our 118 female respondents (in the checklist sample) whether they had experienced
any interruption in their paid employment due to marriage, raising
a family, etc. One-third of them (39) had. Most of them - 30 in
fact - had been out of the labour market for more than five years.
A much larger proportion of *married* women in the sample (50 per
cent) had been 'outside' the labour market and these women constituted all but four of those experiencing career interruption
(three of the remaining were widowed, separated or divorced).
For women employees in our study there was a strong association

between both marital status and grade, and employment interruption and grade; all but two of the women with more than a year's employment interruption were on Clerical grades.

The impact of a break in paid employment is threefold. Apart from the way it might inhibit working for professional examinations there is also the effect on length of service with the organisation, and on the women's own expectations. Long service appears to guarantee some career progression, albeit limited, and can also compensate for lack of qualifications. For both men and women there were no employees with over 15 years' service still on Clerical grades. Conversely, almost half (49 per cent) of the men, and slightly less (45 per cent) of the few women in AP grades had over ten years service. The women on Administrative grades are characterised by absence of career interruption rather than any possession of qualifications. Eighty-three per cent have over four years' continuous employment with the local authority, and the three women on AP grades who are unqualified all have long unbroken service.

As married women are the most likely group to have had some considerable time out of the labour market, they will return to employment with neither qualifications, training nor service. Whereas almost all highly graded men are married (e.g. 97 per cent of the Principal Officers) the reverse is true for women, the most highly graded being single. Clearly, for both sexes, this relation is mediated by *age*. But marital status adds another dimension to this picture: 11 of the 15 women on Administrative grades (73 per cent) are either single or widowed, separated, or divorced, and, although the figures are small, a higher percentage of separated and widowed women are on Administrative grades than of married women (25 per cent against 6 per cent). This distinction does not, we should note, hold for male employees.

The young woman entering employment with the organisation with GCE qualifications (i.e. not into a 'balkanised' labour market) begins, apparently, as an equal to her young male colleagues. It is the intervention of her socially defined domestic role as a wife and mother which upsets this equal relationship most damagingly and permanently. Marriage and absence from full-time paid employment act to disqualify women from access to higher grade posts. This, we have suggested, is due to their lack of key elements in the competition for promotion - post-entry qualifications and/or long service. Women without qualifications entering or re-entering the labour market after raising a family are recruited as a particular category of employee; they constitute a distinct pool of labour from which - with few exceptions - clerical staff are recruited, and for whom avenues of career mobility are no longer open.

Table 3.3 shows the pattern of female employment rather well in terms of employment interruption. Women up to 25 years have had continuous employment, as have most of those still working up to 35 years. But this (25-35 years) is the smallest age group numerically and signifies the point of departure from the labour market.

Women over 35 are far more likely to have left work at some time, so that only around a third have remained in continuous employment.

Table 3.3: Age and extent of employment interruption (%)

Length of interruption	Up to 25 years	Age 25-35 years	35-50 years	Over 50 years
None	98	80	35	35
Up to 1 year	2	15	4	4
1-5 years	0	0	7	4
5-10 years	0	0	21	26
10-15 years	0	5	24	22
Over 15 years	0	0	10	9
	100	100	101	100
No.	(44)	(20)	(29)	(23)

However, this cannot be the whole story, for there are women who remain in employment, and although they tend to do better than their counterparts who have left work at some time, they still fare worse than the men. Two factors can be suggested as contributing to this: direct discrimination against women in selection for jobs, and unwillingness among women to take on higher graded jobs.

Neither of these factors can be easily quantified, but our interviews with managers and women clerks provided evidence of both. Ten of the women we interviewed made comments indicating that they thought being a woman would impair their promotion prospects:

> 'Being a woman doesn't help – unless you have a degree in which case you can do no wrong! They prefer men here – no doubt about it. Because I'm a woman and married they think I'm going to have children.'

> 'I'd like to be head of my section – if I had a sex change!'

On the whole, managers were conscious of the fact that few women occupied senior positions, which was viewed as mildly embarrassing. Both legislation and the women's movement have probably had an impact to the extent that the lack of promotion amongst women was seen, by some managers, as a problem requiring justification. However, even if the expression of concern did reflect the beginnings of a change of attitudes, this had not been reflected in any positive intervention on behalf of women.[4]

The career aspirations of the women we interviewed differed markedly from those of the men – whereas 87 per cent of men expressed an interest in promotion, and over half of these (54 per cent) expected to be promoted, only 54 per cent of women said

they were interested and, of these only 36 per cent expected it.
The explanations the women gave for their aspirations and expectations reflect both a realistic appraisal of the situation in which
they found themselves, and a strong commitment to the domestic
role. One woman of 45 saw the situation very clearly:

> 'Previous occupants of [my] post have moved on quickly due
> to the difficulty of [my] job. I couldn't really progress further
> without accountancy qualifications. In our department [they]
> would rather see the young men in the section, who are train-
> ing, getting on.'

Another woman of 36 said:

> 'No, I'm not really interested in promotion. I've worked for
> quite a few County Councils – the only way to get promotion is
> to take exams and I'm not prepared to start doing that now.'

Domestic role commitments were most frequently cited as reasons
for the very real ambivalence many women expressed about promotion:

> 'I'm intending to have a family in a year or so – I would want
> to get on if I wasn't doing that. But I'm quite happy here and
> might be leaving soon to start a family.'

> 'I don't honestly know. Now that I'm getting older I do not feel
> [that] you can work at the expense of [a] family – but if you
> were team leader you would get torn between work and family.'

> 'Yes but I'm not sure if I'm interested in the overall responsi-
> bility. I've got a home to run as well – I wouldn't want to stay
> late in the evenings.'

Clearly, promotion raises particular difficulties for women which
are not present for the men (none of whom referred to domestic
problems when considering their promotion prospects). Nevertheless, it must be remembered that despite their difficulties over
half of the women *did* want promotion:

> 'Obviously I'd like to [be promoted] – I'm good at my job – I'd
> like to have it recognised. [There would be] more money, more
> responsibility.'

Geographical mobility
This was the third factor we identified as being associated with
higher graded posts. Many of the more senior posts (i.e. Principal
Officer level) had been filled by outside recruits, and managers
emphasised that, in general, they could only be achieved by moving between different local authorities. Our evidence certainly
confirms this, for 37 per cent of the men on PO grades had had
no previous jobs with the local authority, and average length of
service was lower in the PO than in the AP group.

We asked the people we interviewed about their willingness to move in order to pursue a career. Sixty-three per cent of the women said that they would not do so, even for a better job. Even more markedly, only 6 per cent of the women said unambiguously that they *would* be prepared to move for a better job, compared to 33 per cent of the men. Altogether, 28 women specifically referred here to family and domestic commitments - usually the husband's job. For many women, these constraints on mobility were unproblematic:

'My husband's job is more important. I'm not a career woman - I don't want to stay at work.'

'No - I'd go wherever my husband's job is - I would move with him but not for myself.'

'I'm not really career-minded - a "camp-follower" on my husband's job.'

However, for other women, the question revealed the kinds of conflict experienced between work and family:

'I'd be a bit tied - I would have to separate from my husband! If I was single I would but it would have to be a very special job.'

'I would - I don't mind where I live - but there would be problems with my husband. His job is a little more important than mine because we *may* start a family - but if we could both move I would.'

'No. I would have to discuss it with my husband but - very reluctantly - I would have to decline.'

In summarising our discussion of the reasons for the lack of promotion amongst women, we would emphasise a number of points. Firstly, the female clerical labour force is not an homogeneous mass. We identified only one group - young, unqualified women in data preparation - who corresponded to what may be regarded as the 'stereotype' of the female clerk, i.e. 'recruited to carry out the most menial tasks with limited opportunities for promotion'. Younger, qualified women - the group we have characterised as the 'bright school leavers' - were not doing noticeably worse than their male colleagues in career terms, and it seemed that such women were beginning to acquire post-entry qualifications. This raises the question as to whether they will be 'available' for clerical work - like their older female colleagues - in the future.

The older women, with the exception of a small group with long unbroken service, were, unlike older men, largely on Clerical grades. Lack of promotion seemed to be a consequence of the interrelationship of three factors: lack of formal (especially post-entry) qualifications, broken service, and a reluctance to move for domestic reasons. In addition, the women's career expectations were considerably lower than those of the men, especially among those returning to work after raising a family. Indeed, none of the women we interviewed who had been out of paid employment

for more than a year expected promotion. Low expectations
seemed to result from a combination of women employees' realistic
appraisal of their own situation, and a genuine reluctance to
seek a career due to the actual or expected demands of domestic
commitments. For some women, the tension between domestic and
work life was very real. Actual direct discrimination against women
probably plays only a small part - although there is no doubt
that some of the women in our study felt that they had less chance
of getting desirable jobs simply because they were women.

THE JOBS THE WOMEN DO

In our discussion of women clerks and their promotion prospects
(or lack of them) we have emphasised the heterogeneity of the
female clerical labour force. In our discussion of the work carried
out by the women, we would similarly emphasise that the range of
tasks designated as 'clerical' is extremely heterogeneous. Although
women's work is overwhelmingly clerical work, it would be a serious
error to assume that, as a consequence, women simply perform
routine, undemanding tasks requiring little or no initiative. As
we discovered in the course of our research, 'clerical' work in the
local authority setting - for men and women - covered a range
from rule-bounded repetitive jobs, say data entry, to jobs which
were both varied and required considerable discretion and responsibility.

Recent commentators have pointed to the 'deskilling' of clerical
work - a process which, although in process from almost the
moment the occupational category first emerged (Hakim, 1980),
has been enormously accelerated by the widespread introduction
of computer technology and electronic data processing (EDP)
(Braverman, 1974; Crompton, 1979). Indeed, it has been suggested
that 'feminisation' and rationalisation or 'deskilling' of clerical
work are inextricably bound together; that is, that women clerical
workers are recruited specifically for routine 'deskilled' tasks
(Braverman, 1974). In general, there can be little doubt that EDP
has effectively 'deskilled' much 'traditional' clerical work (Hoos,
1961; Stymne, 1966; Whisler, 1970). However, what is less frequently noted is that the impact of EDP varies considerably between
different sectors of clerical employment. In some sectors (e.g.
banking and insurance) the impact of EDP on both work and organisational structure has been profound. However, in others -
including local government - the impact, although considerable,
has been less total than in the financial sector. Although accounting procedures *have* been mechanised, there are many areas of
local government work, particularly those concerned with providing
a service to clients, where the 'computer impact' is apparently
minimal. In addition, in the local authority we studied, expenditure restrictions meant that computer applications were held back
because of capital costs. These factors no doubt contributed to
the heterogeneity of local government clerical work.

The presence of this heterogeneity raises the thorny problem of how 'clerical' work is defined – in particular, that of establishing the boundary between 'clerical' and 'administrative' or 'managerial' work. (This problem is analogous to that of establishing a definition of 'skilled' work, which is discussed in other contributions to this volume.) Officially, the nature of the work involved should be the major factor in determining a 'clerical' job. According to the Purple Book, the Clerical Division 'is to cover posts with *duties* (our emphasis) of a clerical character. Grade 1 is to be used as the general recruitment grade and for staff who undertake a range of tasks which can be carried out in accordance with well-defined regulations, instructions, or general practice.'

AP grades, on the other hand, are described as 'posts involving professional work or concerned with the general administration of the Authority's work or the improvement of its organisation and to posts of a specialist nature not appropriately graded within other Divisions.' In the words of a senior Personnel Officer:

'If you sit and process bills then you're a clerk, if you service a small committee, or draft letters to be sent to clients – that's administration.'

In practice, however, the nature of the work itself plays a rather less important role in defining a job title – whether clerical or administrative – than is given by the 'official' version. A considerable 'grey area' exists between 'clerical' and 'administrative' work – a situation which is to some extent recognised by the fact that the top end of 'clerical' pay scales at times overlap with the lower ranges of the 'administrative' pay scale. The aim of management is to ensure that a particular job is adequately carried out by a suitable individual. Management will, of course, be under pressure to minimise labour costs. If a post can be adequately filled at the clerical level, there will be (from a managerial perspective) little incentive to designate a position as 'administrative' whatever the actual work content – and vice versa. As one manager put the situation:

'You might advertise a job at Clerical 2/3 and get nowhere – adding an extra £100 to the job by making it AP2 gets you the right person.'

We found, therefore, that grade level was not always an accurate guide to work content. To be sure, clerical jobs in general tended to be more routine than AP jobs in general, but there was also evidence of considerable overlap in work content.

With some notable exceptions, there was no clear pattern in the distribution of the various categories of female clerical labour we have identified in this paper amongst the range of jobs in the many sections and departments of the local authority. The exceptions were, first a predominance of young, less well-qualified women in

computer operations (discussed on p. 48), and second a predominance of older women in the divisional offices of Highways
and Social Services (this will be discussed further below). Apart
from data preparation, therefore, there was no evidence that
women clerks were carrying out only the most routine, dead-end
clerical jobs. The range of the work is perhaps best described
by the job descriptions given by two individuals. For one clerical
officer the work entailed:

'Transferring figures from areas onto computer sheets and
checking that it comes back correct. [It] comes in on set
forms . . . [I] send forms off in batches for computer input.
Output comes back to me with corrections and I have to follow
up on corrections - [the] computer indicates anything out of
the ordinary.'

In reply to whether or not she found her work interesting, she
was adamant:

'No. I don't think anyone could. Its the most boring job I've
ever done.'

While at the other end of the spectrum another clerical officer was:

'In charge of abnormal loads which move through the county -
clearance of bridge structures - weight and routing of abnormal
loads. [I] also do general clerical work for the office - a lot of
odd jobs. [I] also work for the Traffic Census - help collecting
figures for that Section. Collate minutes, do typing - a whole
range of clerical tasks. [I] also deal with Public Utility Street
Works - effects of road works on the street - lighting, etc.'

When asked whether she found her job interesting she said:

'Yes, very. [I] like contact with the public, the challenge of the
job. [Its] not repetitious as each application is different in its
own right. [I] enjoy the work.'

Of the 53 women we interviewed, only 16 were occupied in routine
clerical jobs in the sense described in our first example above, 17
were in jobs which were extremely varied and demanded the
exercise of considerable discretion and initiative, and the remaining 20 had jobs which, although containing a substantial element
of routine, were 'leavened' by non-routine elements. One such
job was described in the following terms:

'I have a main index, I keep the filing system up to date. On
each file there is a front sheet which is supposed to keep you
up to date - I work from forms. The Social Worker fills in the
form, we take the information from it and transfer it to the index.
There's lots of phone calls - [I'm] the first point of contact for

members of the public. I also do odds and ends like looking
after children, acting as escort, etc.'

For this clerk work interest was clearly more problematic:

'Um . . . I like my work, I like dealing with the public. But
it can be pretty boring and routine when you see the basket
of forms in front of you. The telephone work I like.'

Local authority 'clerical' work, therefore, includes an extremely
varied range of tasks. In many cases, clerical jobs (as they were
described to us) seemed to have a substantial 'administrative'
component. We have seen how the pool of clerical labour available
is also heterogeneous. Because of their lack of formal qualifications
and/or necessary work experience, older women will predominate
over older men in the clerical labour pool. (Many of the older men
available for clerical work are experiencing a second 'career' -
ex-servicemen, insurance agents, policemen, etc.)
Women's domestic commitments and responsibilities also keep
women 'available' for clerical employment long after their male
equivalents have moved out of clerical grades. Although some
minor managerial complaints were voiced concerning married women
clerical workers (in particular, their unwillingness to work overtime at short notice), in many other respects they were considered
highly suitable employees. That is they could be counted on to be
steady and reliable, yet not to have 'unrealistic' expectations
regarding their work - as we have seen, women's career expectations were considerably lower than those of the men. In particular, older experienced women seemed to be widely relied upon in
the small area and divisional offices of the Social Services and
Highways Departments. Although we are working here with rather
small numbers, 31 (or 66 per cent) out of the 47 women employed
in divisional and area offices were aged 35 or more, as opposed to
the 45 per cent of all female employees who were in this age category. Because of the size of these offices, 'clerical' work often
included a sizeable administrative component, and in addition
required considerable interpersonal skills. As a 37 year-old clerk-
typist at an Adult Training Centre put it when asked to describe
the qualities needed to do her job:

'A lot of it is patience. You'd have to be more mature - one
previous clerk came straight from school but she didn't cope
with it very well.'

A look at her job description explains why:

'Reception work. Quite a lot of clerical work - wages for trainees
items purchased by public, dinner money (paid daily); floats
for any social events. Quite a lot of money handling. Work out
hours of hourly-paid staff (drivers and children's staff). Quite
a lot of figure work for Head Office - attendance figures and

dinner figures. Also write up details of trainees and parents for Head Office. Spend a lot of time on the telephone. Also invoice companies with whom ATC deals. Keep stockholding records. Responsible for ordering stationery. Take minutes on staff meetings, write reports. Type assessment reports. Type correspondence. Responsible for mail and posting. Staff holiday records.'

In addition, she also supervised a mentally handicapped adult trainee for two days a week.

CONCLUSIONS

The educational characteristics of the women workers in our study reflected the characteristics of the population as a whole; and whereas the younger better-qualified women were as successful as their similarly qualified male colleagues, older women (who had failed to gain relevant post-entry qualifications or the necessary length of service) were largely on Clerical grades. This was also true of older men without the necessary qualifications or experience, but, for what may be described as social structural reasons, only a handful of older men fell into this category. Although there was some evidence of overt discrimination against women, for the most part, the fact that women did not reach the higher echelons of local authority employment can be ascribed to their lack of 'success' in acquiring the relevant 'promotion qualities'. Domestic role commitments were obviously a major factor contributing to this lack of 'success', which has had the effect of keeping older women in the clerical labour pool. There was some evidence that the women in the youngest age group (under 25), unlike their older colleagues, were gaining the post-entry qualifications which seem to be so necessary to career development. It is always possible, of course, that past generations of young women have obtained these but have failed to return to local authority work after a break in paid employment. However, national figures suggest that, in the recent past, women have not gained relevant post-entry qualifications (Byrne, 1978; Bird, 1980). If the findings of our case study are repeated elsewhere, therefore, this would obviously indicate a trend rather than 'simple reproduction' (Stewart et al., 1980, p. 277). In any case, this is clearly an area which requires further research.[5]

Finally, we would stress that it is mistaken to assume that women clerical workers are confined to only the most routine, lower-level clerical jobs. Many of the women we interviewed were doing jobs which required the exercise of considerable skill and initiative. In some cases, it seemed to us that the designation of a job as 'clerical' depended not so much on the nature of the work involved (the 'official' basis for classification), as on the nature of the incumbent. This calls into question the basis and nature of occupational classifications (Davies, 1980; Stewart et al., 1980). Local

government is perhaps unusual in that, partly as a consequence
of long-term trade union involvement, job specifications apper-
taining to various grades of employment are precisely defined.
Nevertheless, as we have noted above, many jobs graded as
'clerical' seemed to have a sizeable administrative component, and
conversely, many 'administrative' jobs seemed to be largely
clerical in work content. One feature of contemporary society
which has attracted considerable comment is the growth of 'administrative, technical and managerial' occupations and consequent
'upgrading' of the occupational structure (Goldthorpe, 1980).
Again, this is an area which requires further empirical research,
but the content of 'administrative and managerial' work might
prove to give reasonable grounds for scepticism as to the nature
of the 'upgrading' apparently revealed by occupational data – as
one senior manager put it, 'Nobody wants to be known as a clerk.'
It is perhaps not too much to suggest that had women not been
'available' (and willing) to perform what were often complex and
demanding tasks on Clerical grades, such posts would have had
to be regraded into the burgeoning 'administrative, technical and
managerial' sector in order to attract suitable male applicants.

NOTES

1 Details of age, gender, grade, length of service and job moves
   within the organisation were obtained for all employees, details
   of pre- and post-entry qualifications and previous employment
   were obtained via a checklist to which there was a response
   rate of 70 per cent.
2 This chapter reports on a single case study carried out as part
   of a larger project financed by the Social Science Research
   Council. Further case studies are in progress in banking,
   insurance, and manufacturing industry.
3 The Purple Book – once known as 'The Charter' – is the formal
   agreement between management and NALGO regarding terms
   and conditions of service. The recommended levels of educational qualifications for Clerical grades are described in
   Section 3, paragraph 25(d).
4 It may also be suggested that public sector managers are,
   relatively speaking, under greater pressure to appear as 'good
   employers' than those in the private sector. Census figures
   are suggestive of this. In 1971, of all women in administrative
   and managerial positions, 29 per cent were in public service.
   The corresponding figure for men was 16.4 per cent (Economic
   Activity Tables, part III, Table 19).
5 Unfortunately, the national figures available do not provide
   any clarification. The most recent figures (at the time of writing) for students on day release are for 1976. As the group
   concerned was aged 25 years and under, this data is clearly
   not sufficient to discern whether or not a trend exists.

4 NEW TECHNOLOGY AND WOMEN'S OFFICE WORK
Jackie West

The introduction of new technology is a key element in the restructuring of the contemporary office, through displacing labour and transforming the inefficient organisation of office work. This article is about its impact on women clerical workers who, in the 1970s, made up around a quarter of all working women.

Microelectronics is in many ways very different from earlier computerisation. First, microprocessor-based systems are used extensively to handle text (not just non-verbal data) and, along with developments in telecommunications, can potentially integrate all functions at the core of office work - the collection, production, storage, manipulation, retrieval and distribution of information. They also 'collapse' the number of stages through which information has to pass (for example direct access via visual display units - VDUs - to a mini or even mainframe computer). The capacity for more 'intelligent' programmes requires high-level computing skills, but it can also enable non-computer specialists to operate equipment performing sophisticated functions and can reduce the need for knowledge and discretion. Second, microelectronic technology is increasingly cheap and its office applications tend to be less complex and costly than in manufacturing. In the office particularly, substantial productivity gains can be translated into economic returns over a very short period with little or no risk.[1]

Put rather abstractly, the automation of manual processes can cheapen 'production' in a number of ways - by absolutely reducing the number of workers for a given output, and by dequalifying (and cheapening) labour power. It can also increase efficiency by intensifying labour both in terms of speeding up the labour process and increasing control over it. The office is a prime target for new technology for it has become too much of an unproductive drain on individual capitals and capital generally (Braverman, 1974; Mandel, 1975). Labour productivity has been especially low - so too capital investment - and wage-to-total costs have been high. The 'social office' with its 'wasteful' proliferation of personal secretaries and social relationships has contributed to this (Barker and Downing, 1980). Office work is estimated at around 30 per cent of employment in manufacturing alone (ASTMS, 1979a, p. 22). And while secretarial labour constitutes only around 9 per cent of all office-based occupations (ibid, p. 28) and clerical labour generally only a small proportion of total office labour costs, it is clear that administrative and even senior management levels are in the 'firing' line, particularly in the long run. However, a good

deal of new technology is being applied, and in some instances
first, to areas of the office in which women predominate, and it
is this that concerns me here. The transformation of the office
involves a restructuration of female office employment as such
and perhaps also a more particular restructuring of jobs by way
of deskilling.

I begin by considering – in respect of office work – one major
example of the dominant orthodoxy on microelectronics and employment: the Department of Employment report published in late 1979
(Sleigh et al.). This is far more comprehensive than earlier
government reports (Advisory Council of Applied Research and
Development, 1979; Central Policy Review Staff, 1978a), though
sharing their overall perspective, and its case study approach
draws on 'help' from an extensive range of UK companies. This
report clearly represents managerial objectives, hidden within
a broader argument that 'new' technology will not have devastat-
ing effects. It plays down the labour-saving effects of microelectronics which along with control are the most obvious advantages
to management. Instead it stresses that increased productivity is
the key to competitiveness and growth – new technology then is
the only way to preserve jobs and promises to create more of them.
In addition, the use and development of the new technology is
seen to require specialist skills, currently in short supply. It thus
entails, by implication, an increase in, not dispossession of, the
knowledge and experience of workers. I examine the logic of this
position in the light of both the evidence its authors adduce to
support it and other material. Women's work emerges in fact as
highly vulnerable, particularly to a real contraction of job opportunities within the office – something that is obscured by the
orthodox concern, not to say obsession, with 'overall' employment
effects within the economy.

Trade union concern about new technology, including its introduction in a period of generally rising unemployment, has taken
various forms, not least the call, since at least 1978, for a radical
shift in government policy to promote economic expansion (TUC,
1979b). They have also called for major reforms in education and
training, without which women especially cannot benefit from the
limited areas of job growth that are occurring. I consider at the
end of the paper one aspect of the trade union response to microelectronics – 'new technology agreements'. These are a major
plank in the strategies of individual unions to win conditions
(including 'no redundancy') and benefits. But there are specific
problems presented by the fact that women's unemployment, even
without the recession, is particularly concealed.

CONVENTIONAL WISDOM AND EVIDENCE FROM THE CIVIL
SERVICE AND FINANCE SECTOR

The orthodox view suggests a number of reasons for believing that
the blueprint of the electronic office, however 'convincing', is

merely a 'hypothetical' scenario, a blueprint 'inherently unsafe
to accept . . . at face value'. It is held that the move from a fully
manual to a fully electronic office will be a 'slow steady evolution',
characterised by constraints – on the implementation of what is
technically feasible – and compensating effects (Sleigh et al.,
1979, pp. 55-6). The argument rests crucially on the view that
the automation scare of the 1950s and 1960s with its predictions
of dire employment effects proved unfounded.

It is in relation to this that reference is made to the 'lessons'
of computerisation in the Civil Service. For though staff saving
here was the rationale for computerisation, between 1970 and 1977
staff numbers actually rose by 30,000 (43 per cent) in just those
categories expected to be affected. The example is intended to
show how an explosion of information itself generates possibilities
for new and improved services through exploiting new information
and that 'there is never any shortage of demands made upon
government to provide new services' which cannot materialise
without the freeing of resources by computer applications (ibid.,
p. 56).

This argument is, first, politically and economically decontex-
tualised. As the union CPSA have made clear (1980, pp. 132-3),
new technology is being introduced 'against a background of
savage cuts in the size of the Civil Service . . . part of the means
of achieving this reduction . . . is new technology'. The bulk of
reductions in the year January 1979-80 were in clerical and
secretarial grades: a loss of 12,500 such jobs, 3.7 per cent in
typing and secretarial, 5.3 per cent in clerical officer, and 6.9
per cent in clerical assistant posts. What also matters analytically
is to estimate not what changes have actually occurred following
computerisation, but what the divergence is from what would have
occurred. Without computerisation, projected staff levels in one
government department for 1990/1 represented an increase on the
5007 jobs in 1979/80, of nearly 35 per cent overall and around
that in most categories (with 38 per cent in clerical and almost
25 per cent in executive). With computerisation – including word
processing – the overall staff level would be virtually constant
(a rise of 3.7 per cent), with increases in the management level
of 5 per cent, executive 22 per cent, data processing 719 per cent
(on a very small base), clerical 1.25 per cent. Those in typing
grades were expected to reduce by 95.9 per cent (figures com-
puted from TUC data quoted in APEX, 1979, p. 16).

The implications of past computerisation in the Civil Service
have been neatly expressed by the head of the Department of
Industry's Computers, Systems and Electronics Division. Although
stating that 'generally there has so far been no problem in terms
of displacement of clerical labour', he continues, 'such savings as
have taken place have been generally among the lower clerical
grades' with some increase in higher level staff (Atkinson, 1978,
p. 347). Nor are relative job savings the only consideration. For
whereas he tells us that 'the computer has eliminated some of the
more tedious and repetitive clerical jobs in departments', he also

concedes that 'at the same time, [it] has created others - for example in data preparation'. And, he adds, 'it has certainly altered the form and tempo of the work of many clerks.' Indeed Atkinson himself identifies the three major trends (though 'perhaps more muted in the Service than in other fields') as follows: the reduction of the clerical hierarchy; the polarisation of staff into one group with low-level qualifications doing 'predominantly mechanical work', and a group of higher qualified ADP personnel; and changes in the organisation and pace of work. Future developments will continue to affect clerks, among others (ibid., p. 349).

It might even be that some new jobs in information usage will be created once automation replaces manual filing, a system which currently involves a high loss of information. But examples cited, for the Civil Service at least, point to the fact that 'creative and imaginative work' like faster and more comprehensive retrieval of information to help ministers answer parliamentary questions, will need 'a higher calibre of *staff* than is required in most current clerical jobs' (Sleigh et al., 1979, p. 56; my emphasis). And there is no suggestion that most clerical work could be transformed in this way.

Similar trends can be identified in the finance sector. Already computerisation has been the major reason for employment growth stagnating or lagging behind the vast expansion in business (ibid., pp. 63, 67). Insurance business has doubled, while the labour force has remained virtually static since 1959, that is in twenty years. Banking employment rose between 1970 and 1978 by 29 per cent (to 331,500) while business doubled in that period, but even these DE figures are misleading since they conceal considerable fluctuations: for instance an overall fall in employment of nearly 17 per cent between 1971 and 1976, and in the London Clearing Banks a drop of 4 per cent in the numbers of women, with a 2.4 per cent increase in men, between 1974 and 1976 (see Labour Research Department, 1978, p. 105; CSE Microelectronics Group, 1980, pp. 106-8). None the less women are now around half the labour force in the finance sector (55 per cent in banking). And the implications of 'new' technology in this area are considerable, despite the DE expectation (Sleigh et al., p. 67) that there will have been further business expansion in banking and 'modest' employment growth by the time that employment stabilises after 1985 (and possibly declines after 1990 once the market for personal accounts has been saturated).

Banking provides an interesting example of the argument that adoption of new technology and corresponding labour displacement will be constrained in various ways, offsetting the imminence of the automated, and in this instance 'cashless', society. For example, there are potential legal and political problems with automatic cheque clearing. Self-service machines are in short supply and also costly (ibid., p. 66), though it is hard to see why dramatic price reductions will not follow in this area as they have done with word processing equipment.

Electronic funds transfer (EFT) is not thought to be economically

viable while only half the adult population have bank accounts
and given the high proportion of transactions still made in cash.
However, although its introduction would mean the loss of interest
on overnight deposits, instant crediting for retailers would offset
their otherwise relative advantage over the banks (ibid., p. 66),
and there are clear signs of co-operation rather than competition
between the banks on which to some extent a fully efficient EFT
system depends (since it would have to handle all bank cards).
In late 1979 a consortium of eleven banks was examining the
possibilities (CSE Microelectronics Group, 1980, p. 106).

In short in banking, as perhaps in other sectors, the 'constraints' to which reference is so often made may not prove as
effective as they sound on first hearing. Developments in banking
also provide an interesting test case of the 'logic' according to
which labour-saving is not the main motive, if relevant at all, for
the introduction of microelectronic technology.

Explaining developments in banking to its staff in 1979, National
Westminster management services justified the need for further
automation in terms of 'the ability to cope' physically with large
increases in business:

> If we do not push ahead with . . . ideas like magnetic stripes
> activating terminals [which read customer information from
> cheque cards], if we do not continue to fight and win this
> battle against paper, there will not be a building large enough
> to hold the people who will be required to handle the volume of
> vouchers which will emerge in ten years time if the current rate
> of growth . . . is maintained (quoted in BIFU, 1980, p. 12).

But the 'obvious advantages' of managing without 'masses of
bulky equipment' are clearly only one side, the visible half, of
the equation. For when automatic service tills can process 'one
transaction every 4½ minutes for 24 hours a day' they indeed give
'an idea of the saving of cashiers' time'. Nor is time the only
saving. For cashier-operated counter terminals precisely eliminate
the clerical work of entering transactions onto computers. In at
least one UK bank their installation would have equally eliminated
some data-entry jobs but for an increase in bank workload which
absorbed the displaced labour (Bird, 1980, p. 43).

Banking may well continue its hitherto substantial expansion,
at least for a while, but it is automatic cashpoints (credit and
debit) in factories, lobby banking and the like which are likely
to play a major part for the banks in capturing the remaining half,
or more probably quarter, of the UK population who still prefer
to take their cash in hand. It is precisely the increase in small
bank accounts, whose transaction/value ratio is low, which will
stimulate the need for cost-effective methods of 'handling' (Sleigh
et al., 1979, p. 63), along with space restrictions and competition
from other finance institutions which simply lend money. These
developments are a form of satellite, 'two-tier', banking in which
major transactions and 'back office' functions such as standing

orders, remittances and secretarial work, are centralised in area
or head offices, with high-street branches left only with counter
work, small personal loans and service marketing (BIFU, 1980,
p. 13). There has been a net closure of branches in the 1970s.

Although such restructuring may have less short-term impact
in banking on overall job numbers, reduced local opportunities
are inevitable which must particularly affect married women who
need to work near home. In any case, in both insurance and
banking the effects on career structures and prospects are very
clear. They will undoubtedly have a differential impact for men
and women – despite the almost total silence on this in the official
account.

The DE see the prototype two-tier system – also developed in
insurance – as both a reflection and reinforcement of changing
labour needs and the recruitment base (Sleigh et al., 1979, pp.
63, 67). Both industries are apparently faced with a shortage of
school leavers with good O if not A levels, who are seeking jobs
rather than entering further or higher education.

While the traditional career path (of starting with a clerical
'apprenticeship') is expected to remain in insurance, if not banking, data processing specialisation is seen to offer an alternative
and entirely separate career path (without the need for specialist
professional examinations) for 'those who expect to spend their
lifetime' working in the industries. And just as there is more
demand 'for small numbers of highly qualified staff to organise
and plan work, including computer based procedures', so for
'larger numbers to process information and operate procedures on
a day to day basis' (ibid., pp. 66, 68). The separation of conception and execution within the office itself.

Of banking the DE refer to the way 'growing short term participation in the labour market makes it inevitable that the banks
will abandon any pretence of a common potential career expectation
for all recruits'. Also to the way low-grade clerical jobs are, unlike in insurance, likely to be retained but transferred to 'operations centres' in the two-tier system with 'some increase in full
time clerical jobs but with few expectations attaching to them'
(ibid., pp. 66, 67).

The opaque and euphemistic references to women – a feature of
virtually the entire report – are only made explicit when dealing
with what is perceived as a real threat of job loss in the insurance
industry. Here the vast majority of women, despite their increase
in the twenty years up to the end of the 1970s to the point where
they are 45 per cent of the labour force, are still in low-grade
clerical and typing jobs, and 'undoubtedly the group most at risk
should new technology lead to reductions in overall employment'
(ibid., p. 68).

This would seem more than a little likely since prospects for
growth in insurance are not identified as great and without it
employment would in any case decline 'perhaps by as much as 15
per cent in the next five years' (ibid., p. 69). Even if overall
employment growth is maintained a shift is expected from lower

grade clerical and data processing to higher grade computer
systems and DP jobs, and perhaps in management services and
marketing.

For women, restricted promotion and concentration in deskilled
work in banking is no new phenomenon (Blackburn, 1967; Mumford
and Banks, 1967, ch. 9; Heritage, 1980, pp. 285, 289). But new
technology can further alter, if not reduce, the skill level or
content of many clerical jobs. This can take the form of simplify-
ing work processes, limiting the need for discretion or knowledge,
increasing routine elements or substituting already fairly routine
tasks for others. (The scope for such 'deskilling' is less where
client servicing and administrative tasks are major elements of
clerical jobs – cf. the discussion by Rosemary Crompton and her
colleagues of clerical skills in local government.)

As Bird explains (1980, pp. 54, 82), the cashier 'freed' by
the automatic terminal from the constraint of laboriously – but
accurately – recording the details of all transactions to be separ-
ately entered on the computer, can devote more time to the potentially more interesting work of interaction with bank customers.
None the less reduced 'responsibility' is recognised by management, and terminal operators 'can acquire the basic operating
procedures in half an hour and become fully proficient within
eight weeks'. In some insurance companies, the more sophisticated
word processing permits automation of the full range of clerical
functions, all intermediate text-handling jobs. Systems can provide
comprehensive data on the percentage of risk underwritten by
different companies on specific items, or transact business between
a company's branches and its brokers by composing and printing
addressed policy documents, and handling premium payments, so
reducing the time taken to issue policies from, in one case, three
weeks to three minutes (ibid., pp. 42-3; ASTMS, 1979a, pp. 26-7).
Many of the clerical jobs affected will not necessarily be particularly
skilled, unlike for instance actuarial work, but in any case they
will be reduced in number and many will involve a good deal of
data input and retrieval on VDUs.

The installation of direct access computers can take over routine
and certain non-routine clerical tasks. As APEX describe just one
area of impact (1980a, p. 37): 'an order entry clerk who previously
completed order forms on paper, including calculating prices and
confirming delivery dates, will find these tasks replaced by keyboarding and reading off the screen'.

The above section has looked at some key areas of office employment. But it is crucial to note that general developments in microelectronics affect all clerical work in stock control, accounts,
wages, personnel, customer servicing, sales and the like. In other
words in manufacturing and retailing as well – as indeed the DE
report reveals.[2]

It is also important to stress that a general tendency for stratification of the white-collar labour force further restricts women's
job opportunities per se. Certainly some new jobs are created
directly as a result of introducing new technology into offices, as

elsewhere, but the extent to which their numbers match those jobs actually displaced is, on current evidence, slight. And even if the overall skill level of the labour force is raised this is quite another matter both from upgrading individual employees, and opening up real possibilities of skilled work for those who would have entered the now declining areas of general clerical employment. (For instance, even while there is a shortage of computer staff, employers tend to demand A levels for programming and a degree or good programming or business experience for systems analysis.[3])

These general tendencies are illustrated particularly clearly in the case of word processing.

WORD PROCESSING

As already indicated, WP does not only affect secretaries and typists. Evidence suggests that already more clerical than 'secretarial' job losses are following its introduction (Bird, 1980, p. 42).

WP's full potential lies in electronic mail based on linked word processors and 'telephone' cables. This also transforms a company's 'internal post' between departments and branches, so dispensing with much filing and message delivery. Even while inhibited from external inter-company use by the GPO's telex monopoly, some early electronic mail systems incorporated this facility, whose widespread use will depend both on the level of office automation itself, and on-going developments in telecommunications.

The jobs of internal messengers and filing clerks will become the more redundant once telex messages can be delivered direct, and much faster to personal executive terminals (Barron and Curnow, 1979, pp. 149-50; ASTMS, 1979a, p. 26). Although by the late 1970s only a minority of Bird's nine case study organisations had already integrated WP and data processing functions and/or installed communicating WP, a substantial number were committed to their introduction within two to five years (Bird, 1980, pp. 70-5).

It is secretarial labour, however, where the impact of WP is most immediate and direct - notwithstanding orthodox scepticism on this too. The basis for this latter view is, first, that there is management resistance to the depersonalisation of secretarial and other resources and the fact that WP is too costly for many small organisations which, though employing only one or two typists, none the less altogether generate a great deal of typing jobs. It is also emphasised that the theoretical productivity gain claimed, for instance, by WP manufacturers, 'does not appear to translate at all easily into actual loss of typing jobs' (Sleigh et al., 1980, p. 118). WP is, it is sceptically maintained, often used to overcome a shortage of typists; WP suggests new areas of work (such as more use of standard letters as in personalised advertising, or use for low-level DP to save mainframe computer time); WP could

increase business (such as faster turnover of solicitors' contracts); and the drafting stages of documents often increase while
real output remains the same (Sleigh et al., 1979, pp. 61-2).

Now it is perfectly true that the first comprehensive survey of
WP use in the UK (Bird, 1980) revealed job losses that were not
very dramatic – they occurred in only a third of the case study
organisations – nor did they always or simply result from increased
productivity.[4] However, low rises, even decline, in productivity
and output due to increased document drafting or equipment problems was related to inefficient use and organisational inexperience
(ibid., p. 34).

Furthermore, a 50 per cent reduction in labour, as well as
increased output/workload, occurred in the two cases where real
productivity gains, in terms of turn-around time, were 100 per
cent or more and the WP function highly centralised. In four
others (in three of which productivity counts were unavailable
or not disclosed), labour savings were concealed by an increase
in workload, that is without any corresponding need to increase
staff, and it is equally significant that in two of these, along
with those where job cuts had already fallen, management were
planning future reductions in clerical, administrative and – for
most – managerial, staff. In any case a majority of organisations
were planning more stand-alone and a third of them more clustered
(shared logic) systems in the next year or two, an extension both
of text-processing capacity as such and of its sophistication and
efficiency (ibid., pp. 32-4, 72-4).

The DE repeatedly note that new technology is 'but one' of the
influences on employment – on employee stratification in finance,
on the loss of jobs in small retailing – the existing trends in
rationalisation being at least as, if not more, important. Of WP
they make the extraordinary observation that high productivity
gains across the generality of typing tasks are not wholly attri-
butable to word processors as such but to the 'reorganisation of
typing tasks in preparation for the introduction of word processors' (Sleigh et al., 1979, p. 61). This is of course to concep-
tually separate technology from the social relations in which it is
embedded. WP tends to be used in existing or new 'typing' pools
and particularly centralised, and its functions specialised, where
shared logic systems are used (Bird, 1980, p. 52; APEX, 1979,
p. 29).

The orthodox view that despite a 'considerable reduction in job
opportunities of typists', productivity gains will 'not inevitably
result in overall reduction' (Sleigh et al., 1979, p. 61) is not
upheld by concrete evidence.

Estimates of labour displacement from new technology and
associated developments in office reorganisation are difficult to
compare because they refer to different occupational groups and
make varying assumptions (see for example Forester, 1980; Bowen,
1980). Bird's forecast is based on cautious interpretations of
productivity measures, estimates of the rate and scale of WP
introduction in the UK, and on associations identified in the case

studies, especially the proportion of organisations where expanded
workload will absorb displaced typists and the proportions of
centralised and decentralised installations. In the light of these
Bird suggests that one in three jobs will be displaced in the short
term - that is 21,000 typing and secretarial jobs by 1985, or 2
per cent of the secretarial labour force. But, with increasingly
efficient use and equipment capacity, one to one substitution of
WP units for jobs is thought more likely by 1990, that is a loss of
of 170,000 jobs, as much as 17 per cent within a decade (Bird,
1980, pp. 36-9).

This kind of impact is expected on a group who currently comprise nearly a third of all women clerical workers. Moreover, a
great deal of the labour displaced is vanishing silently through
'natural wastage' (in Bird's case studies all the jobs lost evapor-
ated in this way). Job opportunities are declining specifically from
new technology while at the same time more women enter the labour
market. Further, clerical *unemployment* (mostly female) was
already rising especially fast in the mid 1970s (by 68 per cent
compared with 42 per cent among all manual and 51 per cent of all
workers between June 1975 and 1978: see Bird, 1980, p. 26).
And the generally increased number and scale of redundancies -
whether or not caused by new technology - affects office workers
in manufacturing too (APEX, 1980b). Finally, there is little or
no evidence of new secretarial and typing vacancies where WP is
introduced, and very few other jobs either, in particular for
women.

Far fewer jobs are created than in effect displaced both in
organisations which have shed labour, and overall (see Bird's
data, 1980, pp. 55-8). As with other instances of microelectronics,
new functions needed are often extensions to or new types of
data processing (programming, systems analysis, management)
or work measurement (especially at the moment of typing/sec-
retarial productivity and workload) with the new, but in a sense
transitional job of 'office technician' to analyse all textual information and ensure its transfer to the new system. These areas
do not represent real work opportunities for those faced with
fewer openings as typists or secretaries - with the partial exception of WP supervision and training. Even in WP distribution itself
jobs are estimated by 1979 to have offset only one in seven of
those displaced by WP; sales representatives, whose jobs have
grown faster than in customer support, are predominantly men;
consultancy work already requires extensive experience of WP
and will need additional skills in the future (ibid., pp. 57, 59).

But what of the new WP hierarchy itself? The closing off of
opportunities for women does not appear on present evidence to
be in any substantial way compensated either by this development
or real improvements in working conditions. Significantly this,
and especially the question of deskilling, is ignored by the DE.

Old skills are certainly lost, notably the typist's skill in producing perfect copy. Word processors automatically indent, justify,
tabulate and paginate but also reduce the need to conceptualise

and determine layout. Correspondingly, more time is spent keying
in, less on handling paper and correcting errors. Those most
suited to routine, repetitive WP are not good copy typists but,
for example, punch operators or young workers with little clerical
experience (APEX, 1979, p. 33; Bird, 1980, p. 50).

Generally operators, unlike their supervisors, have received
just a few days of training - usually provided by manufacturers.
Most see this as inadequate and are in APEX words 'then left to
sink or swim' (1980a, p. 40), though there are signs of more
internal training being developed (Bird, 1980, pp. 77-9). Full
proficiency takes at least three months, even in management's
view, or perhaps six - but this is little different from the requirements of most semi-skilled factory production jobs open to women.
Although operators tend to be paid above copy typists, it is not
always in recognition of their new skills, accuracy and responsibility for equipment. As APEX note, it can, where there is no
job evaluation or union pressure, merely reflect initial shortage
of experienced staff or the tendency to train *first* the most
experienced and already higher paid typists. Salaries are rarely
equal to those of secretaries (Bird, 1980, p. 62) and there is
nothing new about specialist typing grades as such.

True, WP does away with many boring and mundane tasks, such
as continual retypes of drafts and editing, and there is a faster
turnover of work. Despite an increase in pace and pressure this
can increase variety. It may well be these which contribute to the
generally positive reactions, even enthusiasm, reported among
many operators. But dissatisfaction as well as low expectations
are prevalent among routine copy and audio typists (McNally,
1979, pp. 79-80), and there is a certain amount of self-selection
for WP work (Incomes Data Services, 1980, pp. 6, 16). Bird herself suggests that this 'halo effect' is likely to dissipate once WP
itself becomes more conventional and particularly with increasing
use of shared logic systems. These generally entail a detail
division of labour between those who input text, printer operators,
proof readers/editors (the printer for several keyboards can be
located in a separate room). Often then there is no continuity
between the beginning and final stages of the product, whether
or not their operators are distributed within departments or in
fact 'pooled' (unless perhaps small-scale printing is done at input
work stations).

Bird's survey of 57 operators of new technology - which indicates
substantial job satisfaction, variety and little effect on supervision
or social contacts - is problematic. It provides no data to relate
these general findings to type of job, location, experience or
conditions of work; more than a fifth of her final sample were
secretaries, and, most important, for the third who were full-
time WP operators, there is no data on the hours they worked or
on how they experienced work in pools. Other evidence makes
more of the visual and mental strain of working with WP/VDUs
and increased pace of work (Barker and Downing, 1980; Downing,
1980).

Significantly there seem to be few moves to enlarge the responsibilities of operators. The range of WP tasks was distributed in a traditional hierarchy in Bird's case studies (1980, pp. 53, 57), that is with the supervisor or other senior WP staff in charge of maintaining and monitoring standards and output, distributing work, proof reading, liaison with authors, technical advice, work simplification techniques using WP, etc.[5]

I look later at the limits and possibilities of trade union action to prevent deskilling, indeed to create autonomous self-directing work groups. It should be said here that several unions have successfully resisted the use of any new systems/equipment for individual, and sometimes also collective, work measurement. There is little doubt, however, that WP systems being developed are specifically designed for increased management control over the labour process as well as for directly raising productivity. Some centralised systems incorporate sophisticated mechanisms for simultaneously securing both. Audio dictation is automatically fed to the system which holds:

> an exact record of how fast each operator can keyboard and how much work she still has to complete . . . [it] then allocates new dictation work to whichever operator can complete it within a given period, storing it until she is free. Operators are, therefore, continuously plugged in with no idea of how much work they have to do, when it will stop, and when they can maybe sneak a break (CSE, Microelectronics Group, 1980, pp. 48-9).

WP is not used full time, currently at least, by downgraded personal secretaries but it affects their work in two ways. First, it results in offloading some typing. The scope for this is probably greater than is sometimes assumed for there are considerable variations in accounts of how much time such secretaries do in fact spend on typing, from under a fifth, a quarter to nearly half (see Bird, 1980, p. 47; Sleigh et al., 1979, p. 57; Vinnicombe, 1980, p. 24). Second, it increases the administrative components of the secretary's job. Her transformation from personal into administrative secretary may reduce underuse and corresponding frustration but, especially if it increasingly entails working for several bosses, it could well result in overwork and conflicting pressures.

Nor are such shifts in responsibility likely in any way to overcome increasing secretarial frustration over promotion. As it is even 'top' secretaries are not *formally* recognised as the managerial assistants they often clearly are. Their 'gatekeeper' function in controlling and handling correspondence and callers depends on extensive experience, skills and knowledge of the organisation's employees, clients, products and operation. They remain, despite their indispensability, outside of the management hierarchy - even where they do perform 'administrative'/managerial tasks such as ensuring completion of their boss's assignments, compiling material

and reports for management use (Vinnicombe, 1980, ch. 6 and
pp. 66-7).

Administrative secretaries segregated into specialist 'support
centres' are even less likely to be regarded as suitable management material. It is more likely that recruitment out of the female
clerical ghetto will continue to stress the need for additional
qualifications and perhaps draw on those graduates in secretarial
studies (courses which include business studies) currently being
groomed in the UK as in the US (McNally, 1979, p. 51; Bird,
1980, p. 49).

Management resistance to the end of the social office - in particular the one-to-one boss-secretary relationship with its personal
control and dependence - may well impede the rapid development
of administrative support centres, at least at the level of top
management. In either case polarisation of the 'secretarial' labour
force is likely as standardised work goes to WP centres, and with
any real promotion into broader computer operations, data analysis
and the like dependent on new skills or new qualifications (Bird,
1980, p. 64). For most 'typists':

> the [career] limitations which exist already for working class
> girls in particular, will become more visible. [And] in becoming
> tied to, paced by and controlled by machines, typists will not
> simply become deskilled, but will become increasingly subject
> to forms of control whose real nature will no longer be masked
> by the social relations of the 'social office' (Downing, 1980,
> p. 287).

NEW TECHNOLOGY AGREEMENTS

Attempts to control the introduction of new technology have taken
various forms. Shopfloor control, where rank-and-file organisation
is strong, and perhaps official union influence weak, has undoubtedly occurred in some sectors of manufacturing. More generally
there has been reliance on conventional bargaining procedures
(Incomes Data Services, 1980), and, on the other hand, an increasing number of specific 'new technology agreements' negotiated by
unions. However, despite union presence, new technology has
sometimes been introduced with at best management 'advice' and
assurances of no redundancy, or even with no consultation at all.
My analysis of the data from an unpublished NALGO survey in
1980 shows that there was a general agreement on WP in around
a fifth of branches reporting on its introduction. Consultation
was typical, though there was none in at least a sixth and in
some cases it occurred only after introduction or following union
pressure.

Consultation itself and 'no redundancy' clauses are major objectives of 'new technology agreements', but the unions have sought
very comprehensive information - on management plans and the
expected effects on jobs - without which meaningful consultation

and agreed conditions will be impossible. But management have
often resisted such disclosure: in banking, for instance, they
warned NUBE of the confidentiality clauses in employee contracts
when the union asked its members for information (BIFU, 1980).
Some unions, such as CPSA, have won interim 'status quo' agreements on say 'cold storage' for WP equipment following trials, or
on its use in the Civil Service only to replace worn-out automatic
typewriters and their functions, and with no staff reductions
(CPSA, 1979, p. 117). Over a year later there was still no new
technology agreement as such and one major obstacle was management reluctance to agree different rules for changes in earnings
arising from the introduction of new technology from those arising from other causes; another was resistance to the union's
parallel claim for shorter hours (CPSA, 1980, p. 133). Agreements
have sometimes followed refusal to operate new equipment and,
more rarely, industrial action ('Labour Research', 1979b).

It was a walkout and strike by eighteen typists for nearly three
weeks at Bradford Metropolitan Council in 1979 which led to a
new technology agreement between NALGO and the local authority.
Management had been considering new technology as a means of
rationalising resources since 1975 (Incomes Data Services, 1980,
p. 16). A joint consultative committee agreed in June 1976 to WP
in one of the directorates providing for no redundancy, redeployment of typists who did not want to transfer, later determination
of salary grades - and a meeting to inform the affected typists.
The union withdrew co-operation largely following disputed gradings but a study group then set up, comprising three officers,
one union official, one typist and the supervisor, agreed to
implementation which took place in July 1977. The section affected
was reduced from 44 to 22 typists. Management attempts to extend
WP to other areas by unilaterally imposing a time-and-motion
exercise, in February 1979, provoked the walkout, but it was also
a reaction to the methods of consultation and negotiation. The
result was a working party which included elected union members
and a new technology agreement. However, what that entailed
represents, though more explicitly, precisely the limits as well
as possibilities of many such agreements.

At Bradford Met the agreement's purpose was to 'provide a means
of dealing with the application of a reduction in the labour force
brought about by either cutbacks in financial resources or the introduction of new technology' (ibid.). In return for management agreement to 'minimise harm to individuals', the union agreed to 'co-
operate with all reasonable steps, including flexible working practices, to reduce manning levels'. The agreement 'guaranteed' no
compulsory redundancy, offers of 'reasonable alternative employment'
for those displaced, and for those who opted for redundancy, extra
payments on top of statutory provision and a return of superannu-
ation, etc. By local agreement, WP operators were moved to the top
four points of the typist pay scale, an increase in gross pay of 13.3
per cent. However, typists working with automatic typewriters were
already at this level - they got a lump sum payment.

Other new technology agreements have been less specific in their ostensible purposes, many of them referring, for example, to the 'mutual advantages' of improving the efficiency of office procedure and/or company competitiveness, or even of ensuring 'smooth introduction . . . without conflict and with the fullest understanding of the issues involved'. What follows is an attempt to highlight certain features of some negotiated agreements up to 1980. There are limited published sources (principally the fortnightly bulletins of Industrial Relations Review and Report, Incomes Data Services and those of trade union resource centres). Aside from these my account draws essentially on those agreements won in the private sector by two unions, APEX and ASTMS; agreements which have covered large numbers of clerical or office workers, and for the most part in areas where the introduction of new technology is generalised rather than at the heart of the production process as in telecommunications. Both unions were among the first to produce discussion and policy documents on new technology; women are over half of APEX membership and, while only just over a sixth of ASTMS', female membership in that union grew the fastest of all unions between 1968 and 1978 (see Judith Hunt's article, p. 158).

All major new technology agreements have secured 'no redundancy' clauses, but this commitment usually depends at best on redeployment. Such commitments are substantial achievements at a time of deepening economic recession.

However, 'no redundancy' agreements simply redistribute unemployment to school leavers, as unions have emphasised, and also to married women returnees to the labour force. Redeployment provisions frequently specify that no workers affected in this way will suffer loss of pay, status or other benefits if their job no longer exists or is reduced in grade following new technology. Sometimes these guarantees are very specific. In these terms 'no job loss' - however much a crucial but 'very difficult clause to win' (APEX, 1980a, p. 57) - provides for *individual* job security but cannot deal with natural wastage, which in some cases has been specifically written in. Yet this is precisely how many white collar *jobs* have been tending to disappear.

Trade unions have seen a fundamental shift in government economic policy as an essential part of any solution to declining job opportunities. But they have also identified two main ways to preserve or even create jobs at 'company' level (though struggles over both have a far longer history than bargaining on new technology): increased output or services, and shorter working hours (the latter also seen as a way of distributing the productivity gains of new technology to workers). Neither tends to feature in new technology agreements as such.[6] Aside from the way the first is constrained by the tendential decline of industrial output, new technology agreements are in a sense largely consultative frameworks, which always specify what areas will be negotiated before systems are implemented or extended, but vary considerably before actual conditions specified at the time. Some unions, notably ASTMS

(1979b), have in fact drawn a clear distinction between such agreements, which are seen as essentially procedural, and separate collective bargaining on wages, conditions, job evaluation, shorter hours, etc. Others, such as APEX (1980a, p. 50) seek more substantive new technology agreements. But those of all unions, particularly where there are joint bodies, are seen as framework and minimum agreements for later and local negotiation, so there are further limitations in my focus on them. None the less some suggestive inferences can be drawn from their scope.

Certain health and safety conditions, such as eyesight tests for full-time or regular VDU operators, have been won by many unions (Incomes Data Services, 1980). Comprehensive conditions are more difficult to secure. Even where very extensive ones have been negotiated, as for instance by APEX, they do not always match up to a union's own recommendations (for example, on no more than forty minutes' continuous work at VDUs in each hour: APEX, 1980a, p. 59). Basic or general training - in 'appreciation' of the system, operating procedures and health and safety implications - has usually been agreed too, at least for affected staff and allowing for subsequent items in training. Increases in pay for accepting change, or in recognition of productivity rises in practice often take the form of lump sum, flat rate payments (Incomes Data Services, 1980; 'Labour Research', 1979b). The possibility of upgrading jobs or even preventing a reduction in job grade is more problematic. Many agreements specify gradings as negotiable (for example those won by TASS (AUEW), NALGO, ACTSS (TGWU), ASTMS); APEX, like others too, has in some cases won a formal commitment from management to consider revising job descriptions or, though more rarely, to recognise changes in responsibility and flexibility. One of the first major APEX agreements formally acknowledged that 'it is not the intention of the system to deskill or fragment jobs, nor introduce greater routine . . .'. Further to maximum flexibility in working methods, 'an agreed positive programme of manpower and job development will be introduced' to increase 'the responsibility and autonomy of job groups and employees' and enhance job content and personal status; but such moves were 'solely' to create 'the right working environment . . . and [would] not constitute a basis for job grading'.[7]

Increasing job satisfaction, in part to increase productivity, is also sought by management consultants (Mumford, 1979), and involvement in design is seen as one way to increase 'participation'. But such moves depend on a pre-existing climate of industrial relations where consultation is seen as both legitimate and necessary. APEX noted, on the basis of their negotiating experience up to early 1980, that management were 'amenable' to trade union demands for qualitative improvements because the return from new investment is 'heavily dependent on employee co-operation in the reorganisation'. At the same time it argued the need to challenge management pressure towards control and fragmentation, and that the aim of creating autonomous work

groups was ambitious (1980a, pp. 38, 49, 44). Training provisions
are less so, perhaps even job rotation too, bearing in mind employers' needs for adaptability (CSE Microelectronics Group,
1980, ch. 14), and that rotation between several routine jobs is
often itself routinised (printing with WP one day a week say,
keyboarding the rest) and such systems may well be little different from those on factory production lines. The comprehensive
retraining sought by trade unions has rested on a demand of
government for a far greater commitment of resources (TUC, 1980).
Clerical and commercial training, however, will suffer most from
cuts proposed by the Manpower Services Commission (Department
of Employment, 1981).

Management objectives and state priorities are not the only
obstacles to overcome, however. APEX observe that just because
job evaluation schemes simply classify jobs in relation to each
other, 'no amount of juggling . . . can correct deskilling which
often occurs if trade unionists neglect job *content* at the stage of
implementation or extension of electronic systems' (1980a, p. 47).
If it is hard to restructure jobs to build in the need for knowledge,
analysis and judgment, so too is winning recognition of those skills
or 'positive' factors which are associated even with low-grade
jobs transformed by new technology - less supervision, responsibility for equipment or confidential data, working conditions ....
Some, however, as APEX also note, are not included in many job
evaluation schemes anyway   in particular dexterity, mental and
visual stress and fatigue - let alone given substantial weighting.
The bias in such schemes in favour of traditional 'male' skills,
and against those conventionally identified as inherently female
attributes (dexterity, etc.) is itself in part a product of trade
union bargaining. It may well be only when more men's office jobs
are transformed by new technology that much effective pressure
in this respect will be exerted by negotiators, alongside moves
within the unions on positive action for women, described by
Judith Hunt in this volume.

CONCLUSION

The most serious effect for women of new technology and the
rationalisation of office work is undoubtedly fewer jobs. This is
the case even in those sectors where the prevailing orthodoxy
seeks proof of its optimism - finance and the Civil Service. The
saving of clerical and secretarial labour generally is a major
objective and effect of office automation. Deskilling is more problematic, but there is little or no evidence of an overall increase
in skills for affected jobs but rather, at most, the substitution of
certain new ones - though not always recognised - for previous
skills displaced. But there are broader issues too, for example
of control and intensity of work. Workers may 'need' less personal
supervision just because the machine paces and checks their work.
The increased polarisation of office staff and further segregation

of office work along gender lines is also a. definite trend, whatever the real content of low-grade jobs, and promotion more
blocked both for clerks and 'typists'. Traditional office careers
have never been viable for most women and alternatives are not
viable either so long as most women's education and training does
not provide them with the qualifications or higher-level skills
sought by employers.

   Some trade unions have been adamant in asserting women's right
to work and, as APEX put it, their total rejection of the view that
married women should forfeit their jobs (1980a, p. 35). But despite mounting trade union concern about new technology in
general, resistance is severely constrained by the recession. It
is increasingly evident that redundancies attributed to the recession provide capital with a direct opportunity for introducing
new technology (Incomes Data Services, 1980; APEX, 1980b).
This tendency has been most marked in manufacturing, where of
course office workers are not immune. Whether or not such moves
occur on a large scale in the service sector of the economy, trade
union struggles to negotiate conditions - let alone benefits - in
return for technological change run foul of a tendency for restructuring of the labour force through natural wastage. 'No
redundancy' agreements which are hard enough to win cannot offset this. Women's dual role in social and domestic production means
that women workers are the most likely to waste 'naturally'. Any
use of new technology to employ women at home as outworkers
(of which there is some sign: Bird, 1980, p. 67) could only reinforce women's oppression and weak bargaining position. It is
perhaps above all the reduction in women's employment which will
weaken union ability to bargain over the content and organisation
of work and thus resist management attempts to tighten control
over the clerical labour process. It is with good reason that trade
unions have been pressing the government for a massive shift in
resources for retraining and job creation generally. For without
this at least women's future in the office could be bleak.

ACKNOWLEDGMENTS

Thanks especially to Theo Nichols and Angela Coyle for their
comments on earlier drafts of this paper.

NOTES

1   It was noted of the Civil Service in 1978 (Atkinson, p. 348)
    that 'the total cost of a small computer system, including key-
    board, memory and output device, is now less than the cost
    of employing a clerk.' Sophisticated systems are of course
    more expensive, but overall savings are very considerable:
    see Incomes Data Services, 1980.
2   For instance, Sleigh et al. (1979, p. 72) identify clerical back-

up work in retailing as vulnerable to reduction - 'by up to 15 per cent . . . in at least two major retailers' - due to point-of-sale terminals, computerised ordering, invoicing and automatic stocktaking. Even expansion in the sector (through, it is held, improved customer service, faster turnover and redeployment of displaced clerks into sales) will further squeeze small retailers and job opportunities here.

3   Programmers (where women currently number four out of ten) will be in less demand with increasing use of high-level languages and packaged software. Only one in twenty systems analysts are women.

4   Bird's small sample of nine cases none the less represented a wide range of 'variables' including labour-force size, public and private sector services and industries, scale and period of WP investment and trade union presence. The organisations are not named, but the data, e.g. on changes in productivity, secretarial numbers before and after WP, show that only one, Bradford Metropolitan, overlaps with cases cited elsewhere - by Counter Information Services, 1979; APEX, 1979; Incomes Data Services, 1980.

5   The two exceptions where typists and secretaries shared all WP tasks were small (university department, research consultancy) and equipment faults and inefficient use reduced productivity (Bird, 1980, p. 34).

6   At least one TASS agreement (with Rolls Royce, Scotland, 1980) specifies as one of its purposes an increase in job opportunities; a commitment to shorter hours is linked to reductions in systematic overtime.

7   APEX and Plessey Telecommunications, July 1979 ('Industrial Relations Review and Report', no. 215, January 1980, pp. 15-16).

5 CONTEMPORARY CLOTHING 'SWEATSHOPS', ASIAN FEMALE LABOUR AND COLLECTIVE ORGANISATION

Barbro Hoel

INTRODUCTION

There has been a long and extensive debate about the form and character of sweatshops. Basically though, what had come to be called sweating in the nineteenth century was related to the arbitrary nature of demand, liability to rush orders and sudden gluts of production which provided manufacturers with no incentive to stockpile (Hall, 1962). Low wages, low rent and above all reliance on vulnerable female labour, especially that of immigrants, reduced overheads and permitted manufacturers to hire and fire at any sign of expansion or contraction of the business (ibid., and Stedman Jones, 1971). Present-day clothing factories in Coventry, which form the focus of this article, can be reasonably described as sweatshops in terms of both the organisation of the industry and the organisation of the female labour force, in particular, control relationships.

Clothing manufacture in Coventry is a fairly recent phenomenon. It was virtually non-existent until the end of the 1960s when Indian-owned factories were set up. At the time I did my research from 1978 to 1980, twenty-two factories employed between 450 and 500 women and a further 46 as outworkers. Every year a couple have gone bankrupt or closed down but in their place one or two new ones have been established. These factories are on the whole small, and the rent paid for the premises is low due to their condition and situation. The workforce is extremely low paid - often half the appropriate statutory minimum rates laid down by the Wages Council - and has very poor conditions. The labour used is almost exclusively immigrant women workers who are vulnerable socially and have difficulties in obtaining jobs in the better-paying sectors of the labour market (see Castles and Kosack, 1973; Kosack, 1976).

More often than not the 'sweatshops' are hidden from view in backstreets, in garages and derelict warehouses. The great majority are located close to or right in the immigrant residential areas of the city. They are overcrowded, cramped, excessively noisy and often have leaking roofs. Heating is a major problem and during the colder months of the year I saw women huddled up in their winter coats and shawls while working. In many of the factories the women themselves had had to buy paraffin heaters and paid for the daily running cost. These heaters constituted a fire hazard among all the cloth that was lying about on the floor. Many premises had inadequate fire exits for the numbers employed

or exits blocked by boxes and stocks of cloth. The workers had
to supply their own toilet paper, rarely had access to a washbasin
with hot water and had no facilities for eating their lunch except
by standing in a corner of the shopfloor. In most factories the
workers were not allowed to eat by the workbench since food
stains might ruin the cloth. As a result they had no place where
they could talk among themselves.

The main body of the workforce consisted of married women
from the Punjab district in India, predominantly Sikhs. These
women have had little work experience prior to their arrival in
Britain and have a very limited knowledge of their legal rights at
work. Less than twenty women workers were of English, Irish or
West Indian origin. The majority, 92 per cent, were young married
women between the ages of twenty and thirty-six, most of them
with children. Most of the working mothers had a well-developed
system of child care within their own community, using their
mothers, mothers-in-law and other female relations.

Most of the Indian women had tried to obtain jobs in English-
owned factories but had faced problems because of discrimination,
lack of skills and suitable qualifications. The Indian clothing trade
makes few such demands and requires no knowledge of the English
language. The work experience the women gain as machinists,
packers and pressers is disregarded outside the trade, hence
movement into other industries is limited (for further detail, see
Shah, 1975; Wilson, 1978, pp. 54-5).

In this chapter I examine a number of key features of employment in the sweated trades. Firstly, I look at the significance of
recruitment of workers, much of which has been through personal
contacts. Secondly, and of equal importance, is the social organisation of work which is characterised by paternalistic employment
practices, minimal job control, piecework and long working hours
with low pay. The particular insecurity of this employment is also
due to the organisation of the clothing industry itself. Finally, I
show how the form and character of 'sweated' labour has significant consequences for collective organisation of the Indian female
workers employed in the clothing industry. Here I draw on three
case studies in particular.

The data for this article was obtained in 1978-80. Altogether I
visited nineteen clothing factories and all but one were owned and
operated by Asian men. Subsequently I did 100 open-ended, in-
depth interviews with women workers in their homes. I revisited
a number of women to discuss particular matters in more detail
relating to their domestic and work situation. In addition, I was
able to attend union meetings and related activities, a range of
social events attended by the women and for some I became a
frequent visitor to their homes.

RECRUITMENT

The channels of recruitment meant that it was quite likely that
the workforces of these factories would be composed of Asian
women. There were six ways whereby women were recruited.
There were advertisements in the two Asian cinemas and, in
Punjabi, at the Job Centre, as well as lists of previous workers
who had been laid off in the past or who had left because of
family difficulties. The two most common methods, however, were
through existing workers, and through family and friends of the
employer - both by word of mouth - often in conjunction with
applications from workers at the factory door. The women learnt
of vacancies from friends, acquaintances and relatives in food
stores, clothing stores and the like in the Asian community, or
on social visits. The smaller factories relied almost entirely on
this Asian 'grapevine' (see also Khan, 1979).

It was evident from this pattern of recruitment that many Asian
women were tied to their jobs by more than a 'cash nexus'. In so
far as jobs were obtained through family and community connections, there were obligations to accept the job as such. It would
not do to complain about the terms and conditions of employment,
in part because this would reflect badly on those who introduced
the women to the employer. Obviously, this is not a hard-and-
fast rule, but it does serve to point out that cash relationships
can be overlaid with others which tend to reinforce certain types
of work behaviour.

Complementary to this pattern of recruitment was the employers'
unwillingness to recruit English women workers (18 were in fact
employed in four factories but almost all in one owned by a Greek
Cypriot). This was partly because the English women tended to
restrict their relationships with the employers to that of cash -
they did not have any sense of family and friendship obligations.
Of course, the Asian employers were unlikely to have much contact
with English people and women in particular, so the usual methods
of recruitment were not likely to operate. Nevertheless, the Asian
employers had developed a view of English women workers as
undesirable, perhaps dangerous, to employ. While two thought
that English women worked harder and would be best suited as
forewomen, on the whole they felt that English, unlike Asian
women demand higher pay and better conditions, and spend a lot
of money on clothes, cigarettes and general entertainment for
themselves.

This view was supported by opinions to the effect that English
women would feel out of place in an Asian-owned factory - isolated,
and perhaps resentful, in a situation where they were unable to
talk with Punjabi-speaking women. I was also told that the Asian
women were not good mixers, due to their inability to speak English
and the tendency to 'stick with their own kind'. The employers
also did not think that English women wanted to work in clothing
factories, since they could get better-paid jobs elsewhere.

All the same, some had employed English women in the past.

However, they had certain additional and specific complaints
about the English women workers, who created problems for the
control and organisation of the workforce. Although English
women were thought of as good workers, they were found 'inflex-
ible' with regard to tea and lunchbreaks, which they were not
prepared to postpone or skip in the busy season or in rush orders.
Besides the owners found it difficult to make them work overtime,
which is important in this trade as a means of coping with extra
production without taking on extra workers. Asian women, according to the owners, rarely refused any requests regarding changes
in their work pattern, for example reductions in their already
very short tea- and lunchbreaks.

For their part the English women were surprised and unhappy
with the passivity of the Asian women, their servile attitude and
response towards the management. As one said, 'They never
answer back.' Whenever any of the English women questioned a
decision or quarrelled with an unfair practice, the Indian women
looked on in amazement. Compared to English-owned firms, the
workers were more closely supervised, often working with a supervisor standing behind the rows of machinists ordering them to
speed up their work, to shut their mouths and not move from
their seats until lunchtime, etc. - 'They were forever checking
on our output and on us.' One of the older English women was
loudly and abusively reprimanded on the shopfloor for talking.
She felt humiliated and her anger showed: 'I was ready to leave
the job that same evening. But, to my amazement the boss came
up and apologised after work and explained that he forgot I was
not an Indian - implying he was so used to shouting abuse at the
others, it was a habit now.' Although many of the Indian women
do in fact leave due to the abuse from many of the employers,
they never reveal their real reason for leaving.

THE DIVISION OF LABOUR

The factories mainly produce one type of cheap, ready-made
garments, ranging from trousers (eight firms) to dresses and
skirts, underwear, sportswear and, in one case, knitted cardigans.
Two of the four dress manufacturers were subcontractors only
working from already cut material. Shirt manufacture (two firms)
in particular faced sharp foreign competition - in the past four
years two firms had stopped shirt production.

The division of labour within each factory was fairly simple.
Firstly, there were the skilled positions held mainly by men who
did cutting and tailoring. Mostly these tasks were performed by
the employers themselves or occasionally by hired male workers,
neither of whom had previous experience. However, I was told
these jobs had to be performed by men as they needed strength
(but see Angela Coyle's discussion of cutting 'skills'). Moreover,
styles and patterns had to be kept secret from competitors hence
the job was better done by the employer himself in addition to

saving on hired labour. Secondly, there were the semi-skilled
positions held by women only comprising overlockers, seamstresses
and buttonholers. This group mainly worked for piecerates,
except in factories with less than twelve workers, where they
were paid a day rate (approximately 50-60 pence per hour).
Thirdly, there were the unskilled positions which include pressers.
The ironing was done with old-fashioned heavy dry irons on
ordinary ironing boards rather than steam presses. This job was
hourly paid, again around 50p per hour. Finally, there were
threadcleaners and packers who were also paid an hourly rate.
However, in the smaller factories these two jobs were performed
by the employer's wife or close relative who was unpaid.

In the majority of factories the supervisory functions were
mainly done by the employers themselves or their wives. However,
where 'outsiders' had to be considered they were carefully chosen
out of the existing staff for their superior skill, speed and 'quiet'
personality. Most importantly, they were expected to do all jobs
better than any of the other workers and faster. The women
workers' piecerate was worked out against the supervisor's speed
and output per hour; she/he was the standard with which all the
others had to compete.

In all, 15 Asian men were hired to fill positions as cutters,
tailors, 'experienced' machinists, usually very old men, and
supervisors. Very few of the women workers were considered to
be skilled despite many years as machinists. The definition of
skill was used in a very arbitrary manner and left to the personal
interpretation of the employers, who in fact tended to use the
word 'experience' instead. The employers argued that there was
no shortage in Coventry of unskilled women workers for the
clothing trade. The 'real' problem was to obtain experienced
workers, and this shortage was due to the short history of clothing trade in the city, and the only recent entry of Indian women
onto that particular labour market.

There was a very high turnover of women workers and a great
movement between sweatshops of workers trying to improve their
wages and conditions, as well as escape from the constant harassment and abuse of many employers. A great number of women had
moved two to three times during a two-year period. Retraining was
demanded if the worker moved from trouser into shirt maufacture
despite identical machinery. As a result the worker would be label-
led unskilled and paid an even lower hourly wage while in training.

PAY AND OVERTIME

There was no fixed rate of pay for standard jobs adhered to by
all the clothing manufacturers. Every individual employer had his
own view or 'feeling' for what constituted a 'right' wage in addition to what he thought his pocket could afford. They also mis-
trusted what they heard of their competitiors' rates. As one put it:

'Let me say they tell me 20p per dozen pieces completed. I cut this quote in half to 10p per dozen. You see, none of the other manufacturers will let you know how much profit they are making.'

Other employers would use the supervisor's speed and output her hour as the measuring block. Moreover, there are differences in the rates paid to workers within each factory for identical jobs. These individual handouts are one of the obstacles in uniting the women within a factory. Only one factory, the sole one which was fully unionised, paid the statutory minimum wage which was £1.19 per hour up to April 1981, while the vast majority of the workforce in the sweated trades got 50-60 pence per hour. However, the employers (a partnership) of the unionised factory did not fail to bring to my attention how the women's attitude to their work had changed following such 'good' wages. They claimed that, with the weekly fixed rate regardless of output, the women no longer bothered to work as hard.

Not only do they receive poor wages for a long and strenuous week, but in many of the factories which run into financial trouble at various stages, they do not even get their full pay for the work done. One worker described how the boss's wife regularly took insufficient cash from the bank to pay everybody, so that money was taken from several paypackets to make up the missing amount, with 'promises' of the difference (perhaps half their wage) at a later date. Workers would often be sent home after a few hours with no prior notice and no pay for the work done:

'We feel so insecure but we hang on to the job we have managed to obtain. It is difficult to explain but it is a sense of obligation, of helping out even though the boss does not really care for us.'

The organisation of the industry makes the women's work particularly vulnerable to redundancy or layoff. The insecurity of the jobs is caused by the seasonality of production and tendency towards rush orders on weekly bases. Layoffs often occur when the market slumps: no stocks are kept due to the changing fashion styles which in particular affect small dressmaking and skirts factories with small outlets and irregular order patterns. Manufacturers in the same line of trade frequently undercut their competitors' already poor wage rates to offer their products cheaper to the mainly Asian wholesalers. The wholesalers in turn play competitors off against each other.

At the slightest fluctuation in the market the workers are laid off, but during the busy seasons they are requested to do up to 15 hours overtime a week. In the majority of the factories this was compulsory if the women were to keep their jobs. Only three factories in fact paid a higher rate for overtime, but still far below the statutory minimum rates. Generally, these extra hours were not called overtime but extra time, and the women were not paid more for doing it. One employer explained it as follows:

'an extra two/three hours daily just means that they are able to finish a few more pieces than they would normally do and hence earn a bit extra. There is no such thing as overtime when you are on piecerate.'

The Indian women workers are by no means unaware of the difference in wages in the sweated trade and other factories – often they have relatives who work for English firms. However, there are great limitations to any improvement due to their weak and vulnerable industrial position within the sweated trade itself and the lack of alternative employment. When an individual worker complained about her wages or working conditions, she would be told to leave or be reminded of the abundance of others willing to take her place in the factory.

None of the women I spoke to had ever been informed of their pay or holiday arrangements when they took on a new job in a sweatshop. Further, there was reluctance to enquire about one's wages, which arose from fear of being seen as 'greedy', or as 'a troublemaker once you ask about pay'. And there is the relief at finding a job, however low paid, as well as the way 'the employer makes us feel we should be very grateful . . . [for] doing us a favour'.

CONTROLLING THE WORKFORCE

It was a common practice for the employers to interfere in every aspect of the women's life. If they did not turn up for work the employers would phone them at home and question their absence. When they said they were ill they were told to come in rather than 'potter around the house doing housework'. If they felt unwell at work tablets were immediately distributed to keep them working. The fear the female workers had for the employer was universal and they would rarely speak up about their grievances. If the relationship between a woman worker and her employer seriously deteriorated into continuous verbal abuse and threats of violence, the husband or father of the worker would often turn up and make counter-threats.

Although the Asian employers' own dissatisfaction with the low wages, lack of promotion, dirty and hard conditions of their previous work had precisely led them into the sweated trades, they did not see themselves as giving the workers a 'rotten' deal. The following was a view shared by many:

'I see the majority of women working for me as benefiting from my job offer. They are all illiterate and have no skills, hence no British factory will make use of them. The women no longer have the same kind of homelife of the extended family like back home in India . . . . Here in England they are left alone in their homes till either the children or husband comes home, unable to go far as they may not be understood. I see myself providing a little extra for them: a place of work where they meet women in similar situations as themselves. Their £20 a week will help towards the family income, and we are like a big family here.'

One employer admitted the existence of exploitation – 'to a cer-

tain extent' - but blamed it on the women's weak bargaining position in the labour market:

> 'You see, our women [Asian] are exploited due to the fact that
> they are unable to get work elsewhere. They neither mix well
> nor speak the language well, hence they are easy victims of
> this society. They simply have to take what is offered to them'.

All the employers worked with a stereotype of Asian women as
passive. It was not an uncommon claim that the Asian women were
slow in their minds and bodies, and that it took a very long time
to make them into speedy workers. But equally because the women
were cast as unable to think for themselves, 'troublemaking' was
seen as an outside force influencing the women, namely husbands
or male relations. Despite the general belief that the Asian female
workers were too grateful to cause trouble, the employers relied
heavily on their own wives and close female relations to keep an
eye on the workforce. It was crucial for the organisation of labour
that such women were involved in the daily operation of the factories both as machinists and supervisors. In this capacity they
worked alongside the workers the whole day leaving them little
chance to express discontent, or even discuss anything amongst
themselves at all.

However, this was not the workers' only problem. With variation
in pay and the development of favouritism, the workforce was most
often divided. Some women acted as informers on the rest of the
staff in the hope of securing their own position in the factory in
the case of redundancies, or to further a pay increase. Other
women were 'bought off' during a troubled time in the factory,
and helped the employer calm down the potential rebellion or vague
opposition that had developed. In this way the division of the
workforce was kept alive; it tended to make the individuals act
on their own rather than collectively. Four women in different
factories, for example, had in the past taken their individual employers to Industrial Tribunal over redundancies without any
support from the rest of the workforce. They all lost their cases.

All the employers stressed how they discouraged their workforce
from discussing matters of pay or other discontentment among
themselves. When the women were appointed they were told to
come individually to see the employer or his wife with any work
problem: 'It is not good for them to natter amongst themselves.'

The employers dealt with the women on an individual basis when
the workforce had got together over a grievance. One described
how, despite his content workforce who were all keen to do a good
job, and his fairness as a boss, an attempt had been made to
establish a union in the factory while he was away on holiday:

> 'But, you see, it was all Communist inspired through their hus-
> bands. The women who work for me are all illiterate and they
> do not know what a union is. They are unable to read the union
> literature and booklets. Frankly anybody could get them to sign

their names on the union card. These women do not come from
a union background - they are all peasants.'

He had dealt with the 'rebellious' women by calling them into his
office, informing them that they were paid according to the statutory minimum wage set by the Wages Council - 'What more did
they want?' He then called them in one by one:

'By talking to them individually I soon managed to get them off
the whole idea of joining the trade union. The chief instigator
of the trouble got pregnant and left soon after. All it takes is
a couple of women to stir the rest.'

During layoffs or redundancies the women involved in 'troublemaking' activities were often the first to go, if no other reason
could be found to sack them or persuade them to leave voluntarily
It was common practice to induce the women, (especially militants
but also 'unsatisfactory' workers) to leave by making their work
conditions even worse. One employer explained how this was done.
He had talked two women out of joining a union but a third had
been 'adamant':

'I pondered for a long time how I could get rid of her. Luckily
she fell ill and on her return I decided to change her job and
give her one of the less attractive ones for a couple of weeks.
After the two weeks were up I gave her the old job back, you
know, she never raised the union matter again.'

Many of the employers expressed the need for the Asian clothing
manufacturers to stand together and refuse to re-employ workers
who had left an Asian-owned factory due to 'trouble'. It served
too as a deterrent for the existing workforce, for since the women
are very close they would soon realise what was happening to their
'rebel' sisters. One employer showed me a blacklist of all the
unionised ex-workers of the strike-ridden factory that had to
close down:

'The problem is that some of these women are very good workers
which makes it difficult to get rid of them through the disciplinary procedure, i.e. lazy worker, late worker, sick worker.
Hence all of us [Asian owners] keep this list to prevent appoint-
ment of any of them. I only managed to get rid of my [two]
troublemakers when I closed the factory for 5 weeks over
Christmas due to my father's death in India. I refused to re-
appoint them when I opened the factory again. Presently, we
are keeping an eye on one woman who could become troublesome
I cannot sack her as she has had no disciplinary warning.'

Some employers could not even begin to conceive of a strike on
their premises. They viewed their relationship with the workforce
in paternalistic terms, and were somehow unable to relate low pay

poor working conditions and frequent redundancies to the causes
for strikes and general discontent among the women. Every issue
seemed to be personalised, that is they would point out what
wonderful employers they were, and their individual attention
and favouritism to the staff. How could one or two redundancies
affect the other workers? They considered it their privilege as
employers to make decisions regarding jobs, pay and work hours
without the whole workforce 'getting up in arms'. The two manufacturers who had had strikes also regarded the strikes as personal vendettas or victimisation by their workers' relatives. They
hinted at a conspiracy by the communist party and other radical
political groups, such as the SWP and the IWA, who had picked
out two factories as scapegoats for the rest of the Asian entre-
preneurs. They gave me the impression that the issue went further
than the factory floor - their pride and public image as entre-
preneurs in the Indian community was at stake.

Only three employers acknowledged the benefit the women could
get from belonging to a trade union. One suggested, however,
that closure would be inevitable:

'The wages are so low and the margins we operate within are too
small to take a wage rise. We would make no profit.'

Nevertheless, the argument against unionisation always seemed to
hinge on the fact that the workers were women with their role in
the home, i.e. not 'serious' workers, and their general lack of
education. The employers were all quick to point out the short-
comings of the women. One of the least-educated owners, nick-
named 'the villager' by the other Asian employers, had this to say
about women and trade unions:

'Most of our Asian women come from small villages and have
never even heard of unions . . . (and) are easily misled. . . .
Unionism is of little use to the women because they are unable
to read the rules and regulations. As shop stewards, for
example, the women would not know what the grievance procedure was. Moreover, I have pointed out to the women that they
would lose some of their Indian privileges (that is, days off for
weddings and festivals) if they joined.'

As mentioned above, the pattern of recruitment reinforces the
employers' control over the workforce. Where women have been
recruited via friends or relations and later on turn out to be
'troublemakers', a direct phone-call to the husband, father or
uncle is often made. He will be requested to persuade his relative
to change her mind. Several women did in fact mention how they
gave in after pressure from relations and in order to avoid a
domestic row as well as a workplace grievance.

It is clear that the women workers in the clothing factories were
controlled and subordinated in a variety of specific ways (see
Beechey, 1979). Firstly, the relationships of servility, subser-
vience and passivity evident between husband and wife, or mother-
in-law and daughter-in-law in the home were reproduced to an
important extent at work. The relationship between employer and

worker was underpinned by the conventional relationship between man and woman in the Asian community (see Wilson, 1978, chs. 6 and 7). But also this pattern of relationship was complicated by the way in which control in the factories was often exercised via the employer's wife or close female relations. Ironically, this form of control tended to reinforce the dependence of the employer's wife and close female relative on the employer as husband or 'successful' male family member. However, it should be noted that the women workers occasionally resisted these forms of control. Often this resistance was supported, encouraged and mediated through husbands, brothers or fathers. While this was an important development, it nevertheless reinforced the subordinate relationship between husband and wife or older males to younger females.

FORMS OF RESISTANCE

All the same these women workers did act to challenge their situation of domination and exploitation in an attempt to establish a degree of control over their working lives. In two ways - individually and collectively - the women workers questioned the control exercised over them as women and as workers.

The high turnover of workers was one way whereby workers responded to their employment conditions. Nevertheless, the owners refused to see any link with the turnover of female workers and the wages and conditions the women were offered. The women' problems were all seen to be domestic ones that were transferred to work. One employer had this to say:

'Women are a problem whether in the home or at work. Their children also create problems. . . . I feel that women do not have the same responsibility as men in their jobs as they are not the breadwinners. . . . Our Asian women are both irregular workers and irresponsible. Absenteeism is a great problem. The women keep taking a couple of days off now and then, and during child illness they remain at home all the time as their husbands do not help out.'

In general employers felt that the women going sick was due to poor health to start with and their simply wanting time off. These attitudes fail to recognise the problems of women workers arising from long strenuous hours under unhealthy and hazardous working conditions, all the time being closely supervised. A large number of women I talked to told me how they had to leave due to illness which they saw as a direct consequence of the work they were doing. Many developed constant headache, sick feelings, nervous tension and pain in their backs from sitting bent over the machine all day with little rest. The nervous tension was partly the result of abuse by the owner and constant worry about output and threats of dismissal if they did not work fast enough. In addition, some women had problems with their eyes: soreness and pain due to the strain while sewing, plus dust irritation from the cloth.

Several women workers, however, left their jobs because they felt it was no longer worth working in the sweatshops for the appalling wages they took home. With the rising cost of living they found that their wages remained stagnant for years with no prospect of an increase. Only a dozen of the nearly one hundred women I spoke to had ever had any success in their individual requests to the employers for a wage increase.

These responses were a very natural way to cope with problems at work, as the women did have difficulties in seeing themselves collectively in a similar relation to their employer, difficulties fostered by the very individualistic, paternalistic and divisive strategies of their employers.

The most recent response, as individuals, to this employment was for the women to improve their knowledge of English and other skills like typing, accounting and to go back to school. Some of the women who were educated here would join TOPS courses and the women who had had their education in India would go to local part-time courses in English language for 3 months at a time. Unfortunately, given the current economic climate, these women found it difficult to obtain new jobs in better-paying sectors of the labour market although by gaining a better knowledge of English in addition to the confidence to speak up and more knowledge of their rights at work, they may be better able to fight back in the future.

The collective resistance has more potential. However, out of the twenty-two factories only one had been fully unionised since 1977. Unionisation was attempted in at least another six factories since then but three of them were stopped even before the women got in touch with the trade union office and asked the official to start recognition procedure. The remaining three factories had varying levels of success, but the one successful factory nevertheless signified the possibility of collective resistance by these workers.

The fully organised factory was one of two that went on strike over recognition and better wages in 1977. Both were greatly inspired by Grunwick's strike and the Indian women's involvement there. In factory no. 1 (which employed twenty women) the owner made six women redundant in July 1977, three of whom were secret union members. This redundancy angered the women who all united regardless of union membership. During a two-week strike they all joined the union and refused to return to work unless their demands for better wages, working conditions and shorter hours were met. The owner agreed and they all went back. However, by November the owner claimed he had a great reduction in incoming orders and he closed the factory down and sacked the workers. Nevertheless, he carried on with homeworkers for nine months and reopened under a new name in August 1978.

The second strike, at factory no. 2, (which employed twenty-two women), began during the second week of the first strike.

The owner had made nine women redundant. The women had all
unionised in secret and struck. After two weeks the TGWU officials
and the Wages Council took a closer look at the pay and conditions
of the factory. The employers (a partnership) were completely
taken by surprise and gave in to the demands made by the union.
The factory is still open as the only fully unionised Asian-owned
factory in Coventry.

One of the two shop stewards at this factory related to me how
she and the other women went about joining the union, faced with
hostile employers. This shop steward had been crucial in the
initial period and her husband's own involvement with the TGWU
as a bus driver had been an important factor in the unionisation
of the other women. He had obtained membership forms from the
TGWU and explained the procedure to her. She in turn arranged
to meet some of the older women in the city centre. There she
convinced them to join the union in order to gain better pay and
working conditions. All the preparations and meetings had to take
place outside the factory in the evenings or at weekends because
the employers' wives were working amongst them. If the news had
leaked they would have been sacked.

At that time in her factory they all worked five days from 8 a.m.
to 6 p.m. and Saturday from 8 a.m. to 1 p.m., with half an hour
for lunch. A full day on Saturday and Sunday was common during
the busiest time of the year – then she took home £16 to £17. Without the extra it was only £13 for 50 hours actual work. Though
much preferring to stay home with her husband and their four
children, she rarely refused weekend work. Pressure to comply
was a reminder that women who could do the extra could easily
be found.

> 'The wage the employer had calculated weekly was never ex-
> plained on the pay packet or by a payslip. This has now changed
> with our new trade union wages. Every extra hour is accounted
> for in writing. We just never compared our pay packet because
> we had been told not to but we knew we all were paid according
> to different rates. To compare all wages could only lead to con-
> flict and jealousy between ourselves.'

The strike and subsequent trade union recognition was very
important since it showed women workers in similar positions in
other sweatshops what could be done. During the months following the two strikes, women workers discussed the possibilities of
resisting, but as I showed earlier many of the attempts were stopped at a very early stage due to informants or the women's own
handling of the situation. Often they would ask the employer if
he would allow unionisation which then gave him warning and
time to take counter measures. However, the strikes and the
subsequent recognition in one factory did bring about a general
knowledge among the workers in other sweatshops of the proper
rates for the jobs done in clothing manufacture. A better understanding of the workers' rights developed since this became a

topic of discussion among working women after exposure of the appalling conditions and pay in the local English as well as Asian press.

Although the legal arrangements with regard to pay, holidays and overtime as well as an employment contract were settled for the one unionised factory, the struggle did not stop there. The two shop stewards have had a difficult time keeping the workforce united and organised. The employers in factory 2 have since attempted to reinstate the old system of favouritism by offering more to some workers to the detriment of others. Moreover, they have used any dispute among the women to divide them further and in this way to break up their union. Twice, time study experts have been called in to challenge the women's output per day against their weekly wage, in favour of piecerates, although to no avail. On each occasion the shop stewards have threatened to stop overtime work if a piecerate system was introduced.

During the past three years it has been extremely difficult for the shop stewards to handle the situation, as they had no previous union experience or knowledge of procedure and negotiations. They have had to lean more heavily and more frequently on their local trade union official for help than is 'normal' practice. Consequently, the Asian-owned clothing industry has come to be considered problematic and excessively time-consuming for the official. Disputes that would normally be settled between employer and shop steward have required the personal attention and involvement of the official. I was told that it was one of the sectors that nobody within the union wants to take on. Nevertheless, the present full-time official has made an effort to overcome the vast communication problems they work under. With all their trade union material, handbook, rulebook, etc., in English, an inexperienced Asian female shop steward with minimal English knowledge can find her job very difficult to carry out without extra help or encouragement.

Moreover, in this factory the women were denied the right to hold their union meeting on the factory premises during their lunch-hour. This in turn created a problem for the shop stewards in informing members of any developments in connection with collective grievances. Few of the women were in fact willing to come to meetings after work hours because of their heavy domestic responsibilities. This unfortunately created a further division amongst the women as the shop stewards tended to inform the group of women workers they were closest to of any recent developments, to the exclusion of the rest. Similarly grievances and complaints from a steward's own friends tended to be taken to the employer whereas other cases would not be dealt with. In this way, joining the union was important and beneficial to the Asian women workers in terms of their wages, holidays and conditions of work but further divisions along friendship lines have been intensified by the stewards' position and nurtured by management.

After the strikes in 1977 the Asian sweatshop employers formed an association to counteract any future action on behalf of their

Asian female labour force. They contracted a management consultancy firm to deal with their labour problems in case of future
strikes and union recognition issues. They have become better pre
pared for collective resistance and have tended to take immediate
action, often quite successful, to crush any labour unrest.

During the latter part of 1979 two large and very successful
sweatshops were confronted by their workforce demanding trade
union recognition. They both employed between 35 and 40 women
workers and in both cases the women had in secret organised over
half the workforce, the necessary percentage required when asking for union recognition. On reception of the request, the employers in both factories called their workers into the office one
by one, grilling them about union membership, reasons for joining
who instigated the organising, etc. They were then offered individual pay increases in return for giving up their membership cards
to the owner and a promise not to join a union again. Threats of
sacking for non-compliance were made. However, in both the factories the shop stewards had foreseen trouble from the employers
and kept the women's membership cards with them. When it became
clear that the workers were unwilling to give up their membership
and listen to the employers' 'good advice', redundancies of the tota
workforce were issued on the advice of the consultancy firm.

THE PROBLEM OF LEADERSHIP

A dress and skirtmaking factory started in 1978 employing 35
women including 12 English women. One of the older women who
in the past had been self-employed and who spoke fluent English
took it upon herself to organise the Asian women. She started to
read rights at work literature and soon realised how many illegal
practices her boss employed. She related to me how she was fed
up watching the other Asian women leaving the boss's office in
tears and despair after they had made a polite request for some
holiday due or for an increase of a couple of pence in their pay
rates. She went to the TGWU headquarters locally, where she
obtained relevant recruiting material. Her personality was very
forceful and persuasive and she explained to the workers, none
of whom was related to the employer, how they could improve thei
conditions and wages by acting collectively as a union.

Most of the dressmakers were getting £20–£25 gross for a 48-
hour week; no overtime pay, no Bank Holidays and only two week
summer holiday during which time he gave them £12 per week
holiday pay. The main problem for the women had started when
the factory became increasingly successful, that is new orders
for different styles were received every week. This meant that
the workers no longer had time to familiarise themselves with one
style and hence build up considerable speed. This drastically
affected their output per day and their wages. Under the changir
conditions of work a fixed hourly rate was seen by the workers
to be more appropriate.

The local union who were to represent the women requested
recognition. The employer suddenly announced that no more
orders were coming in. Shortly after he proceeded to lay off his
entire staff. However, some of his English employees came back
in to do the packing and pressing. His 'non-existent' orders were
distributed to outworkers via an Asian middleman who arrived
daily and carried the ready-cut materials away in his van. This
was all done under the noses of the laid-off women who stood outside his factory daily for ten weeks hoping he would re-open.
Unfortunately, there was a change in leadership amongst the
women. The steward was due for her six-week unpaid leave to
India. She felt all was going well and the women were united.
Hence, she asked a friend within the factory to take over temporarily as steward. The result was that many of the women lost faith
in the whole affair as the steward did not keep them all informed
or call meetings regularly. Also, many of them had to look for
alternative jobs as they feared long-term unemployment and they
could not manage without a regular income, however low. But the
new steward's position was very weak and she had little following
amongst the younger women and she admitted she was frightened
of the boss. She did not dare picket the factory although she
had the support of many of the women on this issue. She explained:

'I am not familiar with what to do, I only took on the role of
steward because my friend asked me. The Asian community is so
small and if we stand outside creating trouble, the owners of
other clothing factories will drive past here. They will recognise
us so we will never get work again in any clothing factory. I
know our boss is giving our work to others, we have seen the
man coming to pick up boxes of ready-cut cloth. We also saw
the tailor and cutter working inside the factory with some white
people packing it all up. I do not have the strength to do this.'

The first shop steward on her return did in fact suggest picket-
ing and making their demands public. Many women, however, felt
she had let them down by leaving when they most needed her.
She was, after all, the only worker among them who was familiar
with their legal rights. By being kept out for over three months,
several of the women who were unionised gave up and took jobs
in other sweatshops. This meant that the 50 per cent membership
rule required by the union for recognition no longer applied to
the remaining workers. As a result the union dropped their recognition claim.

THE PROBLEM OF LEGAL REDRESS

A trouser-making and undwear-producing factory employed 40
Asian women, many of whom were relations of the owner. The
women's wage varied from £20 to £27 gross for a 47-49½-hour week.
The owner was very abusive - always shouting and cursing, there

was no toilet paper and no eating facility. There were no contracts of employment and their wages packets gave no indication of the date received and the hours worked. Besides no pay for overtime, which had become more frequent, holiday pay was £7 per week for their annual two weeks plus three days.

On many occasions the individual workers had approached the owner about a pay-rate increase. This factory had run for seven years and some of the women had had no increases during this time. When workers asked him for increases he very abruptly replied 'Leave if you don't like it here'. Union organisation was made very difficult since several women had obtained their jobs through the wife of the employer, whose sister-in-law and several cousins also worked there.

Unionisation was attempted by the packers and pressers, none of whom were related to the employer. They were also the worst-paid section of the workforce, paid by the hour whereas the machinists were paid per piece. This created a division among them in addition to their varying work tasks. Sixteen women got together outside the factory to discuss the possibility of getting organised. They received extensive help from one of the older women's husband who was himself a shop steward. This time it was the National Union of Metal Mechanics (general workers section) that was approached and their local full-time official thought this was an important challenge when he realised their pay and conditions. He approached the employer and asked for recognition. Two weeks later the workers were informed that the factory was no longer receiving sufficient orders - a surprise to them as trade had been pretty brisk up until the previous week. All the women were made redundant for two weeks, but a couple of the unionised women received letters offering them their jobs back. When one rang the owner to enquire if they were all going back in, he told her it depended upon their willingness to give up their union membership. All the non-unionised women returned in addition to two unionised workers who were put on three days a week only.

The trade union official took the case to the Industrial Tribunal on the grounds of victimisation because of trade union membership. The official organised several meetings outside the workplace in one of the older women's home. He spent hours listening to their grievances and took great care in encouraging them to keep up the fight. Moreover, he briefed them on the forthcoming Tribunal. They all went to the Tribunal in great spirits expecting to win the case. They lost on a legal technicality. The next day the rumour of their failure and the sweatshop owner's success swept around the other factories. Many of the employers made a special point of telling their workforce and to discourage similar action in the future.

CONCLUSION

The patterns of recruitment into the Coventry clothing industry resulted in a mainly Asian female workforce who were tied to their employers by more than a cash relationship. As a result, the women felt a sense of obligation and gratitude to their employers, which was expressed partly through work patterns. In contrast, the few English women who worked in these factories did not have this sense of obligation: for them a job was a job. But, perhaps of equal importance, the employers expressed a view of English women as workers which tended to reinforce their preference for the more easily dominated Asian female workers.

The Asian women workers found themselves in a vulnerable position due to the insecure nature of the sweated clothing trade in addition to the lack of any alternative employment. Their industrial bargaining position was seriously weakened as a result of the abundance of Asian female labour willing to take the place of employed women who express any discontent or resistance about their wages or conditions of employment. The Asian women workers' ability to organise at all is limited by this as well as the fact that they are tied to their employment beyond the need for cash.

The type of control exerised by the employers of these clothing factories, directly and through the community, was repressive and exploitative and particularly used and reinforced their subordinate position as women. The relationship involved close supervision and inspection at all times; it was expressed through verbal abuse and commands. In turn, the women workers found it difficult to discuss grievances or work problems partly because they often worked alongside the employer's wife or kin.

Furthermore, the employers demanded that every worker should be treated individually, thereby discouraging collective action by the women and weakening their bargaining position. In addition, there was the continual and real threat of sacking if the workers did not comply with the wishes of the employer (see also Dromey and Taylor, 1978, chs 2-4; Wilson, 1978, ch. 3). All the same these women did at various points resist the control exercised over them. There were occasions when the workers organised collectively, principally through trade unions, and challenged the employers.

It was on these occasions that the promise of change as well as perpetuation of their subordinate position became evident. Their action showed women in other sweatshops that resistance can lead to change. The result was that women took important and necessary steps to determine and influence their conditions of employment by joining unions and organising collectively. Nevertheless, it should be noted that trade union organisation and action is not without its difficulties: historically trade unions have not been structured or organised with particular reference to the problems and issues facing working women, even less immigrant women. Consequently, the relevance of unionisation is not always immediately apparent to many women workers. The Asian women workers in the 'sweatshops' were no exception: a number of these workers learnt about union organisation from their husbands or male relatives. Paradoxically, this meant that the women workers emancipated themselves at work by reaffirming their dependence upon males. For these women the struggle has only just begun.

ACKNOWLEDGMENTS

I would like to thank Tony Elger for helpful and detailed comments, and Peter Fairbrother for invaluable help and encouragement throughout the writing of this paper.

6 MIGRANT WOMEN AND WAGE LABOUR: THE CASE OF WEST INDIAN WOMEN IN BRITAIN

Annie Phizacklea

It is only in the last five years that the presence of migrant women in Britain and elsewhere in Western Europe has received any serious attention. A number of recent accounts have described migrant women's dual role in production, (Wilson, 1978; Foner, 1979; and Prescott-Roberts and Steele, 1980) and their triple oppression as worker, as woman and as migrant (Kosack, 1976; Morokvasic, 1980). Nevertheless, there has been little attempt to analyse the class position of migrant women workers, nor the forms of consciousness and action that they have brought into the arena of working-class struggle.

This chapter focuses on a single migrant group, West Indian women in Britain; it considers whether and in what way they occupy a distinct position within the British working class, and goes on to examine the industrial and political consciousness and action of West Indian women in one geographical area, Harlesden in north-west London. The analytic framework adopted here is virtually identical to that used in the collaborative work undertaken by Robert Miles and myself (Phizacklea and Miles, 1980). It is a class analysis which employs the concept of class fraction to identify the bases of stratification within classes. The concept of class fraction is derived from the work of Poulantzas (1975) and refers to an objective position *within* a class boundary which is, in turn, determined by both economic, politico-legal and ideological relations. Thus, while the vast majority of West Indian women in Britain can be unambiguously described as working class by virtue of the fact that they sell their labour power for a wage, their position within that class will be determined by their specific position in these three sets of relations.

In the work referred to above we have made a case for conceptualising female and black migrant labour as class fractions. In terms of economic relations both occupy a subordinate position in the labour market; in terms of politico-legal relations both experience de facto discrimination in spite of legislation outlawing sexual and racial discrimination. Moreover, discriminatory action can be justified by ideological representations which in the case of women take the form of sexism and, for black migrants, racism, so the process then becomes circular and self-fulfilling. In our analysis of the political belief and action of the English and West Indian working class, we were able to identify similarities among the men and women, black and white, which could be explained in terms of their shared class position as wage labourers. But we were also aware of dissimilarities in belief and action which could only be

explained with reference to a specific fractionalised class position.
These ideas will be substantiated and elaborated here in the
following ways. The first section examines the migration of
women in the context of their economic role in the West Indies and
certain economic and political factors in Britain from the 1950s
which are vital to an understanding of the class position of black
migrant labour in the British social formation. I then discuss the
current position of West Indian women in economic, politico-legal
and ideological relations. Finally I consider at length certain
findings drawn from the research carried out in north-west
London which compares and contrasts the consciousness and action
of West Indian women with those of West Indian men, English
women and English men.

WEST INDIAN WOMEN AND MIGRATION

The majority of women in my Harlesden networks were Jamaican-
born migrants, and it is important to understand at least a little
of the social and economic role of women in that society. Jamaica's
history of underdevelopment and continuing economic dependence
on transnational corporations is dealt with in detail elsewhere
(Girvan, 1972; Beckford, 1972) and useful summaries can be
found in Foner (1979) and Pryce (1979). Suffice it to say here
that underdevelopment has meant high levels of unemployment for
men and women and, since the nineteenth century, a steady labour
migration from the island.
   Cultural imperialism was an additional legacy of colonial domination. For example, the role of husband-provider is culturally
valued even though the material basis of fulfilling that role has
historically been denied West Indian men. Marriage (a prestige-
conferring act) is postponed until a man can offer a degree of
financial security, thus a large proportion of children are born
to extra-residential partnerships and normally become incorporated
into the mother's natal household. It is suggested that in a situation where the grandmother takes on the 'social mother' role, the
biological mother is put in a position where she strives to assume
the full parental role, including its economic aspect (Philpott,
1977, p. 104). But women's access to regular paid employment is
even more limited and sporadic than it is for men because they
are confined mainly to sectors of women's work. Money-making
activities include dressmaking, domestic service, small-scale trad-
ing and certain agricultural tasks, but such work rarely enables
a woman to achieve financial independence (R.T. Smith, 1956,
p. 42; Foner, 1979, p. 66).
   Thus for over a century women have migrated in search of work,
from rural to urban areas, to Cuba, to the USA and, in the 1950s,
to what Jamaicans had been led to believe was the 'Mother
Country'. News of job opportunities in Britain resulted in the
rapid development of a chain migration from the West Indies. But
the fact that a woman can be motivated to migrate in order to

achieve her own social and economic goals is an explanation that
is never given credence in the early literature relating to West
Indian migration to Britain. For example, Davison's analysis of a
sample survey carried out in Jamaica in 1961 shows the number
of women and men migrating to be equal. He concludes from this
that the women are 'following' men who had begun to settle down
in Britain (1962, p. 16). The inference is that the women were
migrating as dependants of men, but from a legal and economic
standpoint this must be questioned. The same survey shows that
78 per cent of the women were single (24 per cent of whom were
classified as living in a stable union) and when asked why they
were migrating to Britain, they answered almost unanimously 'to
seek employment' (1962, p. 36). There was a short time-lag in
the equalisation of sex ratios in the migration flow, but this can
be explained in a number of different ways. For instance, Foner
argues: 'Probably most important, women may have had more
difficulty than men in raising the rather considerable funds to
pay for their passage because men received preference as the
expected wage earners' (1979, p. 57). My own research leads me
to agree with Foner that West Indian women, whether or not they
'follow' men, are highly motivated to seek regular waged work in
order to be financially independent and from what women heard
about Britain they believed that their ambitions could be realised
in that country.

The presence of black migrant labour must also be seen in
relation to the demand for labour in certain sectors of the British
economy. Semi- and unskilled labour was required for jobs which
indigenous workers had moved out of in pursuit of higher wages
and more congenial work (Peach, 1968) and also for new jobs
created by the introduction of new technology and the subsequent
deskilling of the workforce (Duffield, 1980). In addition, the
newly created National Health Service was suffering from acute
labour shortages at all skill levels and many women were recruited
in the West Indies as nurses. From the early 1950s until the threat
of immigration control became apparent in 1961, the flow of migrant
labour from the West Indies corresponded with fluctuations in the
demand for labour in Britain (Peach, 1968, pp. 37-50). It was
therefore unnecessary to control this supply for economic reasons
because it was self-regulating. Socio-political justifications for the
passing of the 1962 Commonwealth Immigration Act are also dubious.
The racism used to justify colonial domination and exploitation was
perceived to be counter-productive when it came to be acted out
in violent clashes between black and white residents in the streets
of Nottingham and Notting Hill in 1958. And by passing an Act
which was both racist in intent and effect, parliamentary legit-
imation was given to anti-black sentiment and discrimination. It
is against this background that we will go on to consider the
specific class position of black female migrant labour in Britain.

THE CLASS POSITION OF WEST INDIAN WOMEN IN THE BRITISH SOCIAL FORMATION

In order fully to comprehend the economic position of West Indian women in Britain an account of their position in politico-legal and ideological relations is necessary. All black women occupy a subordinate position in ideological relations in their being subjected to racial and sexual categorisation. As a set of beliefs, racism and sexism can be defined in the same way and relate to those beliefs which set a section of the population apart by attributing significance to some biological or other supposedly 'inherent' characteristic which they are said to possess and which deterministically associate that characteristic with some other feature or action. The possession of these supposed characteristics is then used as a justification for denying that group equal access to material and other resources and/or political rights.

All women are the object of sexual categorisation irrespective of class or national origin. The vast majority of women wage workers occupy a subordinate position in the labour market - in 'women's work' commanding low rates of pay, skill and status - because they are viewed primarily as actual or potential domestic labourers. Ideological representations, particularly that of motherhood, are in complete contradiction with the ideology of wagework and the demand for female labour (see the chapters by Caroline Freeman and Marilyn Porter in this volume). It is women with children who feel the full force of these contradictions. West Indian women's conception of the motherhood role, which entails the provision of financial support for children, does not lessen the concrete effects of these contradictions. On the contrary, it could be argued that they are heightened with the loss of traditional shared forms of child care and the latters' replacement with inadequate substitutes in the migration setting.

However, black women are also racially categorised and we must examine whether this places them in a subordinate position in politico-legal and ideological relations. Until 1962 West Indian women, as New Commonwealth citizens, had the right to live and work in Britain without restriction and had the same rights on entry as the rest of the population, except for the right of certain children to join them. According to British Immigration law the mother of an 'illegitimate' child left behind must show that she has had 'sole responsibility' for the child's upbringing if they are to be re-united and this rule has been harshly applied by Immigration Appeal Tribunals (Hewitt, 1976, p. 21).

Immigration law is only one example of the differential treatment experienced by black migrant labour in Britain. Perhaps more important is the continued existence of widespread racial discrimination in the areas of employment, housing and the provision of services (D.J. Smith, 1977; Hubbuck and Carter, 1980). There is, however, very little information as to whether racial discrimination works to disadvantage black women in the same way as black men. One British study which attempts to analyse the position with regard to employment concludes:

> the gap in terms of job levels and earnings between the minorities
> and whites is much greater among men than among women. The
> explanation is probably that women are already discriminated
> against as women, and this tends to restrict them to more junior
> and less well paid jobs; they are therefore not regarded as a
> threat, and there is less need for employers to discriminate
> against them on the ground of colour as well, in order to keep
> them in a subordinate position (D.J. Smith, 1977, pp. 120-1).

What this suggests is that the labour market was so rigidly segmented along sexual lines by the time black migrant women came
to Britain that there was little room for racial discrimination to
have an additional impact. To examine the validity of this conclusion I will draw on the limited data there is to hand which consists of 1971 Census data, the 1972-5 Political and Economic
Planning (PEP) investigation of racial disadvantage (D.J. Smith,
1977), the more recent Department of Employment (DE) analysis
of the 1977-8 National Dwelling and Housing Survey (NDHS) findings (Barber, 1980), and DE unemployment statistics. From this
data West Indian and other women can be compared on four variables: economic activity rates, hours worked, occupational distribution and unemployment levels.

The first three data sources indicate extremely high economic
activity rates for West Indian women, particularly those who are
married. The NDHS findings for married women are shown below
in Table 6.1.

Table 6.1   Economic activity rates of married women by age and ethnic origin (%)

Age (years)	West Indian	Indian	White
16-24	(65.0)[a]	62.3	58.6
25-34	79.4	48.1	49.5
35-44	88.5	59.8	66.1
45-59	87.1	34.9	61.0

Source: NDHS ½ per cent sample reported in Barber, 1980, p. 842.
[a]   Figure subject to sampling error due to small sample size.

Why do West Indian women have such high economic activity rates?
Studies by the Thomas Coram Research Unit suggest that West
Indian women work from necessity, not choice (D.J. Smith, 1977,
p. 66). Of primary importance is the material disadvantage experienced by black migrant labour in Britain in terms of pay, housing
costs and family size (see PEP Report, D.J. Smith, 1977). But
West Indian women are also highly motivated to achieve a degree
of financial independence, and their conception of 'motherhood'
entails an economic aspect.

West Indian women are more likely to work full time than women of British origin. NDHS findings indicate that only 20 per cent of all West Indian women wage workers are employed on a part-time basis.

According to the PEP study of racial disadvantage, 29 per cent of all working women are doing semi- and unskilled manual jobs compared with 47 per cent of West Indian women, 48 per cent of African Asians and 58 per cent of Indians (D.J. Smith, 1977, p. 77). Taking the 1971 Census statistics, we can compare the occupational distribution of West Indian born women with working women generally (it is important to remember that the latter category includes all New Commonwealth, Irish, foreign migrants etc. who collectively constituted 5.7 per cent of the female work-force in 1971). The DE analysis of 1971 figures, reports that 72.8 per cent of all economically active women are concentrated in four occupational orders: clerical workers, 27.2 per cent; sales workers, 11.6 per cent; service, sport and recreation workers, 22.3 per cent; and professional, technical workers and artists, 11.7 per cent (DE, 1976, p. 121). My own calculations of the 10 per cent sample from this census show that 58.3 per cent of West Indian women are concentrated in these four occupa-tional orders, but that there are major discrepancies in their distribution when compared with working women in general. Only 11 per cent of West Indian women are clerical workers and 1.3 per cent sales workers. 21 per cent are service workers and 25 per cent are categorised as professional, etc. workers. A very high proportion of these 'professional' West Indian women are nurses and in 1968 they constituted 35 per cent of overseas-born student and pupil nurses. There is nevertheless some debate about the status of black female migrant labour within the NHS. Official sources indicate that 'immigrant' nurses are over-represented in the least-desirable sectors of nursing, such as mental and geriatric (Department of Employment, 1976) and the periodical 'Race Today' documents assertions that black female student nurses are steered towards the State Enrolled rather than State Registered Nursing qualification (1974, p. 227). West Indian women are also overrepresented, as compared to working women generally, in engineering and allied trades (9.7 as com-pared to 3.2 per cent), as clothing workers (7.3 as compared to 3.6 per cent) and as labourers and packers, etc.

It has been suggested that black migrants function to some extent as a marginal or reserve army of labour (D.J. Smith, 1977, pp. 71-2) to be brought in and thrown out of wage labour accord-ing to the needs of capital. The same is said to apply to women wage workers in general, which raises the question of whether or not black female migrant labour is a particularly vulnerable section of the workforce.

According to NDHS findings for 1977-8, 7.5 per cent of West Indian women born abroad were unemployed compared to 10.5 per cent of women born in India and 4.9 per cent of white women (Barber, 1980, p. 843; the rates include unregistered unemployed

and those temporarily sick). When unemployment levels begin an
upward trend, unemployment amongst male and female minority
groups increases at a faster rate than unemployment generally
and when employment levels begin to rise, minority men and women
are re-employed at a faster rate than men and women generally
(D.J. Smith, 1977, pp. 71-2). A DE analysis of unemployment
levels during November 1973 to May 1975, a period during which
unemployment was rising overall, shows that the proportionate
increase in unemployment among minority-group women was nearly
three times as large as among the total female unemployed (for
minority men the increase was twice as large as among the total
male unemployed) (Department of Employment, 1975, p. 869). Why
is black female migrant labour more at risk of becoming unemployed
than female labour in general?

There is evidence that women generally are less vulnerable than
they were in the 1950s, probably due to their movement from
declining manufacturing industries into more stable white-collar
employment (Bruegel, 1979, pp. 16 8). As black female migrant
labour (and this applies also to women workers born in India,
Pakistan and Bangladesh) is overrepresented in semi-and unskilled
manual work and underrepresented in routine white-collar, such
as clerical work, then they are less likely than female labour as
a whole to be cushioned from the worst effects of economic recession. The part played by racial discrimination in this process
is very difficult to assess. None the less, a recent longitudinal
study - which matched second-generation West Indian women with
similarly qualified young white women, both with virtually identical job preferences - found that the black women took longer to
secure jobs initially. Further, at times of high unemployment
generally the West Indian women were far more likely than the
white women to be unemployed, whereas when demand improved
their rates were equal or in some cases better (Dex, 1980). The
findings would suggest that all things being equal, black women
are a more vulnerable section of the female labour force than
white women.

What our evidence on employment suggests is that West Indian
women as migrant labourers moved into jobs in sectors of the
economy which had labour shortages due to the fact that indigenous men and women were unwilling to take them. There has been
little movement out of these jobs which indicates that West Indian
women have taken on what could be termed a permanent female
migrant worker role supplying cheap and flexible labour power.
More recently West Indian women have been joined in that role by
a rapidly increasing Asian female labour force. That the majority
of such women have effectively settled permanently in Britain has
done little to change their function within the labour market.

In sum I am arguing that West Indian women occupy a subordinate
position in economic, politico-legal and ideological relations, a
position (shared by the vast majority of black female migrant
labour) which is in many respects similar to indigenous women,

but is sufficiently dissimilar and distinct to warrant the description of a class fraction. Whether or not this fractionalised class
position produces its own corresponding forms of consciousness
and action is a separate issue and must be examined empirically.
The next section attempts to document how a small sample of West
Indian women conceptualise their position as wage labourers and
the extent to which their political and industrial action or inaction
can be explained with reference to their fractionalised class
position.

WEST INDIAN WOMEN AND WAGE LABOUR

The data upon which this section draws is part of a larger body
of findings drawn from research carried out in Harlesden and
Stonebridge in north-west London between late 1975 and 1977
(these areas were undergoing socio-economic decline). The
methods used were a combination of observational work and in-
depth interviewing. The first three months of the project were
spent 'lending a hand' in a local advice centre and observational
work in the area was carried out continuously throughout the
total time period. The interview sample (21 West Indian men, 20
West Indian women, 17 English women and 19 English men) was
randomly chosen within selected areas of both private and public
housing. Any one member of a household who was of either English
or West Indian parentage and aged 25 to 50 years was interviewed
(all the West Indian women are under 45 years of age) in their
home either in the evening or at the weekend. (This 'residential'
sample was quite distinct from my collaborator's all-male factory-
based sample.)
    The occupational distribution of the sample as a whole is shown
in Table 6.2.

Table 6.2 Occupational classification of the sample

	West Indian		English	
	Women	Men	Women	Men
	(N = 20)	(N = 21)	(N = 17)	(N = 19)
Semi and unskilled manual	14 (70%)	13 (62%)	6 (35%)	9 (47%)
Skilled manual	3 (15%)	5 (24%)	–	9 (47%)
Routine white collar	2 (10%)	2 (9%)	3 (18%)	–
Unemployed	1 (5%)	1 (5%)	1 (6%)	1 (6%)
Houseworker	–	–	7 (41%)	–

Five of the English women who were currently full-time house-
workers had been engaged in semi-or unskilled manual work prior
to the birth of their first child; two had continued to work inter-
mittently since then. The two other English women not actively
seeking work had previously been employed in routine white-

collar work. Thus national differences between the types of
'women's' work engaged in by English as compared to West Indian
born women are reflected in this London sample.

With the exception of the small proportion of routine white
collar workers in the sample, experience of redundancy was re-
counted by all as though it was an expected feature of their work
histories. The following account is from a West Indian woman who
now works as a home-help for the council:

> 'I used to work in a factory sewing. I did that for about nine
> years and then I was made redundant. I was unemployed for
> about six weeks and then I went into another job and I was
> made redundant again. I was only there a few weeks and they
> closed down, I don't think that the business was doing well
> enough. Then I went to another factory. I'm enjoying this work
> I'm doing now, though, with these old people, I'm sorry I
> didn't go into it earlier.'

There was in fact little difference between the work histories of
English and West Indian men and women. Their access to jobs was
on the whole limited by their lack of qualifications, the majority
having left school at the earliest possible age, although some had
started and sometimes completed a form of further education or
training. For the West Indians, skills learnt in the West Indies
were usually not recognised or deemed inadequate to the demands
of skilled labour in a more highly developed capitalist economy.

The main differences in work patterns among the sample as a
whole are among the women. Apart from one who had not worked
for some time due to sickness, all the West Indian women worked
at least a 35-hour week (some had two jobs). Only five of the
English women worked a 35-hour week and seven were not actively
seeking work. Child care and domestic responsibilities were the
main reasons given by English women for working part time or not
at all. The same proportion of West Indian women gave child care
as the reason for the particular type, location or hours of their
work, as the following quote illustrates:

> 'I work at a school as a general assistant; I help to cook the
> meals and serve them up and I have a couple of part-time jobs
> as well. . . . I worked in a factory for seven years but when
> my little boy started school it was difficult to get someone to
> take him to school in the mornings because I had to start at
> 7.30 a.m. Then during the holidays I had to pay so much money
> to keep him in the play centre I thought I'd get something that
> would be more convenient.'

Thus both the English and West Indian women's acceptance of the
responsibilities of child care (although there were only 4 single
women with children to support in the sample) further forecloses
what we have identified as the limited employment opportunities
open to the majority of the sample.

Very few of the West Indian women reported experience of
regular waged work prior to migration, which corresponds with
Foner's evidence for Jamaican migrants in London, but the latter
argues that the ability to earn a regular wage in England represents a real improvement in the lives of the women she interviewed
(1979, pp. 63-70). I cannot wholly endorse this view on the basis
of the interviews carried out in north-west London. As just one
of the women explained:

> 'If you look into it you'll see that the working class people
> aren't getting anything, we can just barely make it. My hus-
> band isn't working, I have to pay for everything and they still
> take so much tax from me. Everything keeps rising and I'm
> straining, I can't even buy anything for myself. Tonight I
> went to the shops and I bought a few items and it came to over
> £9, I still haven't bought any meat, I haven't paid the milk
> money and I have to buy more things . . . there are lots of
> men out of work and the poor women have to strain . . . it's
> like slavery really.'

This woman worked a 40-hour week, plus overtime in a hospital
laundry, her husband had been made redundant from a local
engineering firm three months previously (he had still not found
alternative work when I revisited this woman three months later);
she has four children, three of whom are still at school.

Three of the West Indian women in the sample had husbands
who had been made redundant in the six months prior to the
interview, another two were single mothers with children; thus a
quarter of the West Indian women were assuming the role of main
breadwinner for the family some or all of the time. Driver's comments on national trends indicate that this is not an isolated
geographical phenomenon: 'it is now an unspoken assumption
among many West Indian women that they, rather than their husbands or brothers, are the guardians of their family's good name
and the providers of its staple income' (1980, p. 113). He suggests that, due to the high levels of male West Indian unemployment, the socio-economic role of women in the West Indies is being
re-established in Britain.

West Indian women, like their male counterparts, believed that
migration to Britain would improve their social and economic
standing. But, as the following extracts from interviews illustrate,
their hopes have been dashed as they see both their standard of
living increasingly eroded by rising prices and their children's
prospects undermined by racism and racial discrimination:

> 'At first it was a little better, but now, it's terrible'.

And another:

> 'You go to work because you have to nowadays, but they take
> so much out of your wages that you don't have enough left to
> run a home and family.'

And another:

> 'We can only work to pay bills, we can scarcely buy clothes so
> that the children can go to school nowadays. You work and by
> Saturday you haven't got a penny to live off.'

A number voiced their deep concerns about the police-black youth
relationship:

> 'All my worries presently in Harlesden is for my children. I
> mean if my son was walking down the road or at a bus stop and
> there was a mugging nearby, how could he explain to the police
> that he wanted to go because he wasn't one of them, with the
> relationship we have here between the police and black youth.
> The police say "they all look alike", they always say that. I
> would like people to tell my children apart from others because
> of their conduct. The hardest thing for these people is to prove
> their innocence.'

The frequency with which these dual concerns were expressed
by West Indian women is simply a reflection of their dual role in
production as domestic and wage labourers. These roles are integrated in a specific way for West Indian women because of their
distinct conception of 'motherhood'. The economic aspect of that
conception has been modified by migration to the extent that
access to regular waged labour enables them to provide financial
support for their families, but migration has not fundamentally
transformed the socio-economic role of West Indian women. On
the contrary, it has merely modified the forms of oppression to
which they are subject.

West Indian women and trade unions
As wage labourers it might be expected that West Indian women
would look to trade unions as a means of defending and improving
the conditions under which they sell their labour power. But even
though women and black workers have constituted a large proportion of new membership over the last twenty years and there
is abundant evidence to show the extent of sexual and racial disadvantage in employment, trade unions have neglected the
interests of both groups and in some cases have been actively
involved in discriminatory practice themselves (Phizacklea and
Miles, 1980, pp. 90-8; Counter Information Services, 1976).
  Given this record of neglect, it might be expected that both
black and women workers would have a lower level of commitment
to trade unionism than white male workers. Before looking at
levels of trade union membership and participation amongst my
London sample, it should be made clear that the questions asked
in the study were 'colour' and 'sex' blind. This was deliberate,
first, because we were keen to see in what contexts the respondents themselves attached significance to colour or gender.
Second, our pilot work clearly indicated that the asking of blunt
questions was often counter-productive.

Three-quarters of the English men in the sample were trade union members. Although only three of the English women were currently members, this low level of membership can be explained by the fact that four of the nine currently employed were part-timers, the least-organised section of the labour force nationally. Among the West Indians 62 per cent of the men and 60 per cent of the women belonged to a trade union. The most common explanation for non-membership among the West Indians was that they worked in a small non-union firm; only one, a clerical worker, explained her current non-membership in terms of opposition to trade unions.

Well over half of all the union members in the sample reported joining under some form of external pressure, not necessarily because of the operation of a closed shop but in some cases through more informal means, as the following quotes from West Indian women illustrate:

'People can be working there and not belong to the union but in the laundry you have to because the other girls will squeal, they are paying their money and you aren't so they wouldn't like that.'

And another:

'I wanted to be with the majority of the staff and as far as I understood most of the staff were members. So I decided to join.'

But none of the West Indians, men or women, saw such pressure as illegitimate. On the contrary, a high proportion went on to explain what they saw as the benefits of membership. As one West Indian woman put it:

'If anyone tries to push you around, they help us.'

And another:

'If you look at past history in England when the old man could come up to you and say you are fired and that was it. That can't happen any more because of the unions. That's a good thing.'

Those who did not refer to 'compulsion' explained their membership in highly instrumental terms: 'It meant more money', or 'For protection'. The question of trade union membership had never arisen for the majority of West Indians prior to migration, but there is little evidence to suggest that, given the opportunity of joining a union in Britain, they were any less likely than white male workers to become members.

In addition, the reasons given for joining a trade union were very similar across the sample as a whole. The similarity in belief

and action among the English and West Indian women and men is
not surprising if we accept that as wage labourers they all have
certain interests in common which trade unions supposedly exist
to defend.

But participation in trade union activities is a different matter:
English men were the most regular attenders of union branch
meetings and 35 per cent were, or had been, shop stewards,
while none of the English women or the West Indians had held a
lay or full-time position within a trade union. Why the disparity?
Firstly, a high proportion of the English men spontaneously
offered information about a family tradition of unionism and spoke
of becoming a steward as a fairly natural process, even though
several added, 'Well, someone has to do it'. These accounts and
sentiments were never expressed by the West Indian women and
men or the English women in the sample.

A second factor is the role played by direct and indirect discrimination. Only one respondent, a West Indian man, alluded to
racist sentiment and practice in relation to his trade union. None
of the women alluded to either racist or sexist practice. Consciousness of racial and sexual disadvantage in employment and powerlessness within trade unions may, however, rarely be articulated
by black and women workers (Coote, 1980, p. 8; D.J. Smith 1977,
p. 330). None the less my research clearly indicates that such a
consciousness had developed among the black and female stewards
in my local network. Summing up her position as a steward in an
iron foundry, one West Indian woman had this to say:

> 'I want to see the workers get the feel of attending the meetings
> and pass on to each other what is going on - when we've devel-
> oped that I'd like to move on and let someone else take over.
> But as shop steward I've never been higher than going to the
> office and paying the dues, black people are going nowhere in
> the trade unions, we're just dues collectors, no advance.'

Her awareness of racial and sexual categorisation led her to the
conclusion that:

> 'I would take any action to keep jobs, we don't want to be out
> on the street, being black, being a woman, that's two things
> you can't hide.'

Unlike one of the male stewards, who argued that the 'migrant
ideology' was an effective barrier to the active involvement of
West Indian workers in trade union activities, this female steward
saw the problem of non-participation as one of trade union attitude
and practice. Thus she saw the first step in a process of long-
term change as being the introduction of positive action towards
black and women workers, including the provision of special training facilities for both groups so that they could gain the necessary
confidence and prerequisites for advance within the trade union
hierarchy (see Judith Hunt's chapter in this volume).

The powerlessness of women and black workers within trade unions raises the question of whether or not they evaluate trade unions less favourably than white men. The majority of the sample, female and male, black and white, defined the role of a good trade union as improving working conditions or attaining the best return on the sale of labour power and/or protecting workers.

Thus while the majority of respondents had a clear conception of what constituted a good trade union, these conceptualisations made no reference to racism or sexism. This was entirely true of the responses to a related question which asked the respondents to evaluate their own trade union's performance. Firstly, nearly half the sample indicated some dissatisfaction with this, though in only one case, a West Indian man, did this relate to racism. In contrast, two West Indian women who were satisfied with their union explained this in terms of their union's successful fight for equal pay. Secondly, what concerned the critics was that their union did not 'deliver the goods', whether this was better wages or as some of the West Indian women put it, failure to provide protection against 'being pushed around'. The latter response was unique to West Indian women and the sentiment was expressed at different points in the interview. Why should this be so? One possible explanation is that as black women workers in a society where racist and sexist belief remains widespread, they are in fact 'pushed around' more than others. But there are other factors, too, which reach back to the migration setting. For instance, in the West Indies very few women had access to regular waged labour and in turn had limited experience of the control over labour power which the wage relation imposes. (In this respect they differ from the majority of male migrants who had such experience.) Their current views reflect a resistance to management's control of the work process and many expressed concern that their shop stewards were party to that control or did not do enough to resist it. One of my informants, a shop steward herself, explained that it was her refusal to be 'pushed around' at work that had led her fellow workers (mainly other West Indian women) to ask her to stand as steward.

What general conclusions can we draw from these findings on trade union membership and participation? Firstly, there is little evidence to suggest that either black or women workers, given the opportunity, are any less likely than white men to join a trade union. Secondly, there is evidence to show that black and women workers participate less in union activities, including election to a lay or full-time union position. Thirdly, the level of similarity in belief and practice towards trade unionism among the sample suggests that primary significance is attached to their shared position as wage labourers. But having said this, there are apparent dissimilarities in belief, particularly amongst the women, which can be explained by their fractionalised class position, but in this context at least, the latter would appear to be of lesser significance.

Industrial action
It is often argued that women are less likely to be supportive of,
or involved in, industrial action. The findings of this study do
not support this assumption in the case of West Indian women
wage labourers. Over half the English men, but only 18 per cent
of the West Indian men indicated having been involved in any
form of industrial action (these figures correspond exactly with
my collaborator's). Among the women, 33 per cent of the West
Indian, compared to only 12 per cent of the English, reported
such involvement (the differences among the women can probably
be explained by the lower level of participation in the paid labour
force among the English female sample).

Extant evidence suggests that black workers are as willing as
white workers to take industrial action (Brooks, 1975; D.J. Smith,
1977) but the present study found a greater willingness on the
part of West Indian women than men to take such action. The
generalised validity of this conclusion is impossible to assess for
a number of reasons: the sample size is very small; West Indian
men may be more reluctant to admit any involvement in industrial
action; and we would want to consider the record of industrial
action for each respondent's industry.

Having said this, West Indian women wage labourers in Britain
have an impressive record of industrial struggle over equal pay,
state-imposed wage controls in the public sector and (perhaps the
most widely publicised) their forming the backbone of the struggle
over pay beds in the NHS in 1975 (see 'Race Today', May 1975).
What is clear from this national record and the findings of the
present study is that the majority of West Indian female wage
labourers believe industrial action to be a legitimate and necessary
form of action in certain circumstances.

This conclusion is given further support by their responses to
a question about the then current proposal to withdraw social
security payments from strikers. West Indian women were the
only group in the sample in which a majority expressed disagree-
ment with this proposal, as the following extracts illustrate:

'They take their tax money don't they? They strike for better
conditions, so they should get social security.'

And another:

'They should be allowed social security, they're only fighting
for their rights.'

What the evidence here and in the last section suggests is that
West Indian women as wage labourers see themselves as part of
the working class, recognise the benefits of trade unionism and
the necessity of solidarity action with other members of that class.
But trade unions are primarily workplace organisations, by definition they are therefore singularly inadequate in combating basic
sources of disadvantage outside the workplace. Disadvantage in

employment is only one aspect of black women's subordinate position within the working class and it is for this reason that they
are forced to initiate independent political action outside of the
workplace.

WEST INDIAN WOMEN AND POLITICAL ACTION

If we were to examine political activity in the formal sphere, we
would conclude that West Indian women had low levels of political
efficacy, perhaps even that they are politically passive. If attention focuses on the informal sphere of political activity, a very
different picture emerges. West Indian women organise over issues
of concern to them which are both broad class-based issues and
also those which reflect their fractionalised class position. An
example of the first would be the Harlesden Claimants Union,
where a number of West Indian women provided a stable, core
membership along with English women. But black working-class
women also take independent initiatives as the two following
examples illustrate.
     The first is of activity which arose around the issue of edu-
cation. A number of the women I interviewed expressed disquiet
over the type of education their children received. As one mother
put it:

   'I don't think the teachers or even the labour exchange is helping the kids at all and I think the reason for this is the majority
   of kids around here are coloureds. I hear that they say why
   worry about the coloureds. That's very bad.'

Very few West Indian women spontaneously referred to racism
and racial discrimination as it applied to themselves. This is not
to say that they do not experience either, but most have developed
mechanisms to cope with racism at least. One of my informants
explained:

   'If they say something that offends me, like go back where you
   came from, I give them back something that will offend them
   from now until tomorrow'.

But the situation is quite different when they perceive racism and
racial discrimination acting as an obstacle to their children's
advancement in British society, particularly in relation to police
harassment and education. A few months after I left the research
area it therefore came as no surprise to learn that West Indian
women had been instrumental in forming a successful pressure
group called the Association for Black Educational Advance.
     The second example is the formation of the West Indian Women's
Association (WIWA) in Harlesden. This initiative came from a
woman who had been active in workplace activity for fifteen years.
In forming the WIWA with the help of several colleagues she was

not turning her back on workplace organisation (she remains a
member of the Trades Council and the WIWA was quick to support
Asian women at a local factory who took strike action to protest
about pay and union recognition), but she believed that the most
pressing issues for the West Indian community, particularly
women, were comminity-, not work-based issues. In addition, she
had experience of working within West Indian voluntary organisations where women had been denied the opportunity of taking
any real initiative. The WIWA has established practical schemes,
such as supplementary education classes, has fought for better
child-care facilities and in some cases set up their own schemes.
The association has made a very rapid local impact.

DISCUSSION

This paper began by putting forward a case for conceiving of
West Indian female labour as part of a racially and sexually
categorised fraction of the working class. Their subordinate position in economic, politico-legal and ideological relations is to some
extent shared by women generally, but is nevertheless distinct.
Racial categorisation and its concrete effects is the most obvious
difference, but socialisation in a culture with a different interpretation of gender roles and, in particular, 'motherhood' is also
highly significant.
   Life in the Caribbean is tough for women, and migration offers
an escape route from persistent poverty and the struggle to attain
the full parental role, including its economic aspects. Whether a
woman migrated as a single or a married person, she came with
the expectation of finding waged work in order to improve her
social and material standing. Fifteen to twenty years later she
instead finds her living standards increasingly eroded and per-
ceives her children's prospects to be undermined by the persistence of racism. Some might expect that in these circumstances
West Indian women would react with withdrawal, possibly return
to the homeland, but neither strategy is in keeping with their
tradition of self-reliance. This self-reliance is not an inherited,
biological characteristic, but a response to a certain set of structural features and related experience. Thus as wage labourers
in Britain they have recognised the need for trade union protection and solidarity action with fellow workers, but they have also
recognised their specific fractionalised position within the British
working class and have acted to counteract some of the disadvantages inherent in that position.
   As the economic crisis in Britain deepens, West Indian women's
resilience and ability to fight back are being put to their severest
test since migration. Semi- and unskilled workers are taking the
brunt of job losses; public spending cuts mean hospital closures;
playschemes and nurseries are closed down. All of these constitute a direct attack on the working class as a whole, not just
black female migrant labour. But black migrant labour is being

subjected to specific additional threats as racist-inspired political violence once more increases and as young blacks are identified as a 'law and order' problem. It is imperative that the whole of the British working class recognises that these are direct attacks on class unity and acts to curb the sexism and racism within its own ranks.

ACKNOWLEDGMENTS

The interview and observational data referred to in this article was gathered while the author was employed by the SSRC Research Unit on Ethnic Relations at the University of Bristol. I would like to thank Bob Miles for his comments on an earlier draft.

7 STANDING ON THE EDGE: WORKING CLASS HOUSEWIVES AND THE WORLD OF WORK

Marilyn Porter

Women's position in the labour market cannot be fully understood without taking account of the complex connections between waged labour, sexual divisions, and the structure and ideology of the family in capitalist society. The theoretical connections, and the specificity of women's position in capitalist society is a continuing problem in feminist debate (Bland, Brunsdon, Hobson and Winship, 1978; Beechey, 1978; Molyneux, 1979; West, 1978 and 1980). Here I want to focus on how those theoretical connections are actually experienced in the lives of working-class women.

Other papers in this collection look at the experience of specific groups of women in the labour market. Questions about that experience - about women's participation in trade unions, about women as 'strike-breakers', or about the development of women's radical activity - often rest on an understanding that we cannot answer them without taking account of women's domestic responsibilities. The material in this paper demonstrates the validity of that position. It shows how the ideas that women have about work and collective action are concretely related both to their ideas and to their experience of the material reality of their place in the family. Class consciousness is constructed within the specific context of people's experience. This means, among other things, that we cannot 'read off' women's position, ideas or consciousness from men's. Women's experience of work is significantly different to that of men, and I want to suggest that that difference rests upon a sexual division of labour rooted, outside work, in the family. Of course women construct their interpretation of the world, and their class consciousness from *both* these areas of experience, but it is one of the underlying themes of this paper that the divisions between men and women and between home and work crucially fracture working-class experience and consequently working-class consciousness.

THE SEXUAL DIVISION OF LABOUR

The sexual division of labour describes the objective differences between what men and women in our society are primarily defined as and are primarily (regarded as) responsible for. It constitutes an actual role and an actual area of responsibility. Despite increasing challenges to the status quo, men are still the designated 'breadwinners', while women's place is still first and foremost 'at home'. Women are defined primarily in terms of their relationships;

117

men by their activity, as is clear from the official classification
of women according to their husband's or father's occupation
(Oakley and Oakley, 1979) and representations in popular par-
lance and advertising (Berger, 1972; Winship, 1978).

There is of course a distinction between the sexual division of
labour and sexist ideology.[1] Sexist ideology lays down what
should happen, and what is held to happen, even when reality
does not tally with ideology. This means that even when the
majority of women *do* work - as indeed they do - they feel they
have to justify doing so. It also means that women who have husbands and children feel that these responsibilities must take pre-
cedence whether they work or not. So regardless of what the
actual sexual division of labour is, the power of sexist ideology
is that it imposes its own reality on people. The women in this
study bear witness to an imperative that makes a majority of
women (who are not in fact solely occupied with domestic responsibilities) regard themselves as deviant. The sexual division of
labour and its associated ideology also goes some way towards
explaining the sanctions imposed on women when they deviate
from their 'traditional role', sanctions such as low pay, unequal
pensions and social security provisions.[2] But most of all it means
that when women enter the labour market they do so as migrants
from the domestic domain (whether they have husbands and children or not), and it is this fact that crucially differentiates their
experience of work.

The women in this study[3] are in no way exceptional, and as
such can be seen as representing the paradigm situation of all
women, but especially working-class women in capitalist society.
They were all married with dependent children under the age of
sixteen. None had full-time jobs and all were dependent on their
husband's wage. Of course all of them had worked before they
had children, and most intended to return to full-time work as
soon as they could - an intention that was going to take some of
their husbands by surprise. Even at this stage in their lives -
and this is far from unusual - most (14 out of 25) did some part-
time work.[4] But however much or little they worked outside the
home, and regardless of their intentions to return to the labour
market, all these women saw their *primary* focus as the home. It
was only when that was satisfactorily disposed of that they could
turn their attention to the world outside. At the same time the
inadequacy of the 'family wage' paid to their husbands created a
constant pressure on them to earn some more money in order to
make their task *in the home* easier.

These women, therefore, exemplify the integral connection
between the two spheres of production and reproduction. As has
been pointed out (Coulson, Magas and Wainwright, 1975; Bland,
Brunsdon, Hobson, and Winship, 1978) - and these women were
well aware of it - in times of recession the downward pressure on
men's wages results in increased work for the women at home.
Cheaper food, on the whole, takes longer to prepare and they may
also have to take extra waged work to maintain their standard of

living. In this way, women's part-time work, and their work in
the home, is a flexible element in capital's productive relations.
It can be exploited by capital; it also forms part of the working
class's defensive strategy. 'For women as wives . . . are situated
in a state of permanent transition' (Bland, Brunsdon, Hobson and
Winship, 1978). Women at home are part of several cycles or inter-
locking spheres; that of production, consumption and reproduction; that of the sexual division of labour organised around the
family; and that of their own lives where they enter and leave
the labour market at different points.

'WOMEN'S WORK'

These women's experience of their work in the home was determined by their husband's wage. In 1974 the factory, ACL, paid
a basic wage about one-third below 'average', and even men who
worked a lot of overtime were unlikely greatly to exceed that.
The couples had an average of three children each, although
family size varied from one child to eight. Half of them lived on
a typical large, barren, post-war housing estate four miles south
of the city. The rest lived closer in, in more traditional pre-war
working-class areas. Most lived in council houses or flats. Fifteen
were living in council houses - either rented or transmuted into
a council mortage. Two were in council flats and the rest had
private mortgages. All had lived in council property at some point.
Their accommodation was adequate but not spacious. They had the
basic labour-saving facilities, like running water and electricity,
but by no means all of them had vacuum cleaners or washing
machines. Only two had a telephone. The outer estates were
typically deficient in amenities such as shops, playgrounds or
buses, as most working-class estates of that period are.
   None of the women was in any doubt what her real 'work' consisted of. The task was, essentially, to maintain, service, and
take responsibility for the care of their homes, husbands and
children. The stress should be on 'responsibility', for the sexual
division of labour does not rest on sealed compartments of activity
for each sex, but rather on the ultimate responsibility. So, if a
wife goes out to work, it does not threaten her husband's 'breadwinner' role; and if he 'helps' with the washing up it does not
relieve her of the responsibility of making sure it gets done (as
Oakley, 1974, and more recently P. Hunt, 1978, have made clear).
The main components of 'women's work' were housework, feeding
the family, and looking after the children. All of these tasks
were seen as substantial and necessary, and whether the women
liked doing them or not, it was generally recognised as 'a hard
job' by both the men and the women. Discussion usually focused
on aspects of cleaning - the physical toughness, the boredom and
the repetitious nature of it.

'When you're doing housework it's nothing - you can do it over and over again' (Felicity Skinner).

'It's so boring - you're stuck home all day' (Veronica Grimshaw).

'It's far harder. On Saturday she stayed in bed, and I worked harder than I ever do in here. It's murder' (Don Grimshaw).

'There's no holidays or rest. The wife was on all day yesterday, with Craig. I went home at 10.00 and back in here at 5.00, but she went to bed at 12.00, and up again at 4.00, and she was on the go all day' (Fred Fletcher).

Indeed, it was quite clear that, above all, 'women's work' meant 'housework', rather than cooking or child care (the reverse of the usual middle-class priorities of child care first and tidyness a poor last, at least in theory - see Oakley, 1974, and Gavron, 1968).

'When you're looking after children, and trying to cope with your 'work', you can't do an outside job as well' (Jane Smith).

'It's [the nursery] helped me. You can get on with your "work" better, can't you? You can't leave it, and you haven't time to sit and play' (Joanna Lee)

It was also the most immediate objection husbands had to their wives taking on outside jobs.

'He wouldn't like to come home and find his bed unmade' (Jean Martin).

'She hopes to go back, but she realises she's got to keep the place clean and tidy' (John Pollard).

'It's all right provided what goes on in the home doesn't suffer' (Michael Lee).

Feeding the family began with the shopping. Indeed it was seen as an advantage of shift work that the men could help with the shopping and see the prices going up for themselves. Although cooking was not rated highly, the difficulties of providing food of any sort at the right times was a recurring nightmare.

'Now the children come in at dinner and you give them a meal. Then he's on 6-2, comes home at 2.00 - give him a meal, and so it goes on. They come home at 4.00 and you've got to prepare another; probably he comes home at 6.00, and that's another. Seems to be all the time with meals' (Felicity Skinner).

Childcare was probably the most flexibly interpreted task. Some women felt they could take outside work throughout their child-bearing years and still cope; a few refused to consider any outside work even when the children were quite grown up.

'She wants to be home with a cup of tea when they come in the door, because that's her job, not being out working, which isn't' (Nigel Martin) (this succinct statement from a man was agreed with by his wife, but with much less enthusiasm.)

However, the children were most often mentioned as the most intrinsically rewarding aspect of 'women's work'.

'It's a nice job with the children. The kids make it. The washing's hard, but when you see them going to school all nice, it's worth it . . . and when they say, "Mum, your bread pudding's marvellous" ' (Ann Davies).

On the whole, although some women liked some aspects of what they did, most found it boring, taxing, exhausting, unstimulating, complicated, lonely and endless. Or as Joanna Lee put it:

'All women are the same. They get married - high ideals. It's going to be lovely to wash the socks, cook the meals and all that for their husbands, but after a few years the novelty wears off. It just becomes a bit of a drudge. Not so much that you mind doing it, but it's the same thing day in, day out, all the time. You get stale yourself. I think - well, if someone was coming to dinner you'd think. "Oh, what will we make for the meal?" and you pull yourself up to do something special - but if it's just your husband you say, "Well, sausages and mash like yesterday". They don't appreciate it anyway. If you put yourself out, they say, "What's this?" '

But, by and large, they shrug their shoulders and get on with it. By marrying and having children they had cut themselves off from certain choices.

'When you're married, you've got to do these things' (Mavis Gray).

'It's my duty. If I didn't want to, I didn't have to get married, did I?' (Jean Martin).

For all this, although domestic labour was hard work, it was not a 'proper job', not like one outside. It was too mundane, too taken for granted, but above all it was not paid. For the men it was the conditions of work in the home that made it not a 'proper job', but for the women it was the lack of pay that was the crucial differentiating factor between work in the home and work outside.

It was clear that the women were not, at least in their own cases, complaining primarily about material deprivation, but about being deprived of economic identity. They could see that in their position as dependent wives they had no economic identity, except second-hand, through their husbands. This might not matter if it were not for the fact that they lived in a capitalist society, where all important relations are reduced to cash relations. In some real sense, if you have no economic identity you have no identity at all.

'Women think independence is important. Men don't I suppose because they don't ever lose theirs. That's important' (Mary Fletcher).

They deeply resented the consequent undervaluing of the work they did at home.

'Men just go to work and come home and get paid, but a woman has to run a house and organise this and that' (Diana Dixon).

'They seem to think you're here all day long and it's a life of leisure. They don't realise there's cleaning to be done, and washing and ironing' (Sharon Thomas).

It is all the more interesting, then, that all these women totally rejected the idea that they *could* be paid for the work they did in the home. Arguments for and against 'wages for housework' have been well rehearsed but these women did not need any preparation.

'Pay? no, because some people don't like doing it, so they'd rather be out at work' (Jackie Young).

'No, it's your own house. It ought to be affection' (Veronica Grimshaw).

'You've got to do it anway, even if you are paid' (Mary Fletcher).

'How can you really? Unless you get it from the government. You can't say to an employer - "Look, I'm looking after my husband's children, you must give him £15 extra"' (Claire Rees).

This last point explores the myth of the 'family wage'. For no employer pays more to a man who has eight children, than he does to one who has two.

They did not, however, object to family allowance. In fact, they saw its continuance in its old form[5] as a direct weekly payment to mothers, as a vital bit of 'money of your own'.

'It's the woman's bit of independence. You know you've got that money there - perhaps to last you the rest of the week; that you haven't got to go to your husband. Some husbands will make you crawl. It just gives you that little bit of independence' (Claire Rees).

Although even such a small sum helped to stretch the housekeeping and the midweek payment made it especially useful, its

real importance was as a symbol of economic independence, and
they reacted with anger at the idea of losing it.

'It's ridiculous to take it away. It's your only means of independence for one thing – even though it's only 90p – but if
you've got a husband who spends money, you'd be lost without
it' (Mary Fletcher).

'Money of your own' was important. They had discounted wages
for housework and regarded any substantial increase in family
allowances as unlikely. It was therefore not surprising to find
these women so determined to acquire money in the only practicable way – by earning it. Nearly all those women (14) who
already had part-time jobs intended to increase their hours as
soon as possible – most of them to full-time jobs. Of the remaining
11, at least half were actively thinking about doing some paid
work in the near future, despite opposition from many of their
husbands.
Let us now look at what happened to them when they enter the
labour market on these terms.

'MEN'S WORK'

Most of the work that has been done on housewives who also
have paid jobs has made several assumptions (Gavron, 1968; A.
Hunt, 1968; Oakley, 1974 and 1976; Fonda and Moss, 1976). One
is that all paid work outside the home, however necessary, *is*
secondary to work in the home and that therefore women must
have a reason for doing it. You only have to imagine asking men
(or women in China) why they work to realise how deep this
assumption goes. When women who work are asked why they do,
they are usually given a number of alternatives that divide into
economic reasons and social or emotional reasons. What these
studies fail to realise is that money *itself* is the primary *social*
reason for working.

'[If you don't work] you can't say you've got anything for
yourself. If I want anything in the way of clothes I've got to
ask Nick to buy it for me. Whereas if you go to work, you've
got some money and you can get it yourself. If you have to ask
for everything, it makes a difference' (Felicity Skinner).

'He's worked for it so I suppose he feels it's his – and sometimes
I used to feel not degraded exactly, but as though I'm getting
a handout. Now, although I'm not earning very much, at least
I earned it and it's my money to do as I want' (Joanna Lee).

When the women took jobs, they recognised that they were
crossing some kind of boundary; that they were operating in a
world that was less 'their own'. (There is a real division between

'women's work' - unpaid work in the home - and *any* paid participation in the labour market. Hence the phrase 'men's work' used
in fact by some of the women, and by which I mean not certain
kinds of work but all 'labour' of which they significantly did not
feel a part.) All the women had worked full time before they
married, and most up to the birth of their first child. A few had
been clerks or typists or shop assistants but the vast majority
had worked as unskilled labour in the large tobacco and fibreboard factories, and wine shippers and in small works producing
pipes and other specialised items. All their experience had been
in a rigidly segregated labour market. Even where they had
worked in the same place as men, e.g. in printing works, or in
the fibreboard factory which employed their husbands, their
jobs, pay and conditions had been quite separate and different.
As we shall see, they also had very little active union experience
from which they could build a labour identity. None of the women
considered the jobs they did in that first phase of their working
life as a lifetime commitment. Their present jobs were noticeably
worse paid and had worse material conditions than their earlier
work. Those whose children had grown up were not returning to
the industrial jobs of their first working phase, but were simply
extending their part-time jobs. It therefore looks as if the third
phase in these women's lives will simply be an extension of the
second.

The kinds of jobs the women were in - overwhelmingly cleaning,
catering and shopwork - are all traditionally low paid. Their
wages were shockingly low, sometimes less than half the average
female wage. They chose such jobs because they were 'handy',
or they had convenient hours or simply because it was not a
factory. Working part time, few of them brought in more than a
quarter of their husbands' wages. They were selling their labour,
in fact, in a clearly differentiated market at lower rates and in
poorer conditions. Their perception of themselves as being in the
labour market on quite different terms from men led to low expectations of both the quality of work and the material rewards they
could get - a fact that employers are quick to take advantage of.

> 'I'm a shop assistant. I also look after a little boy because he's
> always in the shop, and I clean the floors. Its 30p an hour [in
> 1974]. Everyone says I'm mad to do it, but I'm quite happy.
> It's local and the hours suit me. It's not much money. I suppose
> I ought to really . . . I've never made a stand for myself'
> (Joanna Lee).

Women and unions
Most of the women were not in a union. Those who were treated
it as a tedious formality. Some of them were openly hostile. In so
far as they have experienced unions at all, it had not encouraged
them to expect much.

> 'Men expect women to come out with them. But unions don't help

women, except in Wills. We've got a male shop steward. He
doesn't bother' (Gladys Hutchings).

'Well, on Sundays I go round the club and clean up. £1.56 for
4 hours, 39p an hour. I did question it, but it comes under
catering so I can't do nothing about it. I don't know about a
union. That's for full-timers really' (Mavis Gray).

And here is Sharon Thomas, who was one of the few in an
industrial job, giving an account of the work and the union.

'We do finishing of cakes. That's the creaming and jamming and
everything like that. On a conveyor belt. It's all right if you're
allowed to move around, but then if you're stuck sometimes on
the end packer, you're stuck nearly all day long, and it can
drag then. No one seems to come and relieve you. . . . Yes,
I'm in the Bakers' Union, but not before this job. I was in TWU
at Wills, but that was the only one. Everywhere else they
haven't bothered, but this bakery was a closed shop when I
went so you had to join the union. To be quite frank, our union
hasn't done a lot for us. You go to a shop steward with any
problems. They just wave you away and can't be bothered. All
the shop stewards are men. . . . I mean if we've got a real
grievance the best thing to do is go straight to our own manager
- bypass the union altogether.'

In fact, the general conclusion was:

'Unions should be for men, because they do more for men'
(Joanna Lee).

Unions, strikes and even meetings were a distraction from the
simple business of going out, doing a job and getting money as
quickly and painlessly as possible.
    The husbands of these women were all in a union - either
SOGAT or TWU. Half of them were shop stewards, and TWU members had been on strike for two months the year before. This is
discussed more fully elsewhere (Porter, 1978a). Many of the
women had supported the strike more or less enthusiastically.
Some TWU wives had condemned it while some SOGAT wives had
been angry that their husbands had *not* struck. Yet even the
most militant and well informed of the women who supported industrial action for *men*, including their own husbands, rejected
unions for *women*, including themselves. As one of them put it:

'I work in Bolloms [dry cleaners]. It's lovely. There are five
of us and I'm in charge. We've all worked together before. We
were in the union before, when we were up at the factory. I
was a shop steward, but not now. There's no union, and no
reason to have it . . . it's the best wage we've had. That's a
start, and when we've been a year we'll ask for more and that's
when we'll need a union. They don't give way easily . . . I got

a couple of things done (when she was a steward), but I didn't want more. Not enough time to spare. When you have kids, working's enough. If women have families they don't take as much interest' (Val Fennel).

This was the most explicit reference any of the women made to the fact that having children affected the way they thought about their work. It is, of course, the oft-cited reason why women are not so active in unions as men. (See Judith Hunt's chapter in this volume; also P. Hunt, 1980, and Purcell, 1979, who is especially and rightly critical of conventional assumptions about female lack of militancy.) But these women had always regarded their work as secondary and unions as irrelevant, even when they were full-time members of the labour force. Their present position – as part-timers with children – has not changed their attitude, it has simply justified their low expectations of unions.

Equal pay
The women's attitudes to equal pay showed clearly that they re-garded their work as of quite different character to that of their husbands. While they supported the principle of equal pay enthusi-astically, they took the formula 'for equal work' to mean *identical* work. If women did 'men's work' – and in discussion they always chose extreme examples like mining – then, and only then, could they expect the same pay. None of them regarded their own jobs as falling into this category. Although they would have liked 'more money', and felt they deserved it, they wouldn't claim 'equal pay'.

'But [paid] domestic work is hard. I'd like to see the money come up a bit – but for equal pay, I'd have to do a man's job – like the handyman who cuts the grass and so on' (Gladys Hutchings).

Not that a 'man's job' wouldn't sometimes be easier.

'Well there's our charge hand as a start. He does exactly the same as us – half the time he's just stood watching us, and yet he gets more pay than we do' (Sharon Thomas).

In other words, they did not think that the Equal Pay Act affected them, or the vast majority of working women. In this they were quite right, given the discouraging number of cases won since the implementation of the act (Coussins, 1976, and EOC Reports).
More importantly, they had found a formula which enabled them to claim *formal* equality, but which absolved their guilty feelings about working by ensuring that they themselves could never claim it. It was a significant confidence trick.
It was, perhaps, more surprising that they rarely complained about the low rates of pay – but this too can be attributed to the

ambivalence, if not guilt, that these women felt about invading
the men's sphere.

'In one way I don't think women should get equal pay because
the man is the breadwinner. I shouldn't go to work by rights,
because my husband is the breadwinner . . . I just go to work
to help out' (Gladys Hutchings).

This attitude prevents women from pursuing their own claims,
and creates a chasm between two sections of the working class.
For while women are prepared to accept low pay for these kinds
of reasons, the possibility always exists for employers not only
to exploit them as low-paid workers, but to use their existence
to depress *men's* wages, and in any case it creates the potential
for a divided workforce (Nichols and Armstrong, 1976, pp. 85 ff.).

Secondhand jobs: husband's work
The fact that the women regarded their own paid work as of a
quite different nature to that of their husbands meant, also, that
they found it harder to transfer their own experience of work in
an 'imaginative extension' to that of their husbands. It was something that they did not know about because they *could* not know
about it, however much their husbands told them. When they
talked about his work they would add the caveat 'but I've never
done factory work'. Even if they *had* done factory work (like
Sharon Thomas), they would say, 'but I've never worked at
Ashton Containers' (where the husbands worked). A few women
(like Mavis Gray) who had worked in Ashton Containers and did
concede that they therefore 'knew what it was like there', then
added that they did not know what it was like to be a steward, or
work on the big machines. Anyway, 'it's different for men'. (In
connection with this see Peter Armstrong's discussion in this
volume of mutual ignorance between men and women workers in
the same plants.) This made it almost impossible for them to identify with their husband's position as a worker, a weakness made
more important by their *own* lack of identity as workers.
    This situation was not improved by the men's attitudes to telling
their wives about their work. Some thought that they had no
business to know - 'I would say I try not to talk to her . . .
they're outsiders'. More thought their wives wouldn't be interested,
'unless its someone she knew who's had an accident or died'.
    In any case it's part of *their* survival tactics to keep the two
worlds apart.

'Well, I could be wrong, but myself, once I go out this gate,
that's it - that's work finished. I don't take it home. I don't
talk about work at home. I like to forget it' (Tommy Turner).

Most of the men agreed that their wives were interested when
the pay packet was likely to be affected - but only then.

'If anything's going on - wages or union - I usually tell her.
I don't normally discuss it' (Keith Thomas).

'I know the money I bring home interests her, so she has got
an interest in the place' (John Pollard).

'A woman at home minding children - as long as she gets her
weekly money, she doesn't worry a lot' (Fred Fletcher).

So the women were expected to have only the narrowest of
economic interest in their husband's jobs, and no feelings of
solidarity except those implied by marital duty. Any notion of
class solidarity, either between workers in different sectors or
between people affected in different ways by the capitalist relations of production, is completely absent. This becomes a crucial
point in the relationship of women's consciousness of themselves
and class consciousness. Elsewhere (Porter 1978a and b) I have
explored in more depth how women's separation from their husbands' work experience inhibited the development of both their
own and their husbands' class consciousness. And this was true
even when their husbands were involved in a strike. The way in
which the women's own work experience and their perception of their
place in the home enforced the separation between the two worlds
emerges even more clearly from their attitudes to another strike.

The Cowley wives[6]
On 3 April 1974, drivers at the BLMC Cowley plant went on strike.
A week later management withdrew 'normal facilities' from the
shop steward A. Thornley. As a result, by 16 April nearly 12,000
workers were either on strike or laid off. On 23 April there was
a small but vociferous demonstration by some wives outside the
factory against 'the militants'. This union incident was given star
billing by the media, especially the more popular right-wing
dailies. The demonstration had little effect on the course of the
dispute, and a counter-demonstration by wives in favour of the
strikers was rather better attended.
When I talked to the women in this study, this incident was
fresh in their minds. They had followed the matter closely, and
their reactions were forceful. When they talked about their own
husband's wage they acknowledged that it was his because he
earned it, and they were aware (and resentful) of their consequent
dependence. But this dependence, because it was connected with
their role in the home, gave them certain unspecified and indirect
'rights'. It was these that they expressed when they talked about
'the Cowley wives'. They felt that they were entitled to do 'their'
work. If that was imperilled by industrial action then they ought
to defend it.

'It's the women who determine whether the money's good or not'
(Diana Dixon).

'If the family suffers then wives should have a say' (Kate
Wheeler).

'The wives were thinking about the household. You can only
take so much' (Ros Neale).

They saw the issues in very immediate terms. Unions were an
actual threat against next week's housekeeping; not a bulwark
against next year's redundancy. (The irony of some of these
remarks, in view of the subsequent Thatcher government, hardly
needs spelling out.) They clearly perceived the cycle that put money
into pay packets on Friday only to take it out of the housekeeping
purse in the supermarkets on Saturday. Some women expressed
an awareness (often based on family memories of, for example,
the Welsh coal mines) of what life would be like without an organised defence of the working class. All this resulted in a deep
ambiguity which they expressed in their response to the Cowley
incident. For they had caught a glimpse of the fact that they were
a necessary part of the capitalist process, and that they had
certain interests *as housewives*. But they also had an identity
as 'working class', and they did not see how they could intervene
in their own interests *either* as housewives *or* as working class,
nor could they see how their own 'sectional' interests as women
were linked with those of the working class. Their feelings of
ambiguity, and indeed frustration, which from ideas of family
loyalty they repressed in the context of the ACL strike emerged
as 'anti-unionism' in the safer context of the motor industry.
What is being asserted here is some kind of political and economic
identity that has a reality for them but no place in conventional
trade union ideology and practice.

WOMEN AND THE PUBLIC WORLD

One of the notable features of women's work is its private nature.
Each woman, alone in her house, ministers to the needs of her
family. It has long been recognised that one of the difficulties of
organising women at home is that there is no institutional basis
from which they could organise; no parallel to the trade unions
at work. It is sometimes suggested that alternative bases for
political organisation could be found in the community. But this
presupposes that women can, and will, involve themselves in
'public life'. The experience of these women would seem to indicate
that the separation of 'men's world' from 'women's world' dominates
this area of experience as well. It was common to define 'political'
as a male concern. Women, therefore, do not know about politics
because they are women.
    There was general agreement that certain issues - prices,
schools and pedestrian crossings - were an extension of 'women's
work'. And when it was a matter of 'getting things done' locally,
of writing repeated letters to councillors, arranging meetings and
all the time-consuming detail of democratic protest, it was, by and
large, the women who did it - at least those who were not 'too
tied up in their families to join in'. Nevertheless, there was wide-

spread dissatisfaction. They could get petitions up but that
didn't *change* things.

But while the women did see national political life as being male-
dominated, they did not necessarily accept that as being the best
arrangement. Their comments depended on regarding the point
of *consumption* as centrally important. They never mentioned
production or indeed any other aspects of capitalist relations. It
was women's knowledge of *prices* that qualified them for public
power.

'It's the women who gets the stuff in and knows the prices and
worries about money' (Janet Griffiths).

'It would be better if women had the power. If women ran their
homes the way men run the country, there wouldn't be any
happy homes' (Jane Smith).

'I don't think a man knows enough to run a country. Only a
woman could - it's a woman that keeps the home together'
(Mary Fletcher).

No one suggested that if women had more say in running the
country we'd have a different foreign policy, but they did say
that prices would be lower. Nor did they see any connection between foreign policy and prices. Indeed, while prices are seen
as part of one world, and foreign policy is seen as part of a
quite different world, it is difficult to see how any overall analysis
could be developed.

It also appeared that within 'women's sphere' they included all
of Parsons's 'expressive values' - indeed, almost a monopoly of
'goodness'. Women 'understood people' and care for them, and it
was assumed that they would carry this personalised 'caring'
into public life.

They'd be fairer, more soft hearted' (Gladys Hutchings).

'It would be fairer. They know how things are . . . they'd
look after the old people more' (Diana Dixon).

Now, there are quite enough women in high places who are no
more 'soft' or 'caring' than their male counterparts to disprove
this, but the importance of these ideas is that they amount to a
stance, and one that represents a consistent dissatisfaction with
the conventional wisdom.

Most of the men (18) held a familiar position. Politics was an
entirely male sphere and women knew little or nothing about it.
How could they, except through their men folk?

'She just isn't in a position to know. I don't know what women
talk about when they get together, but I'm pretty sure it isn't
politics' (Michael Lee).

Some of the men, especially those with articulate wives like
Don Grimshaw, cast a quizzical eye at the prevailing chauvinism -
'We don't know more, we just talk more'. But on the whole men
were confident, not only that 'politics' was their concern, but
that it was intrinsically more important than 'women's affairs'.
A few women also respected the male supremacy view that only
men know about politics, and that made them superior because
politics was about 'important' matters.

'He tries to explain it, but I still don't understand' (Diana
Dixon).

'I only know about the home and children' (Ros Neale).

Six women could be described as 'collusionist': i.e. men just
thought they knew more.

'Men do. They like to *think* they do, but half of them don't go
to meetings, and don't know, anyway' (Betty Turner).

This attitude carried with it something rather different than
when men said it. What lay behind it was the idea that men - like
children - lived in an imaginary world where they *thought* they
had the power. And women indulged them because it did no harm
and enabled them to get on with the really important things -
normally left undefined, but centering round the home and personal values. A majority of the women (13) defined politics
simply as what men were interested in (with a stress on industrial
politics), and either maintained that the two spheres were incom-
parable or that women's concerns were more important.
Both these positions invoked a rejection of 'politics' as having
nothing to do with them - like Mavis Gray.

'Men do, I think. They read a lot and they're interested in
politics and all that sort of thing. Women are interested in the
cost of living and things like that.'

And many of the others, having said that they knew nothing
about politics and weren't interested, then went on to include
among *their* interests housing, prices, welfare services, care of
children and old people, local amenities and sometimes even things
like earthquakes or wars. All these things were described as 'not
political' - and that left (effectively) industrial affairs and parliamentary politics: tidy exceptions to be sure, but of a limited
range.
What these women seemed to argue was that yes, there were two
distinct spheres, but in so far as they were comparable the
women's sphere was not inferior. They took strength in their
opposition to the male world, and in their feeling of identity with
other women. 'Other women understand.' Their response to what
they saw, clearly enough, as an attempt to relegate them to the

peripheral, was to band together, not to invade male territory, but to define their own as what concerned them, and to define it therefore as important.

WOMEN'S CONSCIOUSNESS AND CLASS CONSCIOUSNESS

Here, clearly exposed, is the chasm between the two worlds. Incompatible and implacable, there appeared to be no immediate way these men and women could unite in common *class* concerns. The two 'worlds' - men's and women's - each with its own activities and ideologies, discrete, separate and to some extent in opposition, appears effectively to have split the working class. This is an important organising principle in terms of understanding not only how men and women understood 'women's work', but how sexual sectionalism develops in the working class, and how that prevents both men and women from developing full class consciousness. At the same time, the insights that women have come to have helped them to develop a consciousness of themselves as women, and this 'sectional' consciousness has contributory value analogous to trade union consciousness for some men.[7]

So the general theme of this chapter has been the way in which the working class is split into two sharply defined and divided worlds, one inhabited by men, the other by women. The 'second-hand' experience of their husband's jobs is deemed 'irrelevant' to and by the women. Men mediated their experience of the point of production in isolated bursts of explanation at best, through a wall of hostility at worst. Women's own experience of the point of production, whether as full-time workers or as part-time supplementary earners, did not appear to bridge the gulf at all.

I have questioned the rigid separation between women who work and women who don't, for, whatever the place of the domestic labour these women did, they also had a continuing direct relationship with the world of work. Yet their place in the labour market and their response to it derived from their prior identity as 'housewives'. Their low pay, their lack of union involvement, their transitional role as workers, can all be explained in terms of their family responsibilities in the sexual division of labour. The point about these women is that they are not unusual: they simply represent ordinary working-class women at a 'moment' in their working lives.

The search for an adequate account of women's position under capitalism must beware of reifying abrupt analytic categories - worker, housewife, domestic labour, production and consumption. I hope that the complex experience of these real women and the way in which they grappled with the fractured world about them will give us the incentive and confidence to develop an analysis which does take account of the rich and 'other' experience of being a woman, even in a fractured capitalist world.

NOTES

1   'Ideology' and its related concept 'consciousness' are used in
    a wide variety of ways: see Harris, 1971; Larrain, 1979. In
    this paper I shall be referring to ideology as a partial inter-
    pretation of human experience that is externally derived, e.g.
    trade union ideology, sexist ideology. By 'consciousness' I
    mean an understanding that each individual constructs out of
    his or her whole experience with the help of available ideologies.
    The goal of fully active class consciousness can, therefore,
    only be achieved in or after a socialist revolution - but it can
    be built long before.
2   In 1979 women still only earned 73% of what men earned (EOC
    1980a, p. 79). Part-time workers did considerably worse. Pen-
    sions, tax and social security legislation have been criticised by
    Lister and Wilson, 1976; Land, 1976 and 1978b. See also EOC
    1980b, Parts 3, 7.
3   The material in this paper is taken from a larger study carried
    out in Bristol 1974/75. The sample, 25 couples, was drawn from
    a medium sized fibreboard factory where all the husbands
    worked. The focus of that study was an examination of the way
    in which the couples mediated their different experiences to
    each other, and how their experiences operated in their ideol-
    ogy and consciousness. The method was loosely structured
    interviews. I first spoke to the husbands, at work; and through
    them made contact with their wives at home. I was able to main-
    tain contact with both husbands and wives during the full
    year's fieldwork. Other aspects of this study have been dis-
    cussed in Porter, 1978a and 1978b; and Porter, Ph.D. Thesis,
    Bristol 1979.
4   In 1971, on official figures, 18.8% of married women with child-
    ren under 4, and 53.5% of those with children aged 16 or over,
    worked. What is noticeable is that whereas the Department of
    Employment (1974) reports that the proportion of women work-
    ing drops with the size of their family - 43.2% of women with
    one child, and 26.8% of women with 5 or more children - in this
    sample 70% of women with 3 or more children under the age of
    11 worked. The commonsensical reason was the relatively poor
    wages paid to their husbands, and this conclusion is supported
    by Fonda and Moss, 1976.
5   This refers to the proposals embodied in HMSO Green Paper,
    Cmnd 5116, 1972 to replace the family allowance with a tax
    credit paid to the *husband* in negative tax. Such was the outcry
    that the proposals were dropped, and family allowances were
    increased. More recently they have included children's tax
    allowances, with both paid to the mother as child benefit,
    although this is still only a token contribution to the real cost
    of keeping a child.
6   The details of this comparatively trivial incident are taken from
    'Labour Research', Vol. 63, Nos. 6 and 7, 1974, and supple-
    mented by the daily papers. Subsequent incidents during the

lorry drivers strike (1978) and the 'grave diggers' strike
(1979) have shown that the Cowley incident was not exceptional.

7   I am referring here to the discussion around the limitations of
'trade union consciousness', deriving from Lenin (1970). My
argument is that just as some trade union experience can bring
members to a greater awareness of themselves as workers,
(but that this has certain *inherent* limitations in terms of a
transformation to class consciousness), so these women's
awareness of their oppression as women gives them a consciousness of themselves as a section of the working class, which
may enable them to make connections with other 'oppressed'
groups.

8 THE 'UNDERSTANDING' EMPLOYER
Caroline Freeman

INTRODUCTION

This chapter explores some aspects of the reciprocal relationship between the family and the labour market. Trying to think out the mutual determination here has a dizzying effect; it is all too easy to fall into circularity. A truly circular argument put forward by neo-classical economists among others exemplifies the sort of thinking which can seem 'common sense'. Women earn less than men, so it is rational for them to withdraw from the labour force to bear and rear children, and also to invest less of their time in education and training for paid work. And why do they earn less than men? Because they fail to participate in the labour force as continuously as men do, and are inferior in terms of education and training. In Mincer and Polachek's own inimitable words:

> foregone market-oriented human capital of mothers is a part of the price of acquiring human capital in children, and, more generally, a price exacted by family life.

Then an afterthought occurs to them:

> Of course, the greater market specialisation, longer hours, and greater intensity of work and of job training on the part of husbands and fathers can be viewed as a 'price exacted by family life' in exactly the same sense. (Mincer and Polachek, 1980, p. 203).

Of course. Arguments like this one spring from the assumption that capitalist institutions are natural rather than historical. But even if we are well aware that the modern truncated nuclear family and the separation between home and work are not immutable but simply points in a continuing process of change, we can still fall into the trap of invoking the family 'as a final, catch-all explanation of the various characteristics of women's position in different societies and at different times, constantly referred to but still to be analysed' (Kuhn, 1978, p. 44). In what follows I try to avoid both pitfalls by looking in some detail at one of the crucial causal links, women's responsibility for child care and how it affects their position in the labour market.

In the UK, as in many other societies, the work of maintaining the existing labour force and of reproducing a new one is split off from the sphere of production and carried out in private,

within individual families and specialised institutions such as
schools. Consumption is the main link between domestic labour
and the commodity market. The work done in the home is carried
out on a small scale repeated in endless tiny units. For this
reason alone it is inefficient, and in addition inefficiency boosts
consumption and is actually encouraged by the sellers of 'consumer
(non) durables'. The most time-consuming, irreducible and important part of domestic labour is the care of children and other
dependent people. There is nothing 'natural' or eternal about the
privatisation of this work, and many reasons for thinking the
costs exacted by the nuclear family too high.

Domestic labour is carried out behind closed doors: serving the
capitalist economy and yet in a sense remaining outside it. That
is one crucial feature of the relationship between the family and
social production; another is the asymmetry of the sexual division
of labour within the family. Pressures from the material culture
(the actual physical housing arrangements, for example), from
the legal, educational and political systems, and the whole weight
of ideology push people into living in nuclear family units. The
same and parallel pressures allocate the main responsibility for
domestic labour to women, and make this the easiest, the 'most
natural' way to live (see Marilyn Porter's chapter in this volume).

This chapter concentrates on the position of women with dependent children. Most women do become mothers, and restrictions
on their working lives over one or two decades have a long-term
effect on their position in the labour market. In asking how
mothers of young children manage to get and keep paid employment, we are asking a question of relevance to all women. Single
and childless women escape the objective disadvantage on the
labour market entailed by child-care responsibilities (although
they may have other family members dependent on them), but
they tend to be treated through discrimination as if they were
mothers themselves. It is the collective position of women which
is decisive.

Because statistics seem static they can make it hard to grasp
the extent of the restrictions on employed mothers. Women constitute nearly 40 per cent of the labour force (EOC, 1980a, p. 70).
If we think in terms of work experience this figure is an underestimate, since it takes no account of the way in which women
tend to take jobs for short periods, and refers just to one point
in time (Yudkin and Holme, 1963, p. 44). It also fails to include
casual employment paid 'on the side', which women are particularly
likely to take. It leaves out unknown numbers of unregistered
homeworkers and childminders. In these ways it underestimates
the number of women 'economically active'. At the same time the
figure of 40 per cent is misleading in a contrary direction. It
seems that women are well represented in the labour force - but
many of them are working part time. About a fifth of the entire
labour force works part time, and most of these are women.
Between a third and a half of women employees are part-timers
at any one moment, and ' . . . an unknown, though even higher

proportion of women work part time at some point in their lives'
(Hurstfield, 1978, p. 1). So the figure of 40 per cent is mislead-
ingly static, and in both its over- and underestimates covers up
the discontinuity and restricted nature of women's employment.
The trend for increasing numbers of women, especially married
women including mothers of young children, to take paid employment does not signal a slackening of the factors militating against
women's equal participation in the labour force.

CHILD-CARE PROVISION AND NON-PROVISION IN THE UK

Since child care is considered the responsibility of individual
families in this society, it is unsurprising that recent surveys
show that employed mothers usually depend on other family members, and sometimes on friends and neighbours, to look after
their children ('Woman's Own', 1979). Public child-care provision
is split into two types: 'care' and 'education', responsibility for
which rests with the Departments of Health and Social Security
and Education and Science respectively (Hughes et al., 1980,
p. 131). This division has ideological implications, suggesting
that care should really be given by mothers, with local-authority
day nurseries or childminders acting as substitute caretakers if
mothers cannot or will not fulfil this role. Education is treated as
separable, as more legitimately a matter for public provision, but
as only appropriate for children over three.

Local-authority day nurseries are envisaged as 'safety net'
provision for children in 'special need'. They only take 0.7 per
cent of children up to four, and their long waiting lists show that
they do not meet even their own narrow definition of the need.
2.2 per cent of the nation's pre-school children are cared for by
registered childminders, and a further unknown number by unregistered minders. These women work without training, for
appallingly low pay and with bad working conditions which most
local authorities do nothing to improve. If the service '. . . is
to be made good we can see no way in which it can remain cheap.
It is cheap at present because minders are exploited' (TUC, 1977,
p. 49). Yet it is childminding, not the improvement and extension
of day nurseries, which is hailed by successive governments as
the 'solution' to the working mother's problems. It is not only the
low cost which appeals. The whole idea of a mother *substitute*,
of one family replacing another, maintains the ideology of attachment to the mother within the individual family as the key to
normal child development. Increasingly, modern research is
challenging this notion (Hughes et al., 1980, p. 35 on).

For working-class women who work full time, childminders,
relatives or local-authority day nurseries are the only possibilities.
Local-authority day nurseries are free, and childminders are cheap
in the sense that the hourly rate is very low, but can seem
dear when £20 is considered as a proportion of a take-home pay
of, say, £45 or £50. Private day nurseries and nannies are options

only for highly paid women workers. Day nurseries would probably cost £25 a week for full-time care, but rarely accept under-
twos.

Day nurseries and childminders will go on looking after children
up to school age, once they accept them. At the magic age of
three education is supposed to become appropriate, and nursery
schools and classes put together offer places to only 7.06 per
cent of children aged two to four (TUC, 1977, p. 17). Here the
familiar inconsistency crops up again. Since nursery schools are
certainly not intended to benefit working mothers by offering
'day care' (they usually take three-year-olds for $2\frac{1}{2}$ or 3 hours
a day at first, and the maximum length of time is $6\frac{1}{2}$ hours for
only 39 weeks a year), if their stated purpose is to benefit children educationally, why are so few places available?

Voluntary provision in the form of playgroups is available for
children aged three to five, although it is impossible to estimate
how many places are available (Hughes et al., 1980, p. 95). By
its recent decision not to accept children under three in its member playgroups, as if this age marked a dividing line below which
group care was unsuitable, the Pre-school Playgroups Association
implicitly supports the administrative split between 'care' and
'education' (Leach, 1979, p. 76). Their short hours and their
frequent insistence on a rota of mothers as helpers makes playgroups of little help to employed mothers anyway, but in practice,
as with nursery schools, some mothers use them supplemented
with various mutual help or other arrangements.

School-aged children are often described as 'off your hands',
a phrase with an ironic ring for employed mothers. Children are
at school $6\frac{1}{2}$ hours a day, 39 weeks a year. For women who
managed to work full time previously it can actually become harder
to do paid work since nurseries are no longer available and childminders are reluctant to have school-aged children, often because
the children themselves get bored and dissatisfied. Except in
Inner London few holiday play schemes or after-school clubs
exist - probably about 3,000 cater for a tiny fraction of the one
and a half million children who are estimated to need places
(Simpson, 1978, p. 10). Vast numbers of children are either left
alone or inadequately cared for by older brothers and sisters or
through vague arrangements with neighbours. The split between
'care' and 'education' has ensured that responsibility for out-of-
school provision has been bounced between departments without
ever settling for long.

The overall picture makes nonsense of any government's claim
to support equal opportunity for women. Many women respond
by staying at home and becoming 'economically inactive'. Recent data
showed 24 per cent of mothers of pre-school children working outside the home, most of them part time. A further 27 per cent of
the mothers said they would like to work. Once the children go to
school, the proportion of employed mothers increases to over
half. A further 20 per cent would like to have paid work ('Woman's
Own', 1979). This confirms earlier findings that while some mothers

with paid work wish they could give up their jobs, it is far more
common for mothers at home to wish they had the chance to work
outside. Even so, the wish for more and better child-care provision is probably underestimated in surveys which question
mothers about their wishes and intentions in the context of existing child-care provision, which is not only difficult to get, but
also not good enough and necessitates complicated supplementary
arrangements.

HOW MOTHERS WORK

That family responsibilities directly affect mothers' position in
relation to the labour market is sufficiently well known, although
often forgotten. This section draws on interviews (carried out
in 1979 and 1980) with 38 mothers whose children had been going
to an after-school and holiday playscheme in Bristol, not to
establish the facts, but to show how in real cases several inter-
acting and reinforcing factors usually apply at once. This means
that for most mothers to take paid jobs at all involves an enormous
amount of organisation and planning in which men rarely have
much part.
    Few employed mothers work full-time, 'standard' hours. To do
so involves large-scale delegation of child care which is rarely
practicable; and for many women undesirable. The 'standard' 8-
hour working day - let alone overtime - is often experienced by
fathers as keeping them from knowing their children, and in a
society which makes the mother the key figure in a child's upbringing, mothers are inevitably more prone to guilt and more
conscious of what they are missing. The literal 'double shift'
worked by many full-time employed mothers, who have to do the
housework after getting home from work, is an even greater
deterrent. But many single mothers have to choose between depending on benefit which only allows them to earn a few pounds
a week, or working full time or nearly full time. Family Income
Supplement can also pressurise single mothers into working longer
hours, since they have to work at least 24 hours a week to qualify.
    For most mothers, whatever their feelings about it, full-time
work is not an option for some years. As soon as there is more
than one child, usually involving different arrangements for each,
it becomes harder to work long hours. In practice the problem is
solved by working unsocial hours, or part time, or both. In 1965
only 41 per cent of employed women *without* children worked
'standard hours'. Of employed mothers, it was only 14.5 per cent,
while 16 per cent worked within school hours, 6.5 per cent in the
evening, early morning or night, and 59 per cent other hours
or 'no set pattern' (Fonda and Moss, 1976, p. 11). Short hours
in the evening or night working are particularly common solutions
when the children are under two. Some women work as barmaids
or waitresses, others for much longer hours as night cleaners or
nurses, making do with just a few hours snatched sleep during

the daytime and trying to catch up at weekends (Union Place
Collective 1976, p. 14). Evening shifts at factories used to be one
way of working for women whose husbands would get the tea
(often ready prepared) and put the children to bed, but as the
recession bites these are becoming rarer.

The unsocial hours many employed mothers work hardly ever
bring any corresponding recompense in pay (Hurstfield, 1978,
p. 49). Often the jobs involved are casual. Evening work in bars,
cafes and night clubs is an unrecorded cash transaction with no
legal status. Twilight shifts are often temporary, and ignored by
the union. Night cleaning is often unorganised and highly exploited
(Hobbs, 1973). Night nurses who work for agencies are better
paid, but if they eventually return to hospital employment this
period in their working life counts for nothing no matter how
responsible the work.

The awkward and fragmented hours often involved are an obvious drawback of part-time work, but one which is often supposed
to be the price of an overwhelming advantage: the possibility of
dispensing with public forms of child care and relying only on
relatives or friends. Whether or not money is involved, these
individual arrangements are essentially private transactions, and
for this very reason some people think of them as the 'natural'
solution to the problem. They may, of course, be combined with
the use of playgroups, schools and nursery schools, but their
essential feature is that they make use of already existing relationships. Of course, the employed mother then has to fit her hours
to suit those of family members or friends. One woman, Pat, used
to work twilight shifts in a local factory, and before the playscheme
was set up she depended on her mother-in-law to look after the
two children when they came home from infants school. Since her
mother-in-law herself worked every morning, Pat could not get a
daytime job. In practice this arrangement was a constant source
of anxiety to Pat which hung over her at work. The grandmother
allowed the children to go to the park alone, which Pat disapproved
of. The arrangement was also under constant threat because Pat's
father-in-law's state of health was so precarious that he might at
any moment need his wife's care himself. The 'neighbourly' solution
has its drawbacks too. One of the playscheme mothers used to
leave her eight-year-old with a friend who lived in the same block
of highrise flats, and who had recently had a baby. This minder
did not dare let the little girl out to play alone, but was unable to
take her out much herself or keep her happy in the small flat. A
third mother also worked twilight shifts. She used to leave the three
children with their father when he was at home during the day,
although he was trying to sleep some of the time. When he was on
dayshift the grandfather would come over to look after the children. When he in turn could not come because of illness, the children of 5, 10 and 13 had to look after themselves. Private solutions
of this sort are more vulnerable than collective, public daycare.

The argument that 'blood is thicker than water', or that a substitute family is the warmest, most 'natural' form of child care

ignores the difficulty of establishing a good relationship with no
guidelines, in a shifting situation of changing needs on both
sides. Not everybody is good at discussion and renegotiation. In
addition there can be real practical difficulties for elderly people
trying to cope with children in an unsafe environment, and for
families in cramped housing to take in an extra child may be a
source of unforeseen strain. In fact, private solutions are often
so precarious that they add to the employed mother's burden.

However they delegate child-care responsibilities, mothers are
limited in the number of hours they can work as well as in when
those hours can be. Of all employed mothers with children up to
two, 38 per cent in 1976 were working for 0-12 hours a week. A
further 22 per cent were working for 13-21 hours a week, so
that 60 per cent of these employed mothers of babies and toddlers
only worked for up to half the standard 40-hour week. Hours
tend to increase as the children get older, but even so 24 per
cent of all employed mothers of primary school children were
working only 0-12 hours a week, and 30 per cent were working
13-21 hours (Central Policy Review Staff, 1978b, p. 41).

Part-time workers lose out in various ways. They earn less
money by the hour, on average, than equivalent full-time workers,
and this association holds for all industries (Hurstfield, 1978,
p. 29). They are in a weak bargaining position, needing to work,
but restricted in the jobs they can take. Employers have the
stronger hand since they can easily replace part-timers from the
pool of supposedly economically inactive women. Women's economic
dependence on men can both *enable* them to accept low pay and
oblige them to take what they can get. Only union organisation
could change this, but so many part-time workers are employed
in twos and threes in small workplaces that they are out of the
reach of unions who have not the resources to seek them out. In
some cases the workers themselves have taken the initiative and
found the unions reluctant to respond (Hobbs, 1973). Overall,
the factors which oblige women to work part time also militate
against their having time to spend on union matters, and their
conditions of work at home do not lead them to think in terms of
collective strength.

'Institutionalised discrimination against part time workers, with
respect to . . . promotion prospects' is widespread (Hurstfield,
1978, p. 33). Sometimes wage rates are affected even though on
paper no discrimination exists. For example in retailing part-
timers tend to remain on the lowest grades and are treated as
ineligible for increments based on length of service, and for merit
awards (ibid., p. 33). One of the playscheme mothers, Margaret,
works in an engineering consultancy firm as a computer operator.
For two years she worked for 30 hours a week during the school
terms and only 20 hours a week during the holidays. Then she
decided she wanted promotion. Her only chance was to work full
time - in this firm, 35 hours a week on Flexitime. Because her
husband, a low-paid worker, gave her his support by looking
after the four children after school and preparing their tea, and

(before the playscheme) taking the two younger ones with him to work in the holidays, and because the whole family submitted to being drilled as for a military operation, Margaret was able to work the longer hours and got her promotion. Working full time in order to qualify for promotion more often demands a 40-hour week, which is correspondingly harder for the family.

'The Part Time Trap' documents the worse conditions part-timers have to accept in terms of sick benefits, pension schemes and paid holidays. Few are covered by employers' sick pay schemes, so if they are not paying National Insurance contributions they are unprotected. Fewer part-timers are entitled to paid holidays, and they are usually excluded from occupational pension schemes, indicating '. . . the extent to which part timers are treated as a cheaper form of labour' (Hurstfield, 1978, p. 45). The fewer the hours worked, the more part-time workers are relatively disadvantaged. But apart from the difficulties of child care itself, both the tax system and the National Insurance threshold make it in the short-term interests of many employed mothers to work so few hours a week that they are below the 16 hours threshold for rights under the Employment Protection Act (Hurstfield 1978, p. 36; Hurstfield 1980, p. 11). These part-timers have no right to redundancy payments, to reinstatement after maternity leave, to claim unfair dismissal - not even to a written contract of employment. Just as women are the invisible unemployed, so they tend to be the invisible employed as well.

Women with young children change jobs, and go in and out of employment, more than men do. For one thing, child-care arrangements may break down temporarily or permanently, and in any case in order to make viable arrangements in the first place, the mother is likely to have had to take casual or temporary work or part-time work with less job security. When the years of the children's dependence have passed, the history of this sort of work experience becomes a limiting factor in itself, so that women remain stuck in a succession of 'marginal' jobs.

Perhaps this does not matter? In popular myth women are said to look for different satisfactions in work from those which appeal to men. They are supposed to expect less inherent interest from the job, and to tolerate boring and repetitive work much better. Money is supposed to matter less to them, and social contacts more. Of course there is a grain of truth in these phrases which personnel managers produce so glibly. Women's situation in the family obliges them to put those commitments first, to accept lower pay and inferior conditions, and their isolation at home makes the social life at work more valuable. To represent women as innocents indifferent to monetary reward is just another of anti-feminism's many faces. If they did not value money, many women would not go out to work under the conditions open to them. They need the money, but they need other things as a precondition of earning at all: hours that fit in with child care, time off when children are ill, a job close to home or school, and so on. These requirements which are ignored by public society lead employed mothers to seek an individual bargain with their employers.

Christine is one of the playscheme mothers for whom the bargain with her employer is far more relevant to her daily life than any legal rights she has or foregoes. Christine works as a secretary in a small local firm. She used to be a legal secretary in the City Centre, where she earned considerably more than her present £54 gross for a 35-hour week. For her it is worth it. Before the playscheme was set up to care for children after school, Christine's boss used to let her slip out of work to the school, which is nearby, collect her three children and install them in her car to wait for half an hour. He lets her take them to the dentist in working hours, or fetch them if they are ill. He even lets her go to school concerts. If the children's illness necessitates several days off she gets unpaid leave, if it is just a matter of an hour or two she can make it up in her lunch hours. Christine's boss is getting a woman who is overqualified for the job, and on whose loyalty he can rely precisely because of his 'understanding' attitude. He used to have a big turnover of staff, and found it difficult to get qualified people to bus out from other parts of town. By a shift of tactics he has managed to get three local married women tied to their jobs despite low pay. This is the sort of mechanism behind the description of women workers as 'less economically motivated'. These bargains between women and their employers are considered in detail in the next section.

THE EMPLOYER'S BARGAIN

Discrimination against women may take the form of preferring similarly qualified men, or the complementary form of preferring women for certain jobs, but for their supposed negative qualities such as being willing to tolerate boredom or accept low pay. Job segregation by sex results from both forms. The actual level and type of discrimination, and which groups of women suffer from it most, depends largely on the economic situation. A 1960 study of 120 firms almost all employing over 100 people found employers deliberately discriminating against younger married women on the grounds that labour turnover was higher in that group (Klein, 1961, p. 21). Yet despite this preference the shortage of labour forced employers to minimise discrimination against women, often to accept the least-liked group and even 'in order both to attract and keep them, to meet their special needs on a number of points' (ibid., p. 27). More part-time work was made available and evening shifts became commoner. Some firms offered married women a longer lunch break, or half an hour off in the morning or evening. Special unpaid leave for school holidays or family sickness were common concessions to child-care responsibilities, but actual nurseries were rare. So, while continuing to discriminate against all women in terms of the types of jobs offered to them, and against women with children by employing them as a last resort,

employers were actually forced into wooing them when this last
resort was reached.

Fifteen years later such concessions were less widespread.
Employers thought women in general more likely than men to take
days off work and to leave their jobs after a short period. Those
who habitually engaged women for certain jobs usually specified
'no children' (A. Hunt, 1975, p. 78). In the larger of the 223 firms
Hunt studied, the ones employing over 100 workers and thus
roughly comparable with Klein's sample, only a minority made
special arrangements to suit women workers with children. One
fifth had a formal policy of time off when children were ill, usually
unpaid. Flexibility about which hours were worked was sometimes
offered to part-timers, rarely to full-time workers. The general
picture is that by 1975 in the worsening employment situation
there were few 'understanding' employers among medium-sized
and large firms at least.

From the employer's point of view it makes sense to be 'understanding' if, and only if, it seems likely to pay. However, this is
a precondition rather than a guarantee that a strategy involving
'concessions' will be adopted. Other factors determine such decisions; some of them, like 'style of management', hard to pin
down. Empirical research on this question would need to look at
the size and scale of firms, and at how much autonomy they have
at local level and within departments. Formally simple questions
like 'would it pay?' would be approached quite differently in the
multinational, the large national firm and the medium-sized or
small local one. 'Concessions' like nurseries which need high
capital investment would be ruled out in advance for many firms.
Another crucial factor is the union organisation. In organised
firms the relations between workers and management are worked
out collectively, and individual 'bargains' usually discouraged on
both sides. Any special arrangements for women workers with
children would apply to large groups and become established
practice, and this may be true of large bureaucratised firms even
where women workers are not organised. In these cases employers
cannot just opt to be 'understanding' in one or two cases or as a
temporary tactic; they would be committing themselves to a course
of action with wider and longer-term effects (see, for example,
the scale of claims made by APEX to Lucas Industries: APEX,
1980c, p. 4). They may well decide that discrimination is the more
rational strategy, and either refuse to employ women with children
or take them on only if they are satisfied they will not have to
make any special allowances for them.

The commonest exception is part-time work. Why do employers
use part-timers? There are usually a few tasks which only take
up part of the working day, like cleaning and sometimes canteen
work. It is easy to see why part-timers are used for these. But
when part-timers are used in the actual production process, it is
likely to be for one of the following reasons:

1   The labour market is such that they cannot get enough full-

timers. (This certainly does not apply at the present!)

2 If they can use part-timers working less than 16 hours a week, they will be cheaper to employ. (But this seldom applies to large employers.)

3 Even though two part-timers are administratively dearer to employ than one full-timer, especially if training is involved, if they are paid at a lower rate they may still work out cheaper.

4 Some firms employ as part-timers ex-full-timers whom they previously trained, but will not employ women part time from scratch.

5 Most importantly: when flexibility is required, when the work load tends to fluctuate, the insecurity of part-timers' working conditions means that they can be taken on and laid off as required without any repercussions from the unions.

6 If peak periods are in the weekends, evenings or holiday season, part-time women employees are about the only ones who can be recruited.

If some of these considerations apply, the restricted hours which mothers of young children can work outside the home are directly in the interests of employers. In these cases they have no difficulty in overcoming the inertial force of the thinking associated with the standard 8-hour day, 40-hour week.

Employers rarely consider it in their interests to provide workplace nurseries. In the past such nurseries 'have been provided during periods of labour shortage to make more female labour available' (EOC, 1979b, p. 5). But even when there was such a shortage few employers took such drastic steps, as Klein's survey shows. I interviewed personnel managers in a large south-west confectionery firm which used to employ about 2,000 full-time women (now reduced to about 300 on production) and had to scour the countryside for suitable workers. Time and again right up to the early 1970s, the possibility of a creche to solve their labour shortage problems was considered and rejected, although the company was spending comparable sums on youth clubs, sports grounds and so on. In this case the obstacle was ideological. The company was willing to employ women with children for the twilight shift which lasted about three months at a time, but would not willingly consider them for permanent full-time work - even though it would have been an economically rational step. More recently, as the EOC admits, some nurseries might be set up to retain 'trained personnel who otherwise would have been forced to leave after the birth of children' (ibid., p. 5). The workplace nursery in a south-west clothes manufacturing firm, employing nearly 400 women, is an example of this. It opened in 1974 on the company's initiative. This company's policy is to recruit school leavers, trying to attract them during their last year at school. They only take women with children if they are skilled machinists, already trained by the company, wishing to return to work. As the personnel manager said, 'If we get the benefit of these skilled machinists, the increase in productivity is bound to follow.' The firm has made

the strategic decision to specialise in women workers, and to
make special arrangements for those who have children in order
not to lose the investment in training. They allow mothers unpaid
time off if the children are ill, or in the school holidays if they
cannot make alternative arrangements, and during the terms
mothers can adjust their hours so as to take the children to and
from school. Thus where skill is very important and a low labour
turnover is essential to prevent losses of investment in training,
quite heavy investment in 'special arrangements' could be rational
for employers. Nevertheless this seldom happens, perhaps because
for ideological reasons employers are reluctant even to start doing
those particular sums, and unions have rarely taken up the issue.
The EOC's suggestion that a relevant reason for setting up workplace nurseries today would be to conform ' . . . with the spirit
as well as the letter of recent legislation on job security and equal
opportunity' seems extremely sanguine (EOC, 1979b, p. 5).

Larger employers are unlikely to make explicit bargains with
individuals or small groups. However, it can happen. Jane is a
technician employed in a large college of further education. She
was attracted to her job because its description read: 'the working
hours are intended to be suited to married women with children,
as work in school holidays is not required.' Nor is work in school
holidays paid for. Effectively Jane loses her job at the end of every
term and is reappointed as a temporary part-time worker at the
beginning of the next term. This is of course highly convenient,
in one sense, since it fits in with her position as the secondary
breadwinner and primary caretaker of the children in her family
But this temporary status robs her of the legal protection of the
Employment Protection Act, because she now lacks job continuity.
Her typist colleague who is also a 'temporary part-time worker'
is paid less than the permanent part-time typists.

In other cases unofficial bargains are struck between particular
managers and particular workers, within large firms which officially
know nothing about it. One of the playscheme mothers told me of
two such arrangements in the medium-sized engineering design
consultancy firm where she works, and the personnel manager
subsequently confirmed this. One woman, Tina, was allowed to
work shorter hours in the school holidays. However, she claims
that she always got the same amount of work done by skipping
breaks and working so intensively that 'I couldn't have kept it up.
The six weeks summer holidays was exhausting'. Another woman,
Jenny, in the same firm does work classified as semi-skilled, involving about three months training on the job. This job is probably actually fairly skilled, for according to the personnel manager
the variation in quality of work can be considerable. Jenny is a
part-time worker who has been with the company since it was very
small. The bargain struck then has been kept to - she has the
long holiday off. The company wants to retain her because of her
skill, and can afford to do this because the department where she
works only includes about 20 workers, including a few boys and
women of various ages, so the danger of setting a precedent is

small. Unofficial bargains like this are possible in a small non-
unionised office, even in a medium-sized company, and especially
if the flow of work is uneven. In a firm with a production line
and with less skill involved they would be less likely.

On the whole, then, the individual bargains between women
and 'understanding' employers are more likely in small firms, and
exceptionally in small departments or pockets of certain large
ones. These bargains, even the written ones like that in the
college above, are reminiscent of the personal bargain over the
sale of labour power and the conditions of work prevalent in the
early nineteenth century. The boss makes 'special arrangements'
or 'concessions' to meet the woman's family responsibilities. In
exchange he gets something he needs. It may be that she is effectively tied to the job: contrary to what is sometimes said, low
turnover of labour is of great value to small, 'marginal' firms.
They cannot afford to buy job attachment with higher wages, but
that does not mean they do not need it. Minor concessions can be
relatively cheap, and negotiated either in advance or as they
come up. The personal nature of the relationship and the lack of
union organisation makes it unlikely that precedents can be set –
the boss does not relinquish any power in doing his worker a
favour. In any case the employer usually expects and gets some
immediate recompense as well as the notional long-term advantage.
Time off is usually unpaid, or if not it is made up in the lunch
hour or on Saturday. The woman may simply work more intensely.
And this sort of relationship with her employer certainly rules
out any inconvenient union activity, usually even membership.

Employers fall into two broad categories as far as employing
mothers is concerned: either they employ them only when they
are satisfied they will *not* have to make special arrangements for
them and will not find them less reliable, or they do make special
arrangements to a greater or lesser extent, usually for a price.
Women are faced with a corresponding choice. One option is to
try to solve their child-care problems by delegation on a large
scale, in order to achieve the best possible 'pre-entry' conditions
on the labour market. We have seen the difficulties involved.
Several of the playscheme mothers had jobs which they felt they
could only hold down by never admitting their difficulties. As
Christine said: 'Whatever it costs me, I never give them a chance
to say – there, you see, she's unreliable, she has a child.' She
is a single parent, a full-time secretary, whose little girl is looked
after by her grandfather after nursery school and goes to the
playscheme in the holidays. Women in this position cannot afford
to be ill. One woman who works as a cleaner for social services
was asked at the job interview to promise that if her children
were sick she would find someone else to care for them. Naturally
if they are really ill she pretends to be unwell herself, and on
other occasions sends them to school when they should really be
at home. Valerie, who works for an electronics factory which has
a similar policy, described it as 'a very hard firm, it makes no
allowances. A horrible firm to work for if you have children.'

Such firms may, but need not always, pay more. One advantage
they do have over smaller but more 'understanding' workplaces
is that at least the possibility exists of union organisation and of
bettering conditions that way.

It is easy to see why women with children who cannot find more
than a few hours child care a week that they are satisfied with,
or who cannot cope with holidays, look for jobs where the individual bargain applies. Many of these jobs will be in the 'black
economy'; casual work of which there is no written record and
with absolutely no security. Others will be perfectly legal but
below all the thresholds which indicate the active interest and
protection of the state. Some will be full-time jobs with proper
contracts of employment, and this unwritten bargain as an additional feature. The point is that women are driven to make individual bargains with their bosses of a sort which effectively keep
them separate from each other and tied to that one 'understanding'
employer.

Pam has three children, aged $1\frac{1}{2}$, $3\frac{1}{2}$ and $4\frac{1}{2}$. She has to make
separate arrangements for each. When a financial crisis in the
family forced her to look for work she went to twenty interviews
for clerical work, and she says that in each case as soon as they
heard she had three young children their previous interested
attitude changed. Unsurprisingly her present employer's sympathetic attitude was a great relief. She has been working there
30 hours a week for six months, and already in that time has had
to take the middle child into work for a day when he was upset,
and have a few days unpaid leave when the eldest had tonsillitis.
Typically, she is not in a union and does not know if there is one.
How could she afford to jeopardise this relationship with her boss
by even the appearance of confrontation? Another woman, Babs,
with two children of school age has found an employer who told
her he took on the family when he took her on. She is very grateful - 'he's most understanding'.

The extreme form, almost the caricature, of the 'special arrangement' bargain is seen in homeworking. There the restrictions of
child care are 'solved' by reconnecting home and work - making the
home a factory, but one with an individual worker who has to look
after children at the same time. The pressures on many women are
forcefully illustrated by the reluctance of homeworkers to criticise
their employers who super-exploit them, or even to say who they
are, lest they lose jobs which are essential to them. When in
trouble these employers simply deny their employees' status as
workers and claim they are self-employed. The homeworker's
situation is not unlike that of the insecure, badly paid and isolated
part-time worker (Crine, 1979, p. 16). While the homeworker
allows her home to be physically invaded by her paid work and its
tools, many part-time workers look for 'understanding' employers
who allow them to take children with them to work. One of the
playscheme mothers always did bar work before the scheme opened,
and took the children with her during the holidays. As she said
'It wasn't good for them, not at all suitable, but at least I knew

they were safe.' Work in shops, washing up in cafes, cleaning
private houses, schools or offices is all just about compatible with
the presence of one's children. Several playscheme mothers described the strain of trying to keep children happy and non-
destructive while they worked. One woman, Clare, cleans a
mother-and-baby home in the mornings. She used to take her two
children, one a very active epileptic boy, during the holidays.
As he got older and more easily bored she found this impossible.
The employer then allowed her to take the holiday off, unpaid, on
condition that her friend covered *for her for no extra pay*. She
would return this favour when her friend needed it. She considers
her employer very understanding, because of this 'concession'
and because now that she leaves her children at the playscheme
she is sometimes half an hour late for work, but as long as she
does the work they do not complain. She works 15 hours a week,
just under the Employment Protection Act threshold, for £1 an
hour.

Clare pays a particularly high price for her bargain, but the
above examples have shown that *some* price will be exacted in
exchange for such concessions as taking one's children to work.
Dependence on the goodwill of an individual employer is in itself
a high price to pay. That women accept it testifies to the enormous
influence that their unpaid work at home has on the conditions of
sale of their labour power, and the importance of the non-economic
elements of the contract. It is easy to describe women as 'back-
ward' in trade union terms, without the slightest understanding
of why and how their conditions of life tend to cut them off from
each other and from other workers (see also Marilyn Porter's
chapter in this volume). One TUC official told me glibly: 'Women
simply prefer the black economy.' Yet as recently as 1974 the
TUC was still issuing its Charter for Women Workers which called
on employers to 'understand' the problems of working mothers,
and offer more flexibility in hours to suit their needs. This section
has shown that employers can understand as well as anyone else,
but the solution for women workers does not lie in appeals to the
good nature of their employers, which can be bought at too high
a price.

THE CHICKEN AND THE EGG

Which comes first? All the emphasis in this article has been on
factors which disadvantage mothers before they even start, factors
external to the labour market. My approach deliberately rules out
the type of explanation offered by segmented labour market
theorists who see women's oppression as rooted in the labour market itself (Amsden, 1980, p. 21). In the previous section employers' strategies have been described, but treated more as a
response to the position of women with children in society than
as a powerful independent factor. For dual labour market theorists,
in contrast, discrimination is the main mechanism pushing women

into the 'secondary sector' of dead-end, marginal, insecure and low-paid jobs. Some of these analysts argue that women are forced into the secondary sector because employers consciously exploit sexual antagonisms to undercut worker solidarity (Reich, Gordon and Edwards, 1980, p. 239). Of course it is true that it is in the class interests of employers to encourage divisions among workers, and true that this is sometimes consciously done. But employers use, they do not invent, these antagonisms, which have material roots - in this case women's position in the family. Other dual labour market theorists think that women are either inherently more suited to secondary-sector jobs, or that they become so by virtue of being restricted to them. But in order to explain the 'fit' between women and inferior jobs you have to leave the internal dynamics of the labour market and look at the conditions in which women sell their labour power - their situation in the family (Beechey, 1978, p. 180). Employers' discrimination reinforces the far more effective discrimination against women stemming from the conditions of their own lives.

The chicken and egg argument is of more than academic importance. If the main source of inequality of opportunity is in the labour market, then that must be the main place it should be fought. In the UK that is where some progress has been made, in the form of the Equal Pay Act and the Sex Discrimination Act. The fight over these measures is still going on, but already their limited value is clear. The Equal Opportunities Commission has been given the task of promoting equality of opportunity by trying to enforce a law which outlaws discrimination - leaving its most basic causes intact. In the early days of the legislation the EOC pinned a lot of hope on the 'powerful concept' of 'indirect discrimination'.

> Here . . . the law was extended to recognise an important social reality: the fact that as a result of previous discrimination or lack of adequate opportunity, provision or encouragement, one group of persons may, to their detriment, be unable to meet a requirement or condition which is not explicitly discriminatory. The requirement may on the face of it be neutral, but it may have the effect of disqualifying one group more significantly than another (EOC, 1977a, p. 3).

A recent example concerns Ms Durrant, who claimed that, in refusing to pay her removal expenses because she was only a part-time clinical psychologist, the North Yorkshire Area Health Authority was guilty of indirect discrimination since more women work part-time because of domestic responsibilities. Her case was rejected by the Employment Appeals Tribunal, but a case based on similar principles has gone to the European Court of Justice (Labour Research Department, 1980, p. 10). Should the case succeed, it would not be one in which discriminators could simply buy themselves off by payments to individuals for 'injury to feelings' and the like, which has so often been the only result of

small victories in Industrial Tribunals. The principle involved is
obviously the right of part-time workers to equal rates of pay and
benefits. Recently unions have been arguing that the way to overcome the divisive effects of part-time work is to improve its conditions, as by the extension of the Employment Protection Act to
some part-timers (TGWU, 1980, p. 49). Although the tactics are
different, the struggle over the Durrant case would be in line
with this position. But is victory possible?

Fighting discrimination, 'direct' or 'indirect', has at the very
least an educational function. It forces people to recognise possibilities which had not occurred to them, and cases of 'indirect'
discrimination in particular tend to expose the width and depth
of women's unequal position by pointing away from the labour
market to the inequalities current legislation leaves intact. But
for that very reason it is illusory to think that 'indirect discrimination' could be reformed away in a capitalist system. It is right
to struggle for the rights of part-timers, but the gains made can
only shift the borders of the 'black economy' and the twilight
area of casual work, without touching the reasons why women are
segregated in this sort of job. In general, if a requirement which
women can less often meet is relevant to the job, as recent training and continuity of experience may really be in some cases,
employers will circumvent any legislation which instructs them to
discount it. For example, at present personnel managers are likely
to question women about child-care arrangements quite openly.
The personnel manager of an electronics factory employing 100
women on the production line told me:

'I always go into it in depth if anyone with young children
applies. Some don't give it enough thought – they might take
on a job on a temporary basis irrespective of the training we
put into them, and then leave when the summer holiday comes
up.'

The EOC's guidance to employers on the subject of job interviews
seems positively utopian by contrast:

Questions relating to marriage and plans for children are seldom
asked of a male applicant and, even if asked, do not imply that
the job will only be offered if the answers are satisfactory. . . .
The requirement not to discriminate against married persons,
or against women, can best be met by leaving questions relating
to marital status and dependents to be followed up with the
successful candidate . . . (EOC, 1979a, p. 12).

Nothing could be easier for employers than to keep the law by
asking no such questions, but simply avoiding all women in the
relevant age groups – as many already do.

Discrimination cannot effectively be outlawed, but of course it
can and must be fought, using legislation but relying on collective
action. Not only does discrimination in the labour market reinforce

the disadvantaging effect of women's position in the family, it is also one of the main ways in which the destiny of *most* women – to become mothers – becomes a decisive influence on the lives of *all* women, who are treated as restricted by present or future motherhood even when no such restrictions exist. Unions vary considerably in the extent to which they give this question priority, in whether they have published policy which members and others can scrutinise, and in whether they put their policy into practice. Attitudes are uneven: in an otherwise militant booklet TASS says that 'The respect and support of male workers has to be earned', referring to the use of women to undercut the wages of the working class (TASS, 1975, p. 9). The other side of the coin is just as powerful – unions have to win the confidence of women.

Trade unions can unite and strengthen those who were already strong enough to be able to get together in a preliminary way (see also Barbro Hoel's chapter in this volume). Most of those whose situations have been described in this article are unorganised and likely to remain so. When it comes to bargains between individual workers and employers, unions are helpless. It does no good to deplore such arrangements, which are inevitable, but it would be as silly to demand more of them as to demand more homework for housebound workers. The only 'special arrangements' which are in women's long-term interests are ones like nurseries, arranged collectively and over which the workers could have some control if their union took a part in managing them. Small-scale arrangements result from women's situation, not their 'backwardness', and the way to fight them is to change that situation so they become unnecessary. This means fighting women's oppression more generally, not only over the terms and conditions of the sale of labour power. There are encouraging signs that unions are beginning to do this, by becoming involved in action against further restriction on abortion, in the National Child Care Campaign, and other issues (see Judith Hunt's chapter in this volume). But there is still ambivalence even when radical demands are raised.

> If women's particular role as a parent is fully recognised, and if it is accepted that women will need to take fairly lengthy periods of leave to have children and may then work part time afterwards, then they cannot conform to the traditional male pattern of employment. At the moment, however, they are penalised heavily for not doing so . . . (TUC, 1977, p. 108).

But how could the weak *not* be penalised in capitalist society?

We cannot have it both ways. If we restrict our fight for equality to the workplace, aiming for a situation in which men and women are treated equally if they have similar things to offer – which is far enough away – then even the fulfilment of this aim would not bring equality because of 'women's particular role as a parent'. This phrase sounds all right, it even sounds sympathetic, but it

covers a widespread oppression, dependency, lack of status and
of power. Like formal equality in the workplace, improved and
widely available free child-care provision is far away and difficult
to get. But together with the demands for more flexible hours and
a shorter 'standard' working week for both sexes, for paternity
as well as maternity leave for childbirth and children's illnesses,
the demand for child-care provision has the great advantage that
it strikes at the heart of women's oppression. It is also easily
divisible. Every extension, every improvement, has immediate
effects.

Looking at things in the abstract it might seem that the oppression of women could be ended if such legislation as the Sex
Discrimination Act and the Equal Pay Act could be made to work.
If either parent could equally well be the main breadwinner, would
not the result be more families in which *both* shared child care
and other domestic work, or more 'role swaps' between men and
women? In reality the sexual division of labour cannot be changed
in the family without altering the role of the family in society, and
making some of its private work public responsibility. In the
abstract, the only inevitable difference between men and women,
which holds women back so long as we live in a commodity society,
is the need for women to have breaks from productive work in
order to give birth and immediately before and after. These inevitable breaks in continuity are, of course, very short in the context
of a lifetime's work. The rest is culture. That does not mean it
can be dismissed, and 'symmetry' be summoned up by a wish.

Women do not really 'choose' to be housewives now. They acqui-
esce in a system which predetermines their choice. That acquiescence is prepared for by training women as a sex to underestimate
themselves, to have little sense of self, and to believe a lot of
non sequiturs about motherhood. The privatisation of child care
and the care of other dependents, which cuts off children and
the other 'economically inactive' from the rest of society, is
intimately bound up with the ideology of women's oppression. So
is the way a lot of unnecessary and inefficiently carried out housework develops around the task of looking after children and stops
it being well done. However far off it may be, it is good to have
something to aim for. The way forward for women and men in
family life is not merely to try to make men accept for themselves
'women's work' in the home as it is done today, but to transform
that work and take a lot of it outside the home, so that the family
could become personal, rather than private, simply one living
option among others.

ACKNOWLEDGMENTS

Thanks to staff and parents of the playscheme at the Bristol
Settlement, to Miki David and Ellen Malos, and to Dan Lloyd and
Mike Feingold of the Bristol Resource Centre.

9 A WOMAN'S PLACE IS IN HER UNION
Judith Hunt

Women today make up 40 per cent of the workforce. They are
low paid, found in a small number of occupations and are a
minority in the professional and senior positions in all of them.
Over 40 per cent of those working are part time. One-third of
women at work are now members of trade unions.

This chapter explores some of the history that resulted in
women's union organisation being significantly lower than men's,
and the recent developments in women's trade union membership,
union policy and activity towards women.

Of the 117 unions affiliated to the TUC, there are only 14
unions where women dominate numerically. These unions organise
public service workers, textiles and shop workers, local government workers, teachers, Civil Servants and clerical workers. In
all others, women are in a minority. Women are still less well-
organised into trade unions than men, despite the dramatic increase
in their membership in recent years (16.5 per cent of the total
membership were women in 1960, 29 per cent in 1978). But those
$3\frac{1}{2}$ million women are underrepresented in all the major decision-
taking bodies of the trade union movement, including the TUC
Congress, (1980: 115 women, 1,203 men) and there are only a
tiny proportion of female full-time officers (TUC Statistical Statement and List of Delegates, 1980).

The pattern of women's membership and their minority position
is caused by a number of factors. These include job segregation,
the fact that women especially work in areas without a tradition
of trade union membership, such as white-collar, service and
clerical workers and that a high proportion of women work part
time. But there are a number of specific historical influences
too, which are relevant to the contemporary problem of women's
inadequate representation.

IN THE BEGINNING

The early years of trade unionism were hallmarked by the fight
for survival, for the right to organise and for legality, in response to the appalling working conditions imposed by the employers' attempts to maximise profit at all costs. The unionisation
of women must be seen in the context of this, and in that of the
historical subordination of women to men, and the subordination
of her paid work and independence to her role as child-bearer
and rearer. This heritage and fears of female labour undercutting

men's wages, combined with acute competition for jobs, resulted
in many trade unionists, particularly skilled workers wanting to
exclude women from paid employment.

This had two consequences. First, there was the development
of women-only trade unions and second, there was a general lack
of organisation amongst women workers with correspondingly low
pay and poor conditions. The general unions, whose growth was
linked to the Match Girls Strike of 1888 at Bryant and Mays and
the London Dock Strike of 1889, showed a greater willingness to
recruit women, although usually placing them in separate branches
or sections (Boston, 1980; Lewenhak, 1977; Soldon, 1978).

It was during this period that the TUC changed its official
attitude to women workers. Previously, it had sought to improve
men's wages and conditions to the level that they could keep their
wives at home. In 1885, for the first time, Congress took the view
that 'where women do the same work as men, they should receive
equal pay'.

There was a continuing struggle in some unions to win acceptance of women as members. These efforts were supported throughout by the Women's Trade Union League, which from 1886 also
promoted many small unions of women workers and, in 1906,
founded the National Federation of Women Workers.

This was formed on the model of a general labour union and
affiliated to the TUC with 2,000 members. In one year, it grew
to 15 branches. The consequences of separate trade union organisation for women were contradictory. Without the NFWW's fight
for the Trades Board Act in 1909, it is unlikely that minimum
wages would have been established in certain low-paid industries
employing mainly women. But the Federation's collective strength
even on equal pay remained weak because of isolation. Even where
a joint negotiating machinery was set up with the ASE (Amalgamated Society of Engineering Workers) and some improvement
was made in the 'women's rates', the existence of separate bargaining units, and separate women's structures, reinforced an in-built
differential between male and female rates of pay.

The dramatic increase in the number of women workers during
the First World War meant that many more women joined general
unions, but it also changed the attitudes of some previously all-
male unions, many of which set up women's sections (women's
membership rose to over 1 million in 1914, an increase of 60 per
cent over 1910, compared with 45 per cent for men). A few, for
example the spinners and print unions, continued to oppose the
employment of women, and in these areas women had to remain
unorganised or join the NFWW whose membership grew from 11,000
in 1914 to 60,000 in 1919 (J. Hunt, 1976).

The recession, combined with the return of soldiers, rapidly
reduced the employment of women. Collective agreements in many
cases either expressly limited the employment of women, or required the employees to be drawn from the ranks of the trade
union, which did not admit women members. This combination
halved the number of female trade unionists. By 1931, out of

5½ million women employed in Britain, only 500,000 were in trade
unions affiliated to the TUC.

Separate organisation had not arisen as a matter of principle,
but as a result of the refusal of existing unions to admit women.
In 1920, Mary McArthur, the founder of the NFWW, negotiated
a merger with the National Union of General and Municipal Workers.
The Executive believed that it ought to strengthen the organisation
of women workers by becoming part of the collective bargaining
arrangements established by the large general union. Experience
was to show that this did not provide the complete answer.

After the merger, the Federation retained its own executive
council and became a women's section of the then NUGMW. It was
given district status and a special department with extra officers
and organisers to cater for women. Mary McArthur was established
as the chief officer. These were considered to be very satisfactory
terms. However, in 1923 the separate women's district was abolished, the representation of women on committees was reduced,
followed by the abolition of the national women's committee and
the abolition of separate women's representation on the General
Council. Within a brief period the sixteen women officials of the
Federation were reduced to one. The sole voice of the women was
that of the chief women's officer.

Mary McArthur has seen the merger as a step towards equality:

> We are convinced that inside the National Union we shall be able
> to demonstrate the possibility of a great industrial organisation
> of men and women, in which women are not submerged, but in
> which they take as active a part as the men. That will be a
> great thing in the history of this country for it has never been
> done before ('Woman Worker', Aug/Sept 1920).

Similar arguments were used by some unions in the mid 1970s
to disband their special provisions for women (NUT, APEX), or
to justify either non-participation in the TUC women's conference,
or opposition to it whilst present (NALGO, CPSA, NUT, UPW).
The argument is that when women are incorporated into existing
structures their interests will be looked after as part of the
overall fight for improved wages and conditions, and that to
separate women off through special provisions is to patronise them
or to treat them as second-class citizens.

Where a reduction in women's additional or separate provision
has occurred, as in the NFWW/NUGMW and other unions, whatever the intention, the effect has been to reduce the number of
women in senior positions in the organisation and reduce the
numbers of those who actively take part in its activities. Several
unions are now re-tracing their steps. The GMWU in 1979 adopted
a comprehensive women's structure linked to their regional and
national organisation to meet the needs of women. The significant
difference to that of the position created by the merger in 1920
is that the new one links in to the union's decision-taking bodies,
both to advise them and to promote the involvement of women in

the union. APEX and NALGO have also recently taken a series
of structural and policy steps to reinstate or develop special
assistance for the particular needs of women.

These developments, explored further below, must be located
against the background of separate women's representation at
various levels in the trade union movement. During the inter-war
period, the Women's Trade Union League became officially incorporated into the TUC as the women workers group with two places
reserved for it on the General Council. Its task was to organise
women workers and to promote common action.

The first formal conference for representatives of unions which
organised women workers was held in 1931. The annual women's
TUC, together with the national women's advisory committee, to
which conference elects five representatives, and the allocation
of special seats on the General Council, is the same basic structure today. But the local machinery of women's committees and
divisional committees also set up in 1931 has altered considerably
over the years. Recognising that it was essential for women to be
organised if they were to improve their pay and conditions, their
main activity was recruitment, supported after 1938 by the first
woman officer of the TUC appointed specifically to help with this.
These committees were disbanded in the mid-1950s, as their
recruiting role was being undertaken by individual unions. New
committees for the particular problems of women workers have
been re-established during and since the 1970s by many trades
councils and regional TUCs as a response to the growing concern
with the needs of women workers.

Women's trade union membership, static throughout the inter-
war period, was affected by the dramatic increase in the Second
World War of women working and in non-traditional areas of
women's work. More women were admitted into mixed unions than
in the previous war, which led to an improvement in the rates of
pay for women. But campaigns to make room in employment for
'the boys' returning from the war, alongside the withdrawal of
nursery facilities and subsidised restaurants and laundries at
the end of the war, resulted in many women leaving the labour
market and trade unions.

Table 9.1   TUC membership

Congress	No. of Unions	Men (000's)	Women (000's)	Total (000's)	% of Total Members Women
1939	217	4116	553	4669	11.4
1958	185	6950	1387	8337	16.6
1968	160	6959	1767	8726	20.2
1978	115	8454	3411	11865	28.7

Source: Report to 1979 TUC Women's Conference.

The membership remained around 16 per cent until the late 1960s when the take-off in women's membership occurred, partly through the increase in women at work, especially in the service sector, and partly due to the affiliation, and increasing size, of white-collar unions to the TUC (Bain, 1970). But as the report to the 1979 women's TUC commented (p. 37): 'Some trade unions have not yet appreciated that the remarkable and rapid increase in women's membership of unions is more revolutionary than evolutionary, and that as such it requires a new approach.'

The facts are that in the ten years between 1968 and 1978, women's membership of trade unions increased as much again as it had done in the previous thirty years. Furthermore, it can be seen from Table 9.1 that the increase in women's membership accounted for nearly all of the increased trade union membership between 1958 and 1968.

In 1968, not one trade union had more than 200,000 women members. By 1978 there were six in this category, and four of them had more than 300,000 members. This meant that between them they had over 1¾ million women members. Table 9.2 shows those unions which have had the greatest increase in membership and the proportion of women members.

Table 9.2   Unions with largest increases in women's membership

	No. of women members (000's)		Increase (000's)	Per cent Increase	1978 women as % of total
	1968	*1978*			
NUPE	136.0	457.4	321.4	236	66.0%
NALGO	132.1	318.8	186.7	141	44.9%
TGWU	194.7	317.9	123.2	63	15.7%
COHSE	38.9	159.4	120.5	310	75.4%
GMWU	199.9	318.2	118.3	59	33.6%
USDAW	155.6	270.5	114.9	74	61.3%
ASTMS	9.4	77.2	67.8	721	17.5%
CPSA	100.0	158.8	58.8	59	70.0%
AUEW (ES)	97.4	148.3	50.9	52	12.8%
AUEW (TASS)	3.5	27.7	24.2	691	14.0%
APEX	38.7	83.7	45.0	116	55.8%

Source: TUC Annual Statistical Statements.

The dramatic increase in the female membership of unions reflects absolutely the job segregation within industry. In only twenty unions are found 3,097,221 of the 3½ million women members of the trade union movement at Congress in 1980, and ten unions had over 70 per cent of the female membership.

This segregation and consequential pattern of trade union membership means that it was not inevitable that a numerical increase would be matched by an increased attention to policy and

activity of women throughout the trade union movement, other
than in a few unions. Indeed a number of unions which had been
traditionally high in female membership did not begin to develop
their policies on women until the mid 1970s.

It is also important to note that representatives of manual
workers as well as white-collar workers have raised issues of particular concern to women. In fact some white-collar and professional unions have continued to oppose special representation
for women. Mel Reed of ASTMS cogently describes this and puts
the argument for positive discrimination in her reply to a motion
moved by the ABS (Association of Broadcasting Staffs) to the
1980 women's TUC conference. She said:

> This ground has been gone over many times before. Once again
> the motion was moved by those who were relatively privileged
> and from fields of employment where equal pay and better
> opportunities for women did exist. If they glanced backward
> they could think of the position of women in the manufacturing
> industries, in hospitals and schools, in commercial and clerical
> areas and in parts of the country where unemployment rates
> were frighteningly high, where male trade unionists were still
> to be convinced of the justice of the cause for women's equality.
> . . . To abandon the Conference now would not guarantee more
> women delegates at Congress or on the General Council. By
> joining together yearly, women had the opportunity to give
> prominence to matters of particular concern to women, and to
> gain help, support and encouragement from each other. To
> abandon the women's conference, at a time when more than ever
> women were going to need unity and the help and support of
> the women's conference would be the height of lunacy (Women's
> Conference Report, p. 111).

Conference supported her argument by overwhelmingly carrying
an amendment that the conference should only be abolished when
'women have *total equality* with men in all aspects.'

The fact that there has been a widening of policy and increasing
attention to the problems of trade union women is related to the
mushrooming women's movement of the late 1960s and 1970s and
its complex impact on society and therefore trade unions.

THE WOMEN'S MOVEMENT

The influence of the women's movement on trade unions is not in
itself new. There had been few direct or organisational links
between the NFWW and the women's suffrage campaigns of the
turn of the century, but individual feminists within the suffrage
movement such as Emma Patterson, Sylvia Pankhurst and Annie
Besant played a significant role in the growth of women's trade
union membership, and there was undoubtedly a living relationship
between the national women's movement and the organisation of

women workers (Strachey, 1978; Llewellyn-Davies, 1978; Dangerfield, 1966; Liddington and Norris, 1978). The breadth of vision
of some of the early socialists and feminists such as Mary Wollstonecraft, August Bebel, and Olive Schreiner (see Bibliography)
had stressed how women's emancipation required fundamental
changes in law, work and family life. But views such as these
became channelled into the narrow demands of the movement for
suffrage and education, surviving only as elements of radical
organisations, not to reappear as public issues until raised by
the contemporary women's liberation movement (Ramelson, 1972).

The 1970s saw the revival of women's campaigning organisations
for law reform, family reform, tax and social security reform,
and a creation of a wealth of new organisations and groups concerned with tackling problems such as abortion and child care.
At the core of this wide women's movement were the groups and
conferences of the women's liberation movement (WLM).

The local groups and the campaigns of the developing WLM
focused initially around four demands adopted at the Oxford
Conference in 1970. The historic strike of the women machinists
at Fords, Dagenham, ensured that equal pay was one of the demands, the others being equal education and opportunity, 24-hour
nurseries, free contraception, and abortion on demand.

Despite an increasingly sharp and divided debate at national
conferences about the value of 'demands', subsequent ones were
added as the WLM became collectively more knowledgeable of the
depth and complexity of women's oppression and the fundamental
changes in social and individual attitudes that would be required
for the liberation of all women. The added demands included a
detailed approach to the law, social security and taxation, the
right to self-defined sexuality and the right for women to live
free from the threat of violence (Wandor, 1972; J. Hunt, 1975).

Thousands and thousands of women have been directly involved
with the activities of the WLM and many more women became involved in the wider women's movement through older campaigns
which had re-vitalised. These range from the Abortion Law Reform
Association to the Fawcett Society. The renewed support for a
wide spectrum of women's rights campaigns would not have been
there without the activities and the sharpness of the questions
posed by the WLM and the determination to challenge society's
stereotyped and limited view of women.

The consciousness-raising groups of the WLM remained very much
the arena of women who had had some form of higher or further education, and still does. But the issues raised of the ways in which
women are psychologically and socially subordinate to men and the
explorations of ways of combating this has had an effect on many
organisations and individuals beyond the confines of the WLM. Perhaps at its simplest level this is expressed by a recognition that the
problem of building women's confidence in themselves and their own
aspirations is a key to involving more women in public activities and
new areas of work, and to developing the possibilities for women's
liberation, both individual and collective (Rowbotham, 1973).

There are few direct links between the women's liberation movement and trade unions, partly because of the social composition
of the movement, the separatist ideas of some sections of the
movement, and because many of its activities consume time which
is not available to working-class women. Also trade unions traditionally do not have structural links with 'campaigning organisations' and at a local level there was suspicion of the new and
rather challenging movement. But various organisations and
campaigns, both national and local, have involved some women
from the WLM as well as from the trade union movement and community and political groups. This contact resulted in an exchange
of ideas and experiences between activists of the WLM and trade
unionists, and areas of common action, as well as the increasing
volume of writing on all aspects of women's rights and liberation.

The National Council for Civil Liberties (NCCL) held a series
of conferences starting with that in 1974 on 'Women at Work'
which was attended by women with considerable trade union experience as well as members of the women's movement, and its
women's committee has played an invaluable role through the provision of practical books, information and guidelines on women's
rights which have been widely used in the trade unions and the
community.

The national abortion campaign, which grew from local women's
organisations, increasingly looked for support of the trade union
movement at both local and national level. This culminated in a
TUC rally supported by NAC which played a significant part in
the defeat of the Corrie Bill which aimed to restrict existing
abortion rights.

The Equal Opportunities Commission was established in 1975,
and has played a role in the promotion of women's rights to the
wider public. The EOC has been criticised by both trade unions
and the women's movement for its early caution and slowness in
defining its public role, for its regressive policy initiatives on
pensions and protective legislation (EOC 1978b, 1979c; TUC Congress Reports, 1976-80; Coote, 1978; Coyle, 1980). But it has
promoted women's rights, for instance, through its research and
publicity material (see Bibliography) particularly in areas inac-
cessible directly to the WLM or trade unions, it has actively supported claims under equality legislation, and supported conferences
and projects of the women's movement.

There is a need to debate further the extent and significance
of the relationship between the women's movement, the WLM and
the development of a substantial discussion on women's rights in
the trade union movement. There will be different assessments
of that, but what is clear and generally recognised is that there
is a relationship.It has operated in two ways. First, through the
interaction of individuals through 'umbrella organisations' such
as NAC and NCCL, and the increasing number of activists in
unions who have had a history of involvement with some aspects
of the women's movement. Second, through the general impact of
the growing national and international women's movement on social

awareness of women's rights, that in turn influencing trade union concerns.

The impact of the women's movement on trade unions can be divided broadly into two categories. First, the impact on policy and negotiating issues; second, the methods and structures being developed to increase women's involvement in trade unions. I will deal with them in this order as the development on policy focused attention on the internal problems that exist in trade unions as far as the representation of women is concerned, and the significance accorded to women's issues in practice.

THE DEVELOPMENT OF TRADE UNION POLICY ON WOMEN

The 1960s saw the beginnings of an expansion in the concerns of the TUC women's conference. This was reflected by the adoption of a charter which included issues other than equal pay. This was updated in 1968 and widely distributed as a pamphlet, the Six Point Charter for Women at Work. Its points included: opportunities for promotion, apprenticeship schemes for girls, improved opportunities for training, re-training facilities for older women, and a special case for the health and welfare of women workers.

In 1968, there was a tremendous clamour at the TUC women's conference for some real action to implement equal pay in response to the report of a government working party. Pressure continued until 1970, when the Labour government introduced its Equal Pay Bill, which was staged to come into full operation by 1975. Whilst welcoming the legislation, trade unions recognised some of its inherent weaknesses, particularly its criteria of establishing equal pay through a direct comparison between a woman's job and a comparative male job, relevant to only 25 per cent of the female workforce. A resolution was passed at Congress to that effect, and was amended by DATA (now AUEW-TASS) to include a call for industrial action to end 'industrial apartheid' (TUC Congress Report, 1976).

Experience showed that the Equal Pay Act's limitations were substantial and its main success was through the elimination of direct discrimination such as 'women's rates' in collective agreements and through the work of the Central Arbitration Committee (TUC Women's Conference Report, 1977). It also had a general effect on the aspirations of women, who now felt they had a legal right to equal pay even if the Equal Pay Act could not solve their problem. Thousands of equal pay claims were tabled throughout public and private industry. It also acted as a spur to industrial action, Trico being the best known of the disputes where women took on management to achieve equal pay where the Act could not be used.

The problems of the Equal Pay Act have continued to be discussed at TUC women's conferences, a special conference in 1977 and at TUC Congress. Detailed amendments have been agreed to be pressed for with an appropriate Labour government to form

an improved legislative framework to complement improvements
in collective bargaining (TUC Congress Report, 1978). The
anti-discrimination legislation was another focal point for TUC
discussion on equality in the early 1970s. This began to raise the
depth of the problem of job segregation by sex and how to create
opportunity to compensate for past discrimination.

The women's movement had also been exposing the complex
layers of discrimination against women and the roots of that
oppression and had clearly linked the problems faced by women
at work to their domestic role. Many of these issues gradually
became topics of debate within the labour movement. Family planning was discussed by the TUC women's conference for the first
time in 1972 and in 1973 support services to assist working women,
nursery education and one-parent families were on the agenda.
The working women's charter was launched in 1974 by the (old)
London Trades Council. This linked the separate areas of women's
oppression at home and at work in a charter of minimum demands
including child care, maternity protection, contraception and abortion, family allowances, legal equality as well as equal pay and
educational opportunity. This was subsequently adopted by many
trades councils and widely campaigned for throughout the trade
union and labour movement.

The TUC's new charter presented to the women's conference in
1975 (International Women's Year) only differed from the working
women's charter in not containing any reference to abortion. After
a fairly tense debate, this conference resolved that 'abortion
should be available to all women on the NHS'. This became Congress policy in September, from a resolution moved by Terry
Marsland of the Tobacco Workers Union. The working women's
charter was never adopted by Congress, but the 'aims for the
working woman' was reissued in 1976, including a demand for
abortion on the NHS.

The TUC women's conference has become a lively event supported by more unions - more were represented in 1980 than in
any other year - and it has provided the TUC women's advisory
committee as well as the General Council with many more specific
tasks. This can be assessed by the almost dramatic increase in
output of TUC policy and material on the specific problems of
women workers. Detailed policy has been adopted on a wide range
of issues, including opportunity in training, women's unemployment, support facilities, health facilities, women's role at work
and specific problems such as those of battered wives. The various
conference resolutions on child care led to a working party and a
report (TUC, 1977), whose substance was adopted by Congress
in 1978, and 'The TUC Charter on Facilities for the Under Fives'.
Policy has also been developed on homeworkers (TUC, 1979a) and
part-time workers, which have been publicised through pamphlets
and leaflets.

There has been a growing recognition amongst many trade
unionists that women are here to stay in the labour force and
therefore have a right to be protected by trade unions. Not least

because the best way to protect men's rates of pay and conditions
is to eliminate low-paid female areas rather than exclude women
from work because cheap labour (female) threatens the wages of
the total workforce. There is incontrovertible evidence that those
women who are members of trade unions have better pay and conditions than those who are not (although they will not necessarily
have 'equal' conditions or pay to similar male unionised workers)
(Ratner, 1980). Collective bargaining has clearly provided a
mechanism whereby women's pay has been increased on an annual
basis where organised. However, one of the factors behind the
continuing and substantial differential in male and female earnings
is the content and structure of collective agreements. This is
succinctly expressed in the discussion document, 'Equal Opportunities: Positive Action', presented to the TUC conference on
positive action in November 1980:

> By and large, earnings in the UK are established by collective
> bargaining and legislation (whether in the form of wages council
> orders or CAC awards under the Equal Pay Act etc.), plays a
> minor part. This suggests that employers have reacted to the
> legislation by setting up 'women-only' grades and that they have
> not been adequately challenged by the trade union movement,
> and there have been cases where unions, through their pay
> negotiations, may have further magnified the gap between men's
> and women's earnings. Legislative improvements, although
> important, will not close the earnings gap unless accompanied
> by a considerably greater effort by unions to promote equality
> of pay and job opportunity between the sexes.

The resolution of the problem of women's pay raises complex
issues which challenge the existing form of some collective agreements and will require a new approach, but there is evidence that
that is achievable and can be done with the support of male trade
unionists. TASS's 'men's pay for women' campaign was developed
to tackle the limitations of the Equal Pay Act and to compensate
for traditional assessments of female pay. An assessment of the
results of the campaigning (in TASS 'News and Journal', December
1980), indicates a wages gap of 87 per cent as against the national
average of 73 per cent for similar groups of workers in the same
period.
   The variation in collective bargaining arrangements means that
different solutions will be required by different groups of trade
unionists, that there is no one simple panacea to this complex
issue. But it is recognised that further change and development
is necessary (Pat Turner, TUC Congress, 1974, 1978, 1980),
and that this will need to include changes in attitudes of men,
both to women at work and within the home. The question of
domestic responsibilities has gradually been raised both informally
and formally within the trade union movement.
   Marie Patterson's presidential speech at the confederation of
shipbuilding and engineering unions' 1978 conference dealt in

detail with the problems that face women at work. She also referred
to the attitudes that exist within the 'privacy of minds' and the
need to change them as part of the process of establishing equality.
Bill Keys of SOGAT introduced the Report on Equal Rights to
TUC Congress in September 1980 by reference to the need for
unions not only to put their own houses in order but for there to
be change in the individual attitudes of men, not only at work
but in the home. His remarks were echoed sharply by Anne
Spencer of the NUTGW and Anna Coote of the NUJ.

The report on Women in the Trade Union Movement to the TUC
women's conference also highlights this question:

> There is also a family responsibility. Domestic chores, shopping,
> and care of the children should not be assumed to be exclusively
> a responsibility to fall on the mother. Increasingly, therefore,
> emphasis is placed on the joint responsibility of husband and
> wife for the home and where work sharing can enable the woman
> to be active within her union (TUC Women's Conference Report,
> 1979, p. 39).

'A WOMAN'S PLACE IS IN HER UNION'

The inadequate representation of women became a recurrent theme
of conferences from 1974. A report compiled by the Equal Pay and
Opportunity Campaign in 1976 revealed the serious discrepancy
between the increased number of women and their lack of representation at all levels in the trade union movement (see Table 9.3).
This was confirmed by reports from individual unions such as in
the film industry (Benton, 1976) and reports of special working
parties, which include NUPE (1974), NALGO (1975), COHSE,
CPSA (1978), and APEX (1979). So too by recent research (for
instance Stageman, 1980; Calow, 1980; Drake et al., 1980; Fryer
et al., 1974).

Increasing documentation and concern with the numerical lack
of representation of women has not automatically led trade unions
to conclude that some kind of positive assistance is necessary to
increase the provision for women. Some have argued that representatives are elected to serve all who elect them, therefore
the problems of women and men alike will be dealt with adequately
by both stewards and full-time officials and by negotiating committees regardless of the presence of women members. However,
recent experience and the results of the merger of the NFWW with
the NUGMW have shown that the particular problems that face
women at work are not necessarily understood or communicated to
male representatives, that women's issues become submerged and
lost in the bargaining demands of male unionists, and that in some
instances, male stewards have acted contrary to their union's
policy on equality because they themselves do not believe in equal
pay or opportunity (see EOC Report on Electrolux). This is partly
a result of the segregation within the labour force so that very

Table 9.3:   Position of women in unions, September 1976

Union	Total membership		% of women members	NEC		Full-time officials		TUC delegates	
	M	F		M	F	M	F	M	F
APEX	62,438	75,278	55%	11	4	5	1	10	3
ASTMS	351,000	62,000	18%	23	1	65	5	19	1
ATWU	23,122	19,027	45%	16	6	19	5	7	2
AUEW (E.S.)	1,038,720	166,000	14%	9	—	186	1	35	—
Bakers	30,122	20,325	40%	14	4	25	1	10	—
CATU	20,768	23,636	53%	16	2	6	—	7	2
COHSE	42,420	101,059	70%	27	1	35	5	8	—
CPSA	69,451	145,693	68%	18	8	24	4	22	8
CSU	29,108	17,676	38%	21	2	10	1	8	2
EETPU	361,193	52,996	13%	14	—	150	—	13	1
FTAT	73,857	10,243	12%	24	—	40	—	11	—
GMWU	592,073	290,283	33%	30	3	272	10	64	4
IRSF	23,093	31,827	58%	25	3	6	—	9	—
NALGO	357,942	267,221	43%	61	5	174	17	69	5
NAS/UWT	70,000	15,000	18%	35	3	8	—	6	2
NUBE	58,118	48,957	46%	21	3	28	3	13	—
NUDBTW	35,186	20,138	36%	14	1	25	1	6	5
NUFLAT	32,187	30,268	48%	15	1	46	2	13	—
NUHKW	19,887	52,836	73%	23	2	29	2	11	1
NUPE	201,847	382,638	65%	20	6	120	2	29	4
NUT	66,896	197,453	75%	41	7	24	2	30	—
NUTGW	13,359	96,070	88%	10	5	34	6	11	5
SCS	85,000	17,000	17%	22	5	17	3	17	—
SOGAT	123,876	69,928	36%	30	4	67	3	31	5
TASS	128,895	15,571	11%	26	2	36	2	14	4
TGWU	1,511,000	289,000	16%	39	1	480	—	76	2
TSSA	55,600	15,705	22%	28	—	50	10	13	2
TWU	7,318	13,381	65%	18	2	6	3	4	1
UPW	147,679	42,321	22%	14	5	11	1	12	2
USDAW	153,653	223,649	59%	16	1	129	4	21	5

Source: Equal Pay and Opportunities Campaign, 1976.

few men do the same jobs as women, and therefore lack direct
experience of the nature of the job and specific nature of the
grievances that arise from that. Because of the generally different patterns of domestic life for men and women, the additional
requirements of women in negotiations, such as on maternity
leave or the right for time-off to care for children, are not yet
widely recognised as being important issues. Equally, many men
do not yet recognise the depth of the question of inequality that
faces women at work.

There is insufficient space to deal further with these issues
(see the other contributions to this volume; Coote and Hewitt,
1980; and Amsden, 1980). Here I want to look at some of the
responses made within the trade union movement itself to the
nature and demands of women's issues.

Some representatives have attended courses on equal opportunity and do understand the problems that face the female workforce, but there are insufficient of these possibilities to ensure
that all negotiating committees will understand these issues. Thus
the absence of women on many committees often means that their
particular problems are overlooked.

The presence of women in the capacity of lay representatives
and full-time officials symbolises clearly that it is a union that
caters for women. As the International Confederation of Free
Trade Unions (ICFTU) have put it in their charter:

> Women whether organised or not, will judge whether union
> organisation adequately considers the question of equal rights,
> opportunities, and treatment by the way equality is practised
> in their own ranks, i.e. the extent to which the participation
> of women in trade union decision making and responsibilities
> corresponds to the number of women members.

Because of increasing concern on this issue, the women's
advisory committee provided a special report to the 1979 TUC
conference on women's involvement. This outlined in detail the
changes in women's membership, and their lack of representation.

It drew heavily on research and work carried out by the
women's committee of the European Trade Union Confederation
and by the ICFTU and included a proposed charter for trade
unions in the UK. This was debated at the conference and amended
by the women's advisory committee in the light of the conference
debate and it was adopted by Congress in 1979. It outlines the
sort of detailed steps that will be needed if unions are to achieve
the greater participation of women in all activities of the union,
and representation of their wives, through adopting a different
approach to the questions of women's domestic responsibilities
and the impact on women of years of socialisation.

The charter includes the following points: union executives and
conferences should publicly declare the commitment of the union
to involving women; structures of unions should be examined to
see whether they prevent women from reaching the decision-making

bodies; special provision should be made to ensure that women's
views are represented; consideration should be given to setting
up advisory committees to ensure that the special interests of its
women members are protected; committees at regional, divisional,
and district level could also assist by encouraging the active
involvement of women in the general activities of the union; efforts
should be made to include provision in collective agreements for
meetings during working hours; every effort should be made to
provide child-care facilities for use by either parent, where meetings cannot be held during working hours; child-care facilities,
for use by either parent, should be provided at all district,
divisional and regional meetings and particularly at the union's
annual conference, and for training courses organised by the
union; special encouragement should be given to women to attend
trade union training courses; the content of journals and other
union publications should be presented in non-sexist terms (TUC
Charter for the Equality of Women within Trade Unions, 1979).

Jane Stageman's study (1980), which highlights the significance
of the TUC charter, was based on the experience of a selection of
women trade unionists and representatives in six union branches
spread across four trade unions in the Hull area (NALGO, USDAW,
TGWU, and NUPE). The study stressed the problems of communication (alike for both men and women), the specific problems of
confidence that face women and their feelings that 'the union just
doesn't provide enough back-up and information for the women'.
(These difficulties are also emphasised by others, for instance
P. Hunt, 1980.) A recurrent theme of all the investigations was
the problem posed for women by their domestic responsibilities
and social conditioning. The majority of the stewards interviewed
echo the points made nationally, of the need for positive assistance to increase women's participation. One interviewed steward
explains: 'We need to be able to voice our demands. Until we get
there on our own merits through education and experience, then
we must have some provision like this' (Stageman, 1980, p. 110).

A number of unions have already taken action on equality, in
some cases before the TUC's adoption of the 1979 charter, and in
fact steps already taken influenced the content of the charter.
Below is a brief indication of the range of measures that are being
adopted, and an indication of some of the unions which have taken
them. This list cannot hope to be comprehensive and will therefore
regrettably omit some unions and actions. It is important to note
that there is enormous variation in the structures and constitutions
of unions, so that action taken by one union is often totally inap-
propriate for another and unions have created a variety of methods
for their own particular situation.

1 Special committees - to advise on policy matters, etc., and/or
with special responsibility for organisation of women members:
NATFHE, NALGO, COHSE, NUJ, AUEW (TASS), NUT, BIFU,
ASTMS.

2 Giving officials and/or research officers special responsibility
for women: TGWU, GMWU, AUEW (TASS), NUT, BIFU, COHSE.

3 Special conferences: AUEW (Engineering Section), GMWU, TGWU, COHSE.
4 Special education facilities - courses for women, special arrangements to enable them to attend, redesign of general union courses
to include sections on equality, etc: NUPE, AUEW (TASS), APEX,
TGWU, GMWU, BIFU, COHSE.
5 Publicity and information - pamphlets, recruitment literature,
policy statements on equality; special articles or concern for
women's issues in union journals: USDAW, GMWU, TGWU, AUEW
(TASS), NUJ, COHSE, ACTT, APEX.
6 Increasing women's representation - reserved seats for women
on national committees: COHSE, TWU, TSSA, AUEW (TASS),
NUPE.
7 Training of full time officers - special training conferences,
materials for full-time officers on equality legislation and negotiating guidelines on maternity, equal pay, equal opportunities, etc:
GMWU, ASTMS, AUEW (TASS), EETPU.
8 Creche facilities - all parents, but women in particular, have
difficulty in attending conferences, residential courses, evening
meetings, etc. A number of unions now provide creche facilities
in an attempt to overcome this problem: NATFHE, ASTMS, AUEW
(TASS), COHSE.
9 A number of unions have special conferences which discuss
matters of particular concern to women, in some cases only women
are elected as representatives, in others some men attend· AUEW
(Engineering Section), GMWU.

In order for women to be equal at work, there must be effective
campaigning against the employers to eradicate past and continuing discrimination. To achieve this compensatory steps such as
above must be taken within the unions to increase women's participation and ensure that women's voice is heard. It is too early to
make anything other than a preliminary and tentative assessment
of the impact of steps already taken. However, there is clearly
no one recipe for success. The contributions of speakers at TUC
Congress, and women's conferences, indicate some of the possible
ingredients for successful organisation.

First, it is important to provide opportunities for women to get
together both formally and informally, and to provide special
education and training events. But it has also been recognised
that because of women's secondary position in society, simply
providing the facilities is not enough. Officers and activists at
all levels of the union need to see it as being an intrinsic part of
their job to encourage women members into activity, and to deal
effectively with negotiating issues relating to women. A positive
approach to child care and domestic responsibilities is also necessary with appropriate assistance being made available from the
unions. Alongside this, unions will need to assess whether their
existing democratic structures inhibit the involvement of women
and require change, not simply to provide a token presence, but
full participation. The debates from the women's movement on

decision-taking and collective work (Joreen, 1973; Rowbotham, Segal and Wainwright, 1979) have exposed some of the problems that face women inexperienced in procedures but the specific solutions will have to be found within individual unions and organisations.

There must be clear links between any women's committees and groups to committees at branch, regional and national level that have a decision-taking responsibility. This is to avoid the creation of a separate structure as in the inter-war period where women's problems are only discussed by women and the solutions not being pursued through the usual channels within that particular union.

The essentials for change sound easy. In practice it requires detailed and painstaking work, both amongst women and men, and an understanding that traditional structures that have been adequate for representing male trade unionists do not necessarily or easily include women and their problems. Reserving seats for women on leading committees of unions certainly creates an atmosphere where women can identify that these kind of trade union roles are open to them too, but unless there is a clear constituency for those women within the organisation and a constituency which has direct links to all the decision-making bodies, then they may only be token women, with all the problems that involves, not least for the individuals concerned.

The problem is almost a circular one. For women's representatives to be listened to it is a prerequisite that women are visible. Accommodations have to be made to ensure that they have facilities which help to overcome the barriers imposed by society. Such help involves the allocation of resources by organisations that are numerically dominated by men.The evidence suggests that it is those unions that have allocated resources for special provisions that have increased the participation of women at all levels and have a better success rate in negotiating on the specific problems of women ('Labour Research', 1979a; Coote, 1980).

The current political and economic policies being pursued by the Conservative government are ones which attack and undermine what progress has been made towards women's equality, both in terms of the right to work, job opportunity, the elimination of low pay and the provision of rights such as maternity rights, and child-care facilities. Perhaps one indication of the importance of the increased female membership of the trade union movement is that the particular concerns of women have been included in the publicity and campaigns around the TUC's campaign for social and economic advance (see in particular, 'Women's Briefcase', 1980), and that the TUC is continuing to develop work on positive action programmes (TUC Congress 1980). These programmes will aim to eradicate past and continuing discrimination against women and to open up opportunities in areas of work previously done by men. In earlier economic recessions as acute as this one, where women were less well organised and where there was no nationally vocal women's movement, their specific problems have not been included to the extent that they are today.

The discussion on positive action programmes is a response to the experience and knowledge gained in the last ten years, and is an issue which strikes a chord with the vast majority of working women. Progress in such programmes should also accelerate the involvement of women in trade unions. The disputes around the introduction of the Equal Pay Act and the experience of generations of trade unionists (male and female) show that people become involved with the union at work when they feel it is dealing with their problem. 'I got involved over my job description dispute. After sticking my toes in over that I got more interested in union affairs' (Stageman, 1980, p. 107).

This chapter has touched on two linking philosophies, one held by the women's movement of the importance of women 'getting together' to discuss problems and develop confidence and activity. The other, that of the trade union movement, is that the strength of trade union organisation lies within the bargaining strength at the workplace. It is in the linking of these two philosophies that the greatest development will take place. There is no basis for hoping that this current Conservative government will make any impact on women's rights, other than to limit them. There are, however, grounds for optimism in the developments on trade union action and policy on women's rights and the increasing recognition of the importance of providing facilities for women's greater participation in union activity at all levels.

The trade union developments alongside the activities of the women's movement, are the only guarantee that the demands of women will continue to be expressed and heard.

ACKNOWLEDGMENTS

I would like to thank colleagues in the trade union and women's movements for discussion and activities which helped form the ideas in this article.

GLOSSARY

ABS	Association of Broadcasting Staffs
ACTT	Association of Cinematograph, Television and Allied Trades
APEX	Association of Professional, Executive, Clerical and Computer Staff
ASE	Amalgamated Society of Engineering Workers (now AUEW)
ASTMS	Association of Scientific, Technical and Managerial Staffs
ATWU	Amalgamated Union of Textile Workers
AUEW (E.S.)	Amalgamated Union of Engineering Workers (Engineering Section)
Bakers	Union of Bakers and Allied Workers
BIFU	Banking, Insurance and Finance Union (used to be NUBE)
CATU	Union of Ceramic and Allied Trades
COHSE	Confederation of Health Service Employees
CPSA	Civil and Public Services Association
CSU	Civil Service Union
DATA	Draftsmen and Allied Technicians Association (now AUEW-TASS)
EETPU	Electrical, Electronic, Telecommunication and Plumbing Union
EOC	Equal Opportunities Commission
FTAT	Furniture, Timber and Allied Trades Union
GMWU	General and Municipal Workers Union
ICFTU	International Confederation of Free Trade Unions
IRSF	Inland Revenue Staff Federation
NAC	National Abortion Campaign
NALGO	National Association of Local Government Officers
NAS/UWT	National Association of Schoolmasters and Union of Women Teachers
NATFHE	National Association of Teachers in Further and Higher Education
NCCL	National Council for Civil Liberties
NFWW	National Federation of Women Workers
NUBE	National Union of Bank Employees (now BIFU)
NUDBTW	National Union of Dyers, Bleachers and Textile Workers
NUFLAT	National Union of Footwear, Leather and Allied Trades
NUGMW	National Union of General and Municipal Workers (now GMWU)
NUHKW	National Union of Hosiery and Knitwear Workers
NUJ	National Union of Journalists
NUPE	National Union of Public Employees
NUT	National Union of Teachers
NUTGW	National Union of Tailors and Garment Workers
SCS	Society of Civil Servants
SOGAT	Society of Graphical and Allied Trades
TASS (AUEW)	Technical, Administrative and Supervisory Section of the AUEW
TGWU	Transport and General Workers Union
TSSA	Transport Salaried Staffs Association
TWU	Tobacco Workers Union
UPW	Union of Post Office Workers (now Communication Workers)
USDAW	Union of Shop, Distributive and Allied Workers
WLM	Women's Liberation Movement
WTUL	Women's Trade Union League

BIBLIOGRAPHY

Advisory Council of Applied Research and Development (1979), 'Technological Change: Threats and Opportunities for the UK', London, HMSO.

Alexander, S. (1976), Women's Work in Nineteenth Century London: A Study of the Years 1820-50, in A. Oakley and J. Mitchell (eds), 'The Rights and Wrongs of Women', Harmondsworth, Penguin, pp. 59-111.

Alexander, S. (1980), Introduction to M. Herzog, 'From Hand to Mouth', Harmondsworth, Penguin.

Alexander, S., Davin, A. and Hostettler, E. (1979), Labouring Women: A Reply to Eric Hobsbawm, 'History Workshop', no. 8, pp. 174-82.

Amsden, A.H. (ed.) (1980), 'The Economics of Women and Work', Harmondsworth, Penguin.

APEX (1979), 'Office Technology: The Trade Union Response', London, APEX.

APEX (1980a), 'Automation and the Office Worker', London, APEX.

APEX (1980b), New Technology and Redundancies, London, APEX.

APEX (1980c), 'Workplace Attitudes to Maternity and Nursery Facilities: A Case Study', London, APEX.

ASTMS (1979a), 'Technological Change, Employment and the Need for Collective Bargaining', Discussion Document, London, ASTMS.

ASTMS (1979b), Technology Agreements, London, ASTMS, unpublished.

Atkinson, W.R. (1978), The Employment Consequences of Computers: A User View, seminar paper, in T. Forester (ed.) (1980), 'The Microelectronics Revolution', Oxford, Basil Blackwell.

Bain, G.S. (1970), 'The Growth of White Collar Unionism', London, Oxford, University Press.

Barber, A. (1980), Ethnic Origin and the Labour Force, 'Employment Gazette', vol. 88, no. 8, August, pp. 841-8.

Barker, D.L. and Allen S. (eds) (1976), 'Dependence and Exploitation in Work and Marriage', London, Longman.

Barker, J. and Downing, H. (1980), Word Processing and the Transformation of Patriarchal Relations of Control in the Office, 'Capital and Class', no. 10, pp. 64-99.

Barrett, M. (1980), 'Women's Oppression Today: Problems in Marxist Feminist Analysis', London, Verso and New Left Books.

Barrett, M. and McIntosh, M. (1980), The 'Family Wage': Some Problems for Socialists and Feminists, 'Capital and Class', no. 11, pp. 51-72.

Barron, I. and Curnow, R. (1979), 'The Future with Microelectronics', Milton Keynes, Open University Press.

Barron, R.D. and Norris, G.M. (1976), Sexual Divisions and the Dual Labour Market, in D.L. Barker and S. Allen (eds), 'Dependence and Exploitation in Work and Marriage', London, Longmans.

Bebel, A. (1971), 'Women under Socialism', (trans. D.de Leon), New York, Schocken, originally published 1883.

Beckford, G. (1972), 'Persistent Poverty: Underdevelopment in Plantation Economies of the Third World', London, Oxford University Press.

Beechey, V. (1978), Women and Production: A Critical Analysis of Some Sociological Theories of Women's Work, in A. Kuhn and A. M. Wolpe (eds), 'Feminism and Materialism', London, Routledge & Kegan Paul.

Beechey, V. (1979), On patriarchy, 'Feminist Review', no. 3, pp. 66-82.

Benet, M.K. (1972), 'Secretary - An Enquiry into the Female Ghetto', London, Sidgwick & Jackson.

Benton, S. (1976), 'Patterns of Discrimination against Women in the Film and Television Industries', London, ACTT.

Berger, J. (1972), 'Ways of Seeing', Harmondsworth, Penguin.
BIFU (1980), 'Report of the BIFU Microelectronics Committee', Esher, BIFU.
Bird, E. (1980), 'Information Technology in the Office: The Impact on Women's Jobs', Manchester, Equal Opportunities Commission.
Birnbaum, B. (undated), Women's Skill and Automation: A Study of Women's Employment in the Clothing Industry 1946-72, unpublished paper.
Blackburn, R. (1967), 'Union Character and Social Class', London, Batsford.
Bland, L., Brunsdon, C., Hobson, D. and Winship, J. (1978), Women 'Inside and Outside' the Relations of Production, in Women's Study Group, Centre for Contemporary Cultural Studies, 'Women Take Issue', London, Hutchinson.
Blauner, R. (1964) 'Alienation and Freedom', University of Chicago Press.
Board of Trade (1947), 'Working Party Reports: Light Clothing', London, HMSO.
Bone, M. (1977), 'Pre School Children and their Need for Day Care', London, HMSO.
Boston, S. (1980), 'Women Workers and the Trade Unions', London, Davis-Poynter.
Bowen, J.A.E. (1980), 'Armageddon or Utopia? A Brief Survey of the Impact of Microelectronics in Some Sectors of the Service Industries', Occasional Paper, Technology Policy Unit, University of Aston, Birmingham.
Braverman, H. (1974), 'Labour and Monopoly Capital', New York, Monthly Review Press.
Bridges, W.P. (1980), Industry Marginality and Female Employment: A New Appraisal, 'American Sociological Review', vol. 45, no. 1, pp. 58-75.
Brooks, D. (1975), 'Race and Labour in London Transport', London, Oxford University Press.
Brown, M. (1974), 'Sweated Labour: A Study of Homework', Low Pay Pamphlet, no. 1, London, Low Pay Unit.
Bruegel, I. (1979), Women as a Reserve Army of Labour: A Note on Recent British Experience, 'Feminist Review', no. 3, pp. 12-23.
Byrne, E.M. (1978), 'Women and Education', London, Tavistock.
Calow, M. (1980), Women in ASTMS, unpublished thesis, Warwick University.
Campbell, B. (1979), Lining Their Pockets, 'Time Out', July 13-19.
Campbell, B. (1980), United We Fall: Women and the Wage Struggle, 'Red Rag', August.
Campbell, B. and Charlton, V. (1978), Work to Rule: Wages and the Family, 'Red Rag'.
Castles, S. and Kosack, G. (1973), 'Immigrant Workers and Class Structure in Western Europe', London, Oxford University Press.
Census of Great Britain (1971), Economic Activity Rates, 10 per cent Sample.
Central Policy Review Staff (1978a), 'Social and Employment Implications of Microelectronics', London, HMSO.
Central Policy Review Staff (1978b), 'Services for Young Children with Working Mothers', London, HMSO.
Clarke, T. (1977), Introduction: The Raison d'Etre of Trade Unionism, in T. Clarke and L. Clements (eds), 'Trade Unions Under Capitalism', London, Fontana, pp. 7-23.
Clothing and Allied Products Industrial Training Board (1972), 'Annual Report', London.
Clothing and Allied Products Industrial Training Board, (1973) 'In Lieu of School Leavers', London.
Clothing and Allied Products Industrial Training Board, (1974), 'Annual Report', London.
Coote, A. (1978), Equality and the Curse of the Quango, 'New Statesman', vol. 96, no. 2489, 1 December, pp. 734-7.
Coote, A. (1980), Powerlessness - And How to Fight It, 'New Statesman', vol. 100, no. 2590, 7 November, pp. 8-11.
Coote, A. and Hewitt, P. (1980), The Stance of Britain's Major Parties and Interest Groups, in P. Moss and N. Fonda, (eds), 'Work and the Family', London, Temple Smith.
Coote, A. and Kellner, P. (1981), 'Hear This Brother', London, New Statesman.
Coulson, M., Magas, B. and Wainwright, H. (1975), The Housewife and Her

Labour under Capitalism, 'New Left Review', no. 89, January-February, pp. 59-71.
Counter Information Services (1976), 'Crisis: Women under Attack, Anti-Report, no. 15, London, CIS.
Counter Information Services (1979), 'The New Technology', Anti-Report, no. 23, London, CIS.
Coussins, J. (1976), 'The Equality Report', London, National Council of Civil Liberties.
Coyle, A. (1980), The Protection Racket?, 'Feminist Review', no. 4, pp. 1-14.
CPSA (1979), 'Civil Service Annual Report', London, CPSA.
CPSA (1980), 'Civil Service Annual Report', London, CPSA.
Crine, S. (1979), 'The Hidden Army', London, Low Pay Unit.
Crompton, R. (1979), Trade Unionism and the Insurance Clerk, 'Sociology', vol. 13, no. 3, pp. 403-27.
CSE Microelectronics Group (1980), 'Microelectronics: Capitalist Technology and the Working Class', London, Conference of Socialist Economists, CSE Books.
Cunnison, S. (1966), 'Wages and Work Allocation', London, Tavistock.
Dangerfield, G. (1966), 'The Strange Death of Liberal England', London, Paladin.
Davies, C. (1980), Making Sense of the Census in Britain and the USA: The Changing Occupational Classification and the Position of Nurses, 'Sociological Review', vol. 28, no. 3, pp. 581-609.
Davison, R.B. (1962), 'West Indian Migrants', London, Institute of Race Relations and Oxford University Press.
Department of Employment (1974), 'Women and Work: A Statistical Survey', Manpower paper no. 9, London, HMSO.
Department of Employment, (1975) Unemployment among Workers from Racial Minority Groups, 'Employment Gazette', vol. 83, no. 9, September, pp. 868-71.
Department of Employment (1976), 'The Role of Immigrants in the Labour Market', London, Department of Employment, Unit for Manpower Studies.
Department of Employment (1980), Weekly and Hourly Average Earnings, 'Employment Gazette', vol. 88, no. 10, October.
Department of Employment (1981), Training and Job Services Face Cuts, and MSC Corporate Plan, 1981-5, 'Employment Gazette', vol. 89, no. 1, January, pp. 3, 39-40.
Dex, S. (1980), The Second Generation - West Indian Female School-leavers, unpublished paper, Keele University, Department of Economics.
Downing, H. (1980), Word Processors and the Oppression of Women, in T. Forester (ed.), 'The Microelectronics Revolution', Oxford, Basil Blackwell.
Drake, P., Fairbrother, P., Fryer, B. and Murphy, J. (1980), 'Which Way Forward'? An Interim Review of Issues for the Society of Civil and Public Servants, London, SCPS.
Driver, G. (1980), How West Indians do Better at School (Especially the Girls), 'New Society', vol. 51, no. 902, 17 January, pp. 111-14.
Dromey, J. and Taylor, G. (1978), 'Grunwick: The Workers' Story', London, Lawrence & Wishart.
Duffield, M. (1980), The Theory of Underdevelopment or the Underdevelopment of Theory: The Pertinence of Recent Debate to the Question of Colonial Immigration to Britain, unpublished paper, SSRC Research Unit on Ethnic Relations, University of Aston.
Eaton, J., Barrett Brown, M. and Coates, K. (1975), 'An Alternative Economic Strategy for the Labour Movement', Spokesman Pamphlet, no. 47.
Edwards, R.C. (1975), The Social Relations of Production in the Firm and Labour Market Structure, in R.C. Edwards, M. Reich and D.M. Gordon (eds), 'Labour Market Segmentation', Lexington, Mass., Lexington Books.
Edwards R.C. (1980), 'Contested Terrain', New York, Basic Books.
EOC (1977a) 'First Annual Report', Manchester, Equal Opportunities Commission.
EOC (1977b) 'Women and Low Incomes', Manchester, Equal Opportunities Commission.
EOC (1978a) 'Second Annual Report', Manchester, Equal Opportunities Commission.

EOC (1978b) 'Equalising the Pension Age', Manchester, Equal Opportunities Commission.

EOC (1979a) 'Guidance on Equal Opportunities Policies and Practices in Employment', Manchester, Equal Opportunities Commission.

EOC (1979b) 'Setting up a Workplace Nursery', Manchester, Equal Opportunities Commission.

EOC (1979c) 'Health and Safety Legislation: should we distinguish between men and women?' Manchester, Equal Opportunities Commission.

EOC (1980a) 'Fourth Annual Report', Manchester, Equal Opportunities Commission.

EOC (1980b) 'Research Bulletin', vol. 1, no. 3, Spring, Manchester, Equal Opportunities Commission.

Fonda, N. and Moss, P. (eds) (1976) 'Mothers in Employment', Uxbridge, Brunel University Management Programme and Thomas Coram Research Unit.

Foner, N. (1979) 'Jamaica Farewell', London, Routledge & Kegan Paul.

Forester, T. (ed) (1980), 'The Microelectronics Revolution', Oxford, Basil Blackwell.

Friedman, A.L. (1977) 'Industry and Labour', London, Macmillan.

Fryer, B., Fairclough, A. and Manson, T. (1974), 'Organisation and Change in the National Union of Public Employees', London, NUPE.

'Garment Worker', March 1964, May 1970, July 1970, August 1972, November 1974, April 1975, November 1975, January 1976, February 1977, October 1977, January 1979, January 1980.

Gavron, H. (1968), 'The Captive Wife', Harmondsworth, Penguin.

Girvan, N. (1972), 'Foreign Capital and Economic Underdevelopment in Jamaica', Kingston: Institute of Social and Economic Research, University of West Indies.

Goldthorpe, J.H. (with Llewellyn, C. and Payne, C.) (1980), 'Social Mobility and Class Structure in Modern Britain' Oxford, Clarendon Press.

Goodman, J.F.B., Armstrong, E.G.A., Davis, J.E. and Wagner, A. (1977), 'Rule-Making and Industrial Peace', London, Croom Helm.

Goodrich, C. (1975), 'The Frontier of Control', London, Pluto Press.

Gordon, D.M. (1972), 'Theories of Poverty and Underemployment', Lexington, Mass., Lexington Books.

Grossman, R. (1978), Women's Place in the Integrated Circuit, 'S.E. Asia Chronicle', no. 66 (joint issue with 'Pacific Research', vol. 9, nos 5-6), pp. 2-17.

'Guardian', 8 and 9 July 1980.

Hague, D.C. and Newman, R.K. (1952), 'Costs in Alternative Locations: The Clothing Industry', National Institute of Economic and Social Research Occasional Paper, no. XV, Cambridge University Press.

Hakim, C. (1979), 'Occupational Segregation', Department of Employment Research paper, no. 9.

Hakim, C. (1980), Census Reports as Documentary Evidence: The Census Commentaries 1801-1951, 'Sociological Review', vol. 28, no. 3, pp. 551-81.

Hall, P. (1962), 'The Industries of London Since 1861', London, Hutchinson.

Hamill, L. (1976), 'Wives as Sole and Joint Breadwinners', discussion paper, Department of Health and Social Security, Economic Advisors Office.

Hamilton, M. (1941), 'Women at Work', London, Routledge & Kegan Paul.

Harris, N. (1971), 'Beliefs in Society: The Problem of Ideology', Harmondsworth, Penguin.

Hartmann, H. (1979a), Capitalism, Patriarchy and Job Segregation by Sex, in Z.R. Eisenstein (ed.), 'Capitalism, Patriarchy and the Case for Socialist Feminism', New York, Monthly Review Press.

Hartmann, H. (1979b), The Unhappy Marriage of Marxism and Feminism: Towards a More Progressive Union, 'Capital and Class', no. 8, pp. 1-33.

Herding, R. (1977), Job Control and Union Structure, in T. Clarke and L. Clements (eds), 'Trade Unions under Capitalism', London, Fontana.

Heritage, J. (1980), Class Situation, White Collar Unionisation and the 'Double Proletarianisation' Thesis: A Comment, 'Sociology', vol. 14, no. 2, pp. 283-91.

Hewitt, P. (1976), Women's Rights in Law and Practice, 'New Community',
   vol. V, no. 1-2, pp. 19-21.
Hobbs, M. (1973), 'Born to Struggle', London, Quartet.
Hoos, I.R. (1961), 'Automation in the Office', Washington, Public Affairs Press.
Hubbuck, J. and Carter, S. (1980), 'Half a Chance?, A Report on Job Discrimi-
   nation against Young Blacks in Nottingham', London, Commission for Racial
   Equality and Nottingham and District Community Relations Council.
Hughes, M., Mayall, B., Moss, P., Perry, J., Petrie, P. and Pinkerton, G.
   (1980), 'Nurseries Now', Harmondsworth, Penguin.
Humphries, J. (1977), Class Struggle and the Persistence of the Working Class
   Family, 'Cambridge Journal of Economics', vol. 1, no. 3, pp. 241-58.
Hunt, A. (1968), 'A Survey of Women's Employment', London, HMSO.
Hunt, A. (1975), 'Management Attitudes and Practices towards Women at Work',
   London, Office of Population Censuses and Surveys, Social Survey Division,
   HMSO.
Hunt, J. (1975), Women and Liberation, 'Marxism Today', November, pp. 326-36.
Hunt, J. (1976), 'Organising Women Workers', London, Workers Education
   Association.
Hunt, J. and Adams, S.A. (1980), 'Women, Work and Trade Union Organisation',
   London, Workers Education Association.
Hunt, P. (1978), Cash Transactions and Household Tasks: Domestic Behaviour
   in Relation to Industrial Employment, 'Sociological Review', vol. 26, no. 3,
   pp. 555-71.
Hunt, P. (1980), 'Gender and Class Consciousness', London, Macmillan.
Hurstfield, J. (1978), 'The Part Time Trap', London, Low Pay Unit.
Hurstfield, J. (1980), Part Time Pittance, in 'Low Pay Review', no. 7, pp. 1-15.
Incomes Data Services (1980), 'Changing Technology', Study 220, June, London,
   Incomes Data Services Ltd.
Industrial Training Research Unit (1975), 'ITRU Research Paper' SL6.
Joreen, (1973), The Tyranny of Structurelessness, in A. Koedt, E. Levine and
   A. Rapone (eds), 'Radical Feminism', New York, Quadrangle.
Khan, V.S. (1979), Work and Network: South Asian Women in South London,
   in S. Wallman (ed.), 'Ethnicity at Work', London, Macmillan.
Klein, V. (1961), 'Employing Married Women', London Institute of Personnel
   Management.
Kosack, G. (1976), Migrant Women: The Move to Western Europe - A Step to-
   ward Emancipation?, 'Race and Class', vol. 17, no. 4, pp. 369-79.
Kuhn, A. (1978), Structures of Capital and Patriarchy in the Family, in A.
   Kuhn and A.M. Wolpe (eds), 'Feminism and Materialism', London, Routledge
   & Kegan Paul.
Kynaston Reeves, T. (1970), The Control of Manufacture in a Garment Factory,
   in J. Woodward (ed.), 'Industrial Organisation, Behaviour and Control',
   London, Oxford University Press.
'Labour Research' (1979a), Women in Trade Unions, vol. 68, no. 3, March,
   pp. 68-9.
'Labour Research' (1979b, Microelectronics - The Trade Union Response, vol.
   68, no. 6, June, pp. 140-1.
Labour Research Department (1978), The Changeover to Electronics, in (AUEW)
   TASS, 'Computer Technology and Employment', Manchester, National
   Computing Centre.
Labour Research Department (1980), 'Bargaining Report', no. 6.
Land, H. (1976), Women: Supporters or Supported?, in D. Leonard Barker
   and S. Allen (eds), 'Sexual Divisions and Society: Process and Change',
   London, Tavistock.
Land, H. (1978a), Who cares for the family?, 'Journal of Social Policy', vol. 7,
   part 3.
Land, H. (1978b), Sex Role Stereotyping in the Social Security and Income Tax
   Systems, in J. Chetwynd and O. Hartnett (eds), 'The Sex Role System',
   London, Routledge & Kegan Paul.
Land, H. (1980) The Family Wage, 'Feminist Review', no. 6, pp. 55-77.
Larrain, J. (1979), 'The Concept of Ideology', London, Hutchinson.

Leach, P. (1979), 'Who Cares?', Harmondsworth, Penguin.
Lenin, V.I. (1970), 'What is to be Done?', London, Panther (originally published in 1905).
Lewenhak, S. (1977), 'Women and Trade Unions', London, Ernest Benn.
Liddington, J. and Norris, J. (1978), 'One Hand Tied Behind Us: The Rise of the Women's Suffrage Movement', London, Virago.
Lister, R. and Wilson, E. (1976), 'The Unequal Breadwinner: A New Perspective on Women and Social Security', London, National Council of Civil Liberties.
Llewellyn-Davies, M. (ed.), (1978), 'Maternity: Letters from Working Women', London, Virago reprint of 1915 edition.
Lockwood, D. (1966), 'The Blackcoated Worker', London, George Allen & Unwin.
McIntosh, M. (1978), The State and the Oppression of Women, in A. Kuhn and A.M. Wolpe (eds), 'Feminism and Materialism', London, Routledge & Kegan Paul.
McNally, F. (1979), 'Women for Hire: A Study of the Female Office Worker', London, Macmillan.
Mandel, E. (1975), 'Late Capitalism', London, New Left Books.
Marx, K. (1976), 'Capital', vol. 1, London, Penguin.
Mincer, J. and Polachek, S. (1980), Family Investments in Human Capital: Earnings of Women', in A.H. Amsden (ed.), 'The Economics of Women and Work', Harmondsworth, Penguin.
Ministry of Labour (1967), 'The Introduction of Shift Working', London, HMSO.
Molyneux, M. (1979), Beyond the Domestic Labour Debate, 'New Left Review', no. 116, pp. 3-27.
Morokvasic, M. (1980), Yugoslav Migrant Women in France, F.R.G. and Sweden, Unpublished report, Paris, Centre National Recherche Scientifique.
Mumford, E. (1979), Designing Office Automation for Human Needs, paper to Colloquium on Sociological Impact of Computers, December, London, Institution of Electrical Engineers.
Mumford, E. and Banks, O. (1967), 'The Computer and the Clerk', London, Routledge & Kegan Paul.
National Board for Prices and Incomes (1968), 'Payment by Results Systems', Report no. 65, London, HMSO.
National Union of Tailors and Garment Workers (1978) 'Employment in Clothing: A Struggle for Survival', NUTGW.
Nichols, T. and Armstrong, P. (1976), 'Workers Divided', London, Fontana.
North Tyneside Community Development Project (1978), 'North Shields: Women's Work', Final Report vol. 5, Newcastle Upon Tyne Polytechnic.
Oakley, A. (1974), 'The Sociology of Housework', London, Martin Robertson.
Oakley, A. (1976), 'Housewife', Harmondsworth, Penguin.
Oakley, A. and Oakley, R. (1979), Sexism in Official Statistics, in J. Irvine et al., 'Demystifying Social Statistics', London, Pluto.
Panitch, L. (1976), 'Workers, Wages and Control', New Hogtown Press.
Parsons, K. (1974), Women in the Trade Union Movement: Or out of It? unpublished dissertation, University of Liverpool.
Peach, C. (1968), 'West Indian Migration to Britain', London, Oxford University Press.
Phillips, A. and Taylor, B. (1980), Sex and Skill: Notes towards a Feminist Economics, 'Feminist Review', no. 6, pp. 79-88.
Philpott, S.B. (1977), The Montserratians: Migration Dependency and the Maintenance of Island Ties in England, in J.L. Watson (ed.), 'Between Two Cultures', Oxford, Blackwell.
Phizacklea, A. (ed.) (forthcoming), 'Migrant Women Workers'.
Phizacklea, A. and Miles, R. (1980), 'Labour and Racism', London, Routledge & Kegan Paul.
Piore, M.J. (1975), Notes for a Theory of Labour Market Stratification, in R.C. Edwards, M. Reich and D.M. Gordon (eds), 'Labour Market Segmentation', Lexington, Mass., Lexington Books.
Pollert, A. (1981), 'Girls, Wives, Factory Lives', London, Macmillan.
Pond, C. (1977), 'For Whom the Pips Squeak', Low Pay Paper, no. 15, London, Low Pay Unit.

Porter, M. (1978a), Consciousness and Secondhand Experience: Wives and Husbands in Industrial Action, 'Sociological Review', vol. 26, no. 2, 263-82.
Porter, M. (1978b), Worlds Apart: The Class Consciousness of Working Class Women, 'Women's Studies International Quarterly', vol. 1, pp. 175-88.
Porter, M. (1979), Experience and Consciousness: Women at Home, Men at Work, PhD thesis, University of Bristol.
Poulantzas, N. (1975), 'Classes in Contemporary Capitalism', London, New Left Books.
Powell, J. (1976), 'Work Study', London, Arrow Books.
Prescott-Roberts, M. and Steele, N. (1980), 'Black Women: Bringing It All Back Home', Bristol, Falling Wall Press.
Pryce, K. (1979), 'Endless Pressure', Harmondsworth, Penguin.
Purcell, K. (1979), Militancy and Acquiescence amongst Women Workers, in S. Burman (ed), 'Fit Work for Women', London, Croom Helm.
Race Today Black Womens Group (1974), Black Women and Nursing: A Job like Any Other, 'Race Today', vol. 6, no. 8, August, pp. 226-30.
Race Today Black Womens Group (1975), Caribbean Women and the Black Community, 'Race Today', vol. 7, no. 4, April, pp. 108-13.
Raffe, D. (1979), The 'Alternative Route' Reconsidered, 'Sociology', vol. 13, no. 1.
Ramelson, M. (1972), 'The Petticoat Rebellion', London, Lawrence & Wishart.
Ratner, R. Steinberg (1980), 'Equal Employment Policy for Women', Philadelphia, Temple University Press.
Reich, M., Gordon, D.M. and Edwards, R.C., (1980), A Theory of Labour Market Segmentation, in A.H. Amsden (ed.), 'The Economics of Women and Work', Harmondsworth, Penguin, pp. 232-41.
Roche, J. (1973), Future Trends in the Clothing Industry, in M. Barrett Brown and K. Coates (eds), 'Trade Union Register' no. 3, pp. 199-209.
Routh, G. (1980) 'Occupation and Pay in Great Britain', 2nd edn, London, Macmillan.
Rowbotham, S. (1973), 'Women's Consciousness, Man's World', Harmondsworth, Penguin.
Rowbotham, S. Segal, L. and Wainwright, H. (1979), 'Beyond the Fragments: Feminism and the Making of Socialism', London, Merlin Press.
Royal Commission on Equal Pay (1946) 'Report', London, HMSO.
Rubery, J. (1978), Structured Labour Markets, Worker Organisation and Low Pay, 'Cambridge Journal of Economics', vol. 2, no. 1, pp. 17-36.
Shah, S. (1975), 'Immigrants and Employment in the Clothing Industry: The Rag Trade in London's East End', London, Runnymede Trust.
Schreiner, O. (1978), 'Women and Labour', London, Virago reprint of 1911 edition.
Simeral, M.H., (1978), Women and the Reserve Army of Labour, 'The Insurgent Sociologist', vol. 8, nos. 2 and 3, pp. 164-79.
Simpson, R. (1978), 'Day Care for School Age Children', Manchester, Equal Opportunities Commission.
Sleigh, J., Boatwright, B., Irwin, P., and Stanyon, R. (1979), 'The Manpower Implications of Micro-electronics Technology', London, HMSO, Department of Employment Micro-electronic Study Group.
Sleigh, J., Boatwright, B., Irwin, P., and Stanyon R. (1980), How Real is the Threat of Technological Unemployment? 'Employment Gazette', vol. 88, no. 2, February, pp. 115-20.
Smith, D.J. (1977), 'Racial Disadvantage in Britain: The P.E.P. Report', Harmondsworth, Penguin.
Smith R.T. (1956), 'The Negro Family in British Guiana', London, Routledge & Kegan Paul.
Smith, R.T. (1973), The Matrifocal Family, in J. Goody (ed.), 'Character of Kinship', Cambridge University Press.
Snell, M. (1979), The Equal Pay and Sex Discrimination Acts: Their Impact in the Workplace, 'Feminist Review', no. 1, pp. 37-58.
Soldon, N.C. (1978), 'Women in British Trade Unions, (1874-1976), Dublin, Gill & MacMillan.

Stageman, J. (1980), 'Women in Trade Unions', University of Hull, Adult
    Education' Department, Paper no. 6.
Stedman Jones, G. (1971), 'Outcast London: A, Study in the Relationships
    Between Classes in Victorian Society', Oxford, Clarendon, Press.
Stewart A., Prandy K. and Blackburn R.M. (1980), 'Social Stratification
    and Occupation', London, Macmillan.
Strachey, R. (1978), 'The Cause: A Short History of the Women's Movement',
    London, Virago reprint of 1928 edition.
Stymne B. (1966), EDP and Organisational Structure: A Case Study of an
    Insurance Company, 'Swedish Journal of Economics' (Stockholm) vol. 68,
    no. 2, pp. 89-116.
TASS (AUEW), (1975), 'Women's Rights', Richmond, Surrey.
Taylor, B. (1979), The Men are as Bad as Their Masters, 'Feminist Studies',
    vol. 5, no. 1, pp. 7-41.
Toynbee, P. (1980), 'Guardian', 10 March 1980.
TGWU (1980) 'Women's Handbook', London.
TUC, (1975-1980 incl.) Reports of Congress, London, Trades Union Congress.
TUC, (1931, 1968-1980 incl.), Reports of Women's Conference, London, Trades
    Union Congress.
TUC, Positive Action Conference, November 1980, background papers and
    Supplementary Report to 1981 TUC Women's Conference, London Trades Union
    Congress.
TUC, (1978-1980 incl.) Statistical Statements and List of Delegates, London,
    Trades Union Congress.
TUC (1977), 'The Under Fives: a Report of a TUC Working Party', London,
    Trades Union Congress.
TUC (1979a), 'Homeworking: a TUC Statement', London, Trades Union Congress.
TUC (1979b), 'Employment and Technology', London, Trades Union Congress.
TUC (1980), Review of the Employment and Training Act 1973, memorandum
    of evidence submitted to Manpower Services Commission Review Body,
    February.
Union Place Collective (1976), 'As Things Are', London, Bonfire Press.
Vinnicombe, S. (1980), 'Secretaries, Management and Organisations', London,
    Heinemann.
Walker, J. (1978), 'The Human Aspects of Shiftwork', London, Institute of
    Personnel Management.
Wandor, M. (ed.) (1972), 'The Body Politic', London, Stage 1.
West, J. (1978), Women, Sex and Class, in A. Kuhn and A. M. Wolpe (eds),
    'Feminism and Materialism', London, Routledge & Kegan Paul.
West, J. (1980), A Political Economy of the Family in Capitalism: Women, Repro-
    duction and Wage Labour, in T. Nichols (ed.), 'Capital and Labour', London,
    Fontana.
Whisler T. (1970), 'The Impact of Computers on Organizations', New York,
    Praeger.
Williams, N. (1972), The New Sweat Shops, 'New Society', vol. 20, no. 509,
    June, pp. 666-8.
Wilson, A. (1978), 'Finding a Voice: Asian Women in Britain', London, Virago.
Winship, J. (1978). A Woman's World: Woman - an Ideology of Feminity, in
    Women's Study Group, Centre for Contemporary Cultural Studies, 'Women
    Take Issue', London, Hutchinson.
Winyard, S. (1977), 'From Rags to Rags', Low Pay Pamphlet, no. 7, London,
    Low Pay Unit.
Wollstonecraft, M. (1975) 'A Vindication of the Rights of Women', ed. M.
    Kramnick, Harmondsworth, Penguin, originally published 1792.
'Woman's Own' (1979), Fair Play for Children and a Fair Deal for Mothers,
    17 February.
Wray, M. (1957), 'The Women's Outerwear Industry', London, Duckworth.
Yudkin, S. and Holme, A. (1963), 'Working Mothers and Their Children',
    London, Sphere Books.

INDEX